# Northern Ireland's Lost Opportunity

Gerard,

Thanks for your
support & interest!

Hope you enjoy!

All the
best!

Tony
Norvel

# NORTHERN IRELAND'S LOST OPPORTUNITY

## The Frustrated Promise of Political Loyalism

Tony Novosel

**Pluto**Press
www.plutobooks.com

First published 2013 by Pluto Press
345 Archway Road, London N6 5AA

www.plutobooks.com

Distributed in the United States of America exclusively by
Palgrave Macmillan, a division of St. Martin's Press LLC,
175 Fifth Avenue, New York, NY 10010

British Library Cataloguing in Publication Data
A catalogue record for this book is available from the British Library

ISBN   978 0 7453 3310 6   Hardback
ISBN   978 0 7453 3309 0   Paperback
ISBN   978 1 8496 4806 6   PDF eBook
ISBN   978 1 8496 4808 0   Kindle eBook
ISBN   978 1 8496 4807 3   EPUB eBook

Library of Congress Cataloging in Publication Data applied for

10   9   8   7   6   5   4   3   2   1

Typeset from disk by Stanford DTP Services, Northampton, England
Simultaneously printed digitally by CPI Antony Rowe, Chippenham, UK and
Edwards Bros in the United States of America

One of the great lessons out of this whole [Northern Ireland Peace Process] process, which may be incidental to the result, but nonetheless important in human terms, is the capacity for personal redemption. The ability of people who have made serious, tragic errors, violent errors, committed brutal atrocities; to accept responsibility, to be punished for it, to accept their punishment and then to change, genuinely change.

George Mitchell

# Contents

# Acknowledgements

Any time anyone takes on a project of this scope there is no way the author can take full credit for the completed work. I received a great deal of help from many people, from those who supplied me with moral support to those who read various versions of this manuscript. This is my humble attempt to thank them all.

I cannot thank my 'partner', Alice Cottone, enough. She has been amazing throughout the whole writing process over the past two years and she has been a rock. She gave me the space to do my ten- to twelve-hour writing days; many times bringing over food or making sure I stepped away from the manuscript when necessary. Without her support, there is no way I could have finished this book.

A special thanks goes out to all those who agreed to do interviews. They gave up freely of their time, providing insights and first-hand knowledge of this period.

Billy Hutchinson was absolutely crucial to this work. It was my chat in 2007 with Billy that refocused me and convinced me to continue with this work. His intervention was also crucial in getting access to individuals and materials that underpin this work.

I can never repay William Mitchell, Aaron Edwards, Richard Reed and Sean Brennan for the amount of time and work they put in with me. They read through various parts and/or all of the manuscript, even while doing work on their own Ph.D.'s and/or holding down full-time jobs. Each of them also gave up their time to meet and talk at length about this work.

Mark Williamson deserves many thanks. He arranged a talk for me in October of 2009 on the Shankill Road, which then led to a series of talks over the next two years. This proved invaluable as it enabled me to organise and create the structure of this book.

Dawn Purvis deserves special mention here also. Beyond providing me with an interview, she also went out of her way to meet with me and talk for hours with me about this work.

It is safe to say, that without Roy Garland, his work on Spence and his help this book would not exist. Roy's personal encouragement, his comments, and help with materials were essential for this effort.

Graham Spencer and Peter Shirlow deserve special mention. Their work inspired me to begin this project and also informed my analysis. Both provided a great deal of help in the formulation of this work, especially my proposal.

Henry Sinnerton was also a great help. Henry's work on David Ervine helped me a great deal as did the many discussions we had together.

I must also include Graham Walker and Eamon Phoenix here. Graham's friendship, encouragement, and work on Unionism have been invaluable. Eamon's support throughout has been crucial to my staying focused on this work.

To 'Big' Jon McCourt – what can I say? He and I have spent many hours together talking and talking about everything related to the politics and history of Northern Ireland/Ireland. These meetings were so important to my knowledge and my development.

To Jeanette and Mark Ervine, who spent so much time sharing their lives with me, thank you so much. Your friendship and help was invaluable.

I want to thank Monica McWilliams. Her belief in me and her great support over the years has made all the difference. Thank you.

Harry Donaghy and all those around the Messines Project in Belfast deserve special mention. Many is the time I sat with Harry and others at the John Hewitt suffering from self-doubt. Through the intense Friday afternoon discussions over the past four years, Harry, among others, encouraged me to carry on and gave me great insights, thoughts to consider and criticisms I could not ignore. I must also mention Frank, Beef, Joe, Brendan, Joe, Kerry, Gerry, Kevin, Tom, Tommy, Marty, Mark, Danny, Laurence, Florence, Brenda, Andy and the many others who regularly meet at the Hewitt on a Friday afternoon. I hope I have left no one out.

I cannot leave out Mairead Collins. She was instrumental in helping me with the transcripts and without her aid I would still be doing them, and this book would be another few years down the road. Our mutual friend Margaret Hagan deserves mention also. We have worked together since 2006 with Margaret always providing critical and probing questions and forcing me to focus my argument.

Sarah McAuliffe-Bellin has been a great support through this. She has engaged me intellectually from the start and has given me the opportunity to present my research in America.

Louis Edmondson also deserves my thanks. His skeptical views and sharp questions forced me to ensure that my argument was a strong and valid one, and that it could hold up to the harshest criticisms.

I would also like to thank the staff of the Linen Hall Library's Northern Ireland Political Collection and microfiche sections. They were a great help in getting the materials I needed for my research.

Two people who really deserve my thanks are Tony and Karen. Over the past four years, they have given me unlimited use of their house in Belfast and, more importantly, their friendship. Dennis also deserves thanks. In 2007, he provided me with a place to stay and introduced me to some people who became very important in the completion this book.

Special and heartfelt thanks to my brother Mike, sisters Rose and Anita, and especially my father, Tony, for support throughout my life and this project.

Special thanks to my roommates in Belfast in 2009, Erin Hinson, Lisa Monahan and Jasmine Kurjakovic. You were all wonderful and a great source of inspiration.

I must thank everyone at the University of Pittsburgh's Department of History. The support I received in the department helped make this book possible. In particular, four individuals, Bernie Hagerty, Bill Chase, Rob Ruck and Reid Andrews deserve my appreciation for their help and support. In particular Bill, as he has done since I first met him in 1987, went above and beyond the call of duty. He took the entire manuscript, corrected punctuation, grammar and style, and pointed out inconsistencies and weaknesses while also providing very good suggestions for strengthening the book.

Finally, I want to thank all my close friends in Belfast and Derry/Londonderry, many of whom now go back nearly 40 years with me and who wish to remain nameless; thanks for all your friendship and support. For many others in Belfast and Derry/Londonderry who I have gotten to know, thanks so much for your friendship and support over the years. If I tried to list everyone, it would go on for pages.

A final thanks to all the people who saved me from making errors in this work. I appreciate all your help. If any errors do remain, they are my responsibility and mine alone.

# Abbreviations

| | |
|---|---|
| AIA | Anglo–Irish Agreement (also known as the Anglo–Irish Accord) |
| BURC | Belfast Unemployed Resource Centre |
| CRA | Civil Rights Association |
| DUP | Democratic Unionist Party |
| EPIC | Ex-Prisoners Interpretive Centre |
| GFA | Good Friday Agreement (also known as the Belfast Agreement) |
| IRA | Irish Republican Army |
| IUG | Independent Unionist Group |
| MI5 | Military Intelligence – Section Five |
| MI6 | Military Intelligence – Section Six |
| NICRA | Northern Ireland Civil Rights Association |
| NILP | Northern Ireland Labour Party |
| NIO | Northern Ireland Office |
| OC | Officer Commanding |
| OUP | Official Unionist Party |
| OIRA | Official Irish Republican Army |
| PIRA | Provisional Irish Republican Army |
| PRONI | Public Records Office of Northern Ireland |
| PUG | Progressive Unionist Group |
| PUP | Progressive Unionist Party |
| RHC | Red Hand Commando |
| RIC | Royal Irish Constabulary |
| RUC | Royal Ulster Constabulary |
| SDLP | Social Democratic Labour Party |
| UCDC | Ulster Constitution Defence Committee |
| UDA | Ulster Defence Association |
| UDI | unilateral declaration of independence |
| ULF | Ulster Loyalist Front |
| UPA | Ulster Protestant Action |
| UPL | Ulster Protestant League |
| UPV | Ulster Protestant Volunteers |
| US | United States |
| USC | Ulster Special Constabulary |
| UUP | Ulster Unionist Party |

| UULA | Ulster Unionist Labour Association |
| UVF | Ulster Volunteer Force |
| UWC | Ulster Workers' Council |
| VUP | Vanguard Unionist Party |
| VPP | Volunteer Political Party |

# Glossary of Terms

*Beyond the Religious Divide* UDA document published in 1979 putting forth ideas on how to unify the two communities in Northern Ireland.

**B-Specials** Part-time militia originally created under the USC in 1920. The Catholics viewed the B-Specials with great loathing, while the Protestant population tended to view them as their front line against republicanism.

*Common Sense* UDA document published in 1987 calling for a government with proportional representation, a bill of rights and voluntary power sharing.

*Criminalisation* Policy instituted in 1976 by the British government. It sought to portray anyone involved in violent activities as part of the Troubles as ordinary criminals. The goal of the government was to split the paramilitaries, in particular the IRA, from their support base by portraying them as common criminals; not freedom fighters.

**Democratic Unionist Party** Party founded by the Rev. Ian Paisley in 1971. Initially was to be a party that was to the right on the border, but on the left in social issues. It was the party of 'No!' for many years, refusing to compromise with the nationalist population. Eventually supplanted the UUP as the largest unionist political party and went into a power sharing government with Sinn Féin.

**H-Blocks** Cellblocks built in the Maze prison to house prisoners beginning in 1976. They were named because of their shape.

**Long Kesh/Maze** Name of the prison camp used to house paramilitary prisoners throughout the conflict. Located in Lisburn, about seven miles from Belfast.

**Loyalist** Mainly working class Protestants who fought to maintain the Union with Great Britain through the armed struggle. Prior to this conflict, this term was used to refer to all those who wanted to maintain the Union with Great Britain.

**MI5** The British Security Service responsible for national security.

**MI6** The British Security service that deals with UK national security in the international realm.

**Official Unionist Party** See **Ulster Unionist Party.**

**Orange Order** Founded in 1795. Exclusively Protestant organisation its purpose is to promote and propagate biblical Protestantism. It was intimately tied to the Unionist Party throughout much of Northern Ireland's history. Its annual marches are still a source of contention and violence.

**Progressive Unionist Party** Small Protestant working class Party that is aligned with the UVF and the RHC. It has a social democratic ethos based on 'Old Labour' in Britain.

**Proportional representation** Voting system in which the share of seats held by a political party closely matches the share of popular votes that the party receives. The British put this in place at the creation of the Northern Ireland state to ensure fair representation for the Catholic population. Eliminated in 1923 in local elections and 1929 for the National Elections. Now used in elections in Northern Ireland.

**Sharing Responsibility** Policy document developed over a period of ten to twelve years by the UVF, the RHC and members of the PUP that called for a devolved power-sharing government and an end to strictly majority rule.

**Stormont** Seat of government in Northern Ireland. After the 'Stormont' building was opened in 1932, 'Stormont' became a common reference for the Northern Ireland government.

**Tara** Fundamentalist Presbyterian group preparing for the final, apocalyptic struggle with Catholicism, communism, liberalism, etc. Run by William McGrath, a paedophile and suspected MI5 agent.

**Ulster Democratic Party** Small and now defunct Party that was aligned with the UDA.

**Ulsterisation** British Government policy that shifted responsibility for security from the British Army onto the police force (RUC) and the part-time UDR. Modelled after the American policy of 'Vietnamisation'.

**Unionist** Term used for those, mainly middle and upper class Protestants, who supported the maintenance of the Union with Britain though constitutional and political means, and who distanced themselves from working class and physical force Loyalism. Prior to this conflict, the term was interchangeable with 'Loyalist'.

**Ulster Unionist Party** Sometimes called the OUP or 'Unionist Party'. This party ruled Northern Ireland throughout most of its history. It ruled in a formal alliance with the Orange Order. The UUP, under David Trimble, went into the first power-sharing government after the GFA in 1998. Over the past ten years, the UUP has lost a great deal of political ground and is now the second largest Unionist party behind the DUP.

# Preface and Overview

This story of the U.V.F. is not a tale of protestant terrorism. It is the story of how the protestant working class was forced in extremes to take off on a voyage of self-discovery. It is a voyage that is not yet over – indeed, it is barely begun. But that it *has* begun, and that there can be no going back, is the light shining in Ulster's present darkness.

David Boulton[1]

The genesis of this book goes back to Good Friday in 1995 when, through the good graces of a mutual friend, I met with Billy Hutchinson, former member of the Ulster Volunteer Force (UVF), an ex-life prisoner and member of the Progressive Unionist Party (PUP), at the PUP headquarters on the Shankill Road. In this initial meeting, Billy and I engaged in a long, wide-ranging discussion about many topics related to the 1994 ceasefires and his vision for the future, a vision that I found surprising and progressive. This meeting gave me a glimpse into a world I knew little about and left me wanting to learn more about Loyalism; in particular, Loyalists like him.

Before the 1994 ceasefires, I would have had great difficulty getting news and/or information about Loyalism. This changed somewhat after the 1994 Combined Loyalist Military Command – the umbrella organisation that encompassed the UVF, the Red Hand Commando (RHC) and the Ulster Defence Association (UDA) – called the Loyalist ceasefire. It then became easier to learn about people like Billy Hutchinson, David Ervine and Gusty Spence from the UVF, and William 'Plum' Smith, Winston 'Winkie' Rea and Ronnie McCullough from the RHC. These men were the political movers in their organisations and they worked closely with Councillor Hugh Smyth, a member of the PUP and long-time Protestant working class political activist on the Shankill Road.

Before this, I had assumed that unionism/Loyalism was a monolithic bloc and that, at best, Loyalists were nothing more than neo-fascists, Nazis and/or sectarian killers. The more I read and learned about these men and the PUP the more I came to realise that the stereotype that I had of Loyalism and Loyalists, in these cases, did not hold. Instead, I discovered that the PUP was an expressly 'Socialist Unionist Party'.[2] A party that wanted to create a social democratic state where everyone, regardless of religion or class would have their rights protected and would have a role to play in a new Northern Ireland. What made this more surprising for me was that the UVF and RHC founded and took the leading role in the PUP. This fascinated me and eventually led me to begin work on this book.

As my curiosity deepened, I began to work closely with David Ervine in 2004 on my ideas for this book. Over the next two years, we engaged in a series of informal and formal discussions about politics and history in Northern Ireland. Because of these discussions, Ervine had agreed to help me with getting contacts for my work. However, with his untimely death in January 2007, I thought I might never finish this project. Nevertheless, because of our work together I resolved that, come what may, I would write a history of the UVF. Therefore, I booked a two-month trip to Northern Ireland in the summer of 2007 to begin the preliminary research.

Perhaps not unsurprisingly, given the scope of the project I had set for myself, once I began the research my focus changed from trying to write the definitive history of the UVF, a herculean if not impossible task, to writing about the political evolution of the UVF and the RHC in the 1970s and 1980s. This happened as I discovered more and more UVF and RHC documents and realised that there was a story about the UVF, RHC and Loyalism in general that most people, myself included, knew little. That is, I found a story of an armed, violent and, many would say, terrorist movement that sought a way out of the dead end of violence in the 1970s and tried to fashion a political solution for Northern Ireland. However, I still did not have a clear focus of how I could tell this story.

Then, a week before I was to return home in 2007, I ran into Billy Hutchinson. After a brief chat, he told me to give him a ring. I did, and we met at his office in North Belfast after work one day. This meant we could talk without interruption or time limit. For nearly three hours, we talked about his history, the history of Northern Ireland and Ireland, the political history of the UVF and of Loyalism. At the end of that conversation I had a clearer focus, and deeper appreciation of the importance of the history, development, evolution and tragic failure of political Loyalism to end the conflict.

Once focused on this topic, I began my research in earnest in 2008 and then, in 2009, I spent two months in Belfast conducting interviews with many of those who had intimate knowledge of this history. I also spent more time in the Linen Hall Library reading more and more documents from that period. Thus began my study of political Loyalism and what Hugh Smyth calls 'the lost opportunity'.

This refers to that period in Northern Ireland's history, when the UVF, RHC and their political allies put forward proposals, mainly between 1973 and 1987, to end the conflict and create a just and equitable society for all, regardless of class or religion. Theirs was a vision that, in the right circumstances, could have ended the violence in Northern Ireland much earlier than 1994. However, instead of finding acceptance, the political programme of the UVF, the RHC and its allies often found outright hostility and rejection. Therefore, instead of a new beginning, this became a 'lost opportunity'.

The story of this failure and, more importantly, of Loyalism's attempt to engage with politics to end this conflict is crucial now for a number of reasons. For one, this is a story that needs to see the light of day, as it is a 'lost story', an inconvenient truth for many that presents a very different image of Loyalism and Loyalists.

Another reason that makes this study necessary is that many of those crucial to this study are aging or dying. Over the past few years, Billy Mitchell, David Ervine and Jim McDonald, three of the intellectual giants in Loyalism, died taking a great deal of knowledge of this period to the grave. This fact made it crucial to conduct the interviews used in this book now because Loyalists did not keep detailed records or policy documents in the way the republican movement did. Without the extensive written history of what they did, these interviews have been essential to understanding the story of the positive contribution that Loyalism tried to make during the darkest days of the conflict.

It is also important to write this book to challenge the traditional stereotypes of Loyalism that only hinder our understanding of this period and the history of the conflict in Northern Ireland. Only by doing that can we begin the serious study of the development of political thinking and the politics of the UVF, the RHC and their collaborators outside of the organisations. Without this knowledge, we cannot really understand why this conflict lasted so long.

While all these are significant reasons for doing this work, there is a more important purpose to this enterprise. This work will be the first one that puts the political history of the UVF and RHC in the public square. This means that academics, as we always do, can argue about what this all means and if this argument is correct or not. However, that is secondary to the fact that the UVF, RHC and the Protestant working class community can engage with the history and arguments in this book to examine and debate their own histories, while coming to their own conclusions on the evidence presented here.

There is a hunger and a desire within the Loyalist paramilitary groups and the larger Protestant working class community for this history. Beginning in October 2009 and continuing through the summer of 2011, I have given talks to seven groups of the RHC and the UVF as well as addressing the PUP on my preliminary findings. To illustrate the level of interest, 50 UVF and RHC members showed up on a Saturday afternoon in the Northern Ireland Supporters Club on the Shankill Road in October 2009. 70 members of the RHC attended the talk at the Somme Heritage Centre in May 2010. At the other talks, in smaller venues, the average attendance was 25 people, with two of those talks including members of Sinn Féin, and former Provisional IRA (PIRA) and Official IRA (OIRA) members. Then, on 1 March 2012, an event took place at the Spectrum Auditorium on the Shankill Road dealing with the Loyalist prison experience, in which I gave a talk and participated in a panel discussion with the audience. Between the afternoon and evening sessions, 380-plus people attended.

At all the meetings and talks, those who came exhibited a keen interest and desire to learn their own history and what came out of their organisations. For many, it was the first time they had ever heard this history and for others it was the first time they heard anything positive about themselves and their organisations. Now, I do not intend this work to build self-esteem, but the reaction after each of the meetings indicates that there is a great desire to not just learn from this history, but also use it in a productive and constructive way.

It is also important to note that this book can only accomplish so much. I necessarily focused on one wing of Loyalism because of the constraints I operated under due to my work situation. Some of the UDA documents, *Beyond the Religious Divide*,[3] *Common Sense*[4] and its Constitutional Proposals,[5] point towards a necessary reappraisal of the UDA's political evolution; work that I will necessarily leave to future researchers. Time constraints also meant that I could not spend the many hours in the National Archives at Kew Gardens and the Public Records Office of Northern Ireland (PRONI) necessary to verify every claim of those I interviewed, the 'facts' found in the documents, or the preliminary conclusions that arose during my analysis.

This book seeks to answer as many questions as possible, as best it can, based on the interviews with those who were involved in the political thinking of this period, interviews conducted by others, the documents found in the Linen Hall Library, the newspaper archives in Belfast, and in various published and unpublished studies. These answers and conclusions will, in some cases, be incomplete. Finally, this book does not seek to be the definitive study of political Loyalism and its evolution. Rather, its goal is to open the door for the next generation of students and scholars to walk through and begin the serious study of this movement in all its manifestations to prove, disprove, or build on the arguments in this book.

## NOTES FOR THIS MANUSCRIPT

A few technical issues warrant comment here to make sure that there is no confusion in the reading of the text.

Throughout the text, unless otherwise noted, when referring to the IRA, the reference is to the Provisional IRA. When talking about both, I will use 'PIRA' to distinguish it from the 'OIRA'. When quoting, I left it as it appeared in the original source.

I will use 'Northern Ireland' instead of the 'North of Ireland', or the 'Six Counties', which nationalists and republicans would tend to use, as it is the legal political entity.

Being aware of the controversy over its name, I have chosen to use the designation of Derry/Londonderry when writing about the city in the manuscript. If using direct quotes, I left it as it was in the original quote.

In cases where I quote extensively from one specific document, speech or interview, I generally put the endnote at the end of the paragraph in which those quotes appear.

When anyone I interviewed requested anonymity, I respected their wish, but I note this when quoting those individuals in the text and the endnote.

Throughout the text, I use the term 'volunteers' for both Loyalists and Republicans. I do not use this as a 'value' judgement, but use it to reflect the terminology Republicans and Loyalists use and the way in which these men see themselves.

At times, I will relate anecdotes that are from informal conversations. While not normally proper in this type of work, I included them as they flesh out the larger narrative here.

When this study uses the term 'Unionists', it is for the most part referring to those who support the maintenance of the union with

Britain though constitutional, legal and political means. More importantly, 'Unionism' in the context of this study refers mainly to those politicians who controlled the Northern Ireland state from partition in 1921 and came mainly from the middle and upper classes. Gradations exist within unionism, but this will tend to hold for this study. In contrast, when using the terms 'Loyalists' or 'Loyalism', this refers to those who took up arms to defend the union with Britain. They were and still are 100 per cent working class.

There are always problems in works of this type concerning when loyalist, unionist, republican, nationalist should be capitalised. When dealing with unionism and Loyalism I have opted to capitalise 'Unionist' whenever it refers to the elites and middle classes, and to differentiate it from the Protestant working class, i.e. 'Loyalists.' I have kept the original format when quoting from a source. I have capitalised 'Republicanism' when it refers directly to the IRA and Sinn Féin and left it in lower cases when referring to republicanism as an ideology. When dealing with 'Loyalism' I have opted to capitalise it when referring directly to the UVF, RHC and its political allies, but to put it in lower case when referring to the loyalist working class community as a whole.

When talking about the UVF and RHC, the study takes into account that there is only one UVF and one RHC. There are factions and tendencies in both organisations, but when discussing both groups, this work acknowledges that all the actions, the violence and the killings as well as the politics emerged from the same organisations and from many of the same men within these organisations.

# Introduction

> I would say that the [Loyalist] experience is, loved, hated, slapped, hugged. Loyalism
> [is] much maligned and much misunderstood ... it suited people to keep Loyalism
> down, manipulate Loyalism, control Loyalism, demonise Loyalism and hang crimes
> of the century on Loyalism. But no recognition of progressive thinking.
>
> Dawn Purvis[1]

The 'accepted wisdom' concerning the 'peace process' in Northern
Ireland posits that the Irish Republican Army (IRA), Sinn Féin
and the 'pan-Nationalist Front' (Irish-America, Bill Clinton, The
Republic of Ireland, the Social Democratic Labour Party [SDLP] and
even the Pope) created and/or drove the peace process in Northern
Ireland. In effect, their efforts and their efforts alone led to the
ceasefires, the Good Friday Agreement (GFA) and eventual power
sharing in Northern Ireland. This is the thesis of Tim Pat Coogan's
*The Troubles*,[2] Ed Moloney's *The Secret History of the IRA*[3] and
much of the analysis that has appeared in the press and journals
since the 1994 ceasefires and subsequent peace talks.

This narrative has taken on many forms. In one iteration, Gerry
Adams and Martin McGuinness led the Provisionals and the
Republican movement to another phase of the struggle and one
step closer to a United Ireland.[4] Another focuses on John Hume's
engagement with Gerry Adams, which brought the IRA away from
violence and on to the political path.[5] More recently, Ed Moloney
argues that Adams and McGuinness cynically moved the IRA onto
ceasefire in 1994 and the political path, realising that they had
arrived at a stalemate and that a compromise solution was now
the only way forward.[6]

There is some truth in each of these narratives and there is no
doubt that the IRA had travelled a long road from 1969 to power
sharing in 2007. Jim Gibney's Bodenstown oration on 2 June 1992
clearly illustrated this fact.[7] Gibney acknowledged that evolutionary
processes had taken place in Republican thinking over the previous
ten years and that Republicans recognised that the world had
changed since the conflict began in 1969. Furthermore, his statement
made clear that by 1992, the IRA came to realise that one of the
most pressing issues the IRA faced was the need for peace.[8] In a

departure from Republican orthodoxy, he clearly stated that the IRA was now prepared to accept all-party negotiations to end the conflict. Gibney said,

> We know and accept that the British government's departure must be preceded by a sustained period of peace and will arise out of negotiations. We know and accept that such negotiations will involve the different shades of Irish nationalism, and Irish unionism engaging the British government either together or separately to secure an all-embracing and durable peace process. We know and accept that this is not 1921 and that at this stage we don't represent a government in waiting.[9]

With this statement, the IRA had publicly stated that it was prepared to negotiate a peace that fell far short of its goals. More importantly, in a departure with its proclaimed link to the 1918 Dáil as the basis for its legitimacy to lead and rule the Irish nation, the IRA clearly stated that it did not expect to become the state once the British left Ireland. This was a momentous shift.

Observing the development of the peace process that began with Gibney's speech, many writers have accepted that the Republicanism was light years ahead of Loyalism in its political thinking. Citing Chris Farrington's work *Ulster Unionism and the Northern Ireland Peace Process*,[10] Catherine O'Donnell argues,

> For Republicanism it is clear that the starting point for change preceded the peace process and indeed facilitated it. For loyalism and unionism the peace process necessitated change and reassessment.[11]

Farrington and O'Donnell argue correctly that Republicanism, as Gibney had stated, experienced a long period of internal evolution and growth, eventually leading Republicans, or at least their leadership, to the realisation that negotiation and compromise rather than violence would lead to peace and their goal of a united Ireland. According to this narrative, Republicanism led the way in political thinking while Unionism/Loyalism was always 'reactive' and 'behind' the thinking of Republicanism.

While giving the IRA and the Republican movement its due in pushing forward the peace process that led to the ceasefires in 1994, the GFA in 1998 and the power-sharing executive of 2007, this is but one story of paramilitaries moving towards a negotiated peace and trying to lead from the front. Almost unknown and nearly lost in the history of the conflict is what the leading elements within Loyalism, i.e. the Protestant working class, as exemplified by the UVF, the RHC and their political allies, tried to do politically in the 1970s and the 1980s to end the conflict in a compromise peace.[12]

Unlike Republicanism, very little writing exists on Loyalism in this period. Consequently, we know very little about the history of Loyalism and next to nothing about the progressive political thinking it developed in the 1970s. The works that do exist usually reinforce the stereotypes of Loyalists as unthinking, mindless thugs who never had a political thought. Biographies such as *Mad Dog: The Rise and Fall of Johnny Adair and 'C' Company*[13] and *None Shall Divide Us*[14] are prime examples. In particular, Adair's biography validates the negative image of Loyalism and Loyalists. In the introduction to his book, *The State of Loyalism in Northern Ireland*,[15] Graham Spencer referenced the 'hard man' image of Johnny Adair on the front cover of Adair's biography to illustrate our popular perception of the typical Loyalist as nothing more than a pathological gangster.[16] This image tends to hold in most people's minds and the paramilitaries themselves know this. In fact, one Loyalist stated,

> I think the majority of them [Loyalists] are perceived as being thick-headed, knuckles dragging on the ground, long side-burns, dark glasses; you know these are the stereotypes of a gangster hoodlum.[17]

Not all studies perpetuate this stereotype. Much work, mainly academic, has recently appeared examining Loyalism since the ceasefires. In particular, Graham Spencer's *The State of Loyalism in Northern Ireland* examines the development of Loyalist thinking and politics in the 1980s and 1990s, as well as the role this evolution played in the Loyalist contribution to the present peace process. Carolyn Gallaher's *After the Peace* is another valuable study that examines the differing approaches to politics exhibited by the UDA and the UVF.[18] Peter Shirlow's continuing work on all aspects of Loyalism and Loyalist identity is also a welcome addition to the discussion. In particular, his work with Mark McGovern on the edited volume *Who are the People'? Unionism, Protestantism and Loyalism in Northern Ireland*,[19] and Shirlow's *Beyond the Wire: Former Prisoners and Conflict Transformation in Northern Ireland*[20] are important in re-examining the Loyalist experience and evolution. James McAuley's work is also outstanding in this area. Besides publishing a great many articles on Loyalism,[21] his work with Tonge, Shirlow and Catherine McGlynn in *Abandoning Historical Conflict?: Former Political Prisoners and Reconciliation in Northern Ireland*[22] is crucial to understanding Loyalism and moving beyond the accepted stereotypes.

However, as much as these writers have worked to dispel the traditional stereotypes of Loyalism, the legacies of the propaganda put out by Republicans and the British, and the use of Loyalists by the British Army and the Police to do their 'dirty' work, continues to resonate in the popular mind today. Furthermore, the popular press and books such as Stone's and the one on Adair reinforce the stereotype. One personal example of this perception makes this point clearly. In a June 2007 conversation with a moderate nationalist, I explained that this project focused on the evolution of Loyalist political thinking in the 1970s. This person immediately responded: 'Do they think?'[23]

Furthermore, the violence carried out by the UVF and the RHC that resulted in the deaths of 555 people during the conflict provides ample evidence to validate this negative perception.[24] The ruthlessness that these groups are still capable of was on display again in May 2010, when the UVF carried out a particularly vicious killing on the Shankill Road on a busy Friday afternoon, and its role in the riots that took place in June 2011 around the Short Strand area of East Belfast. Regardless of any positive work done by Loyalism in any period, this killing and the 2011 violence reinforced all the negative stereotypes people have of Loyalism[25] while validating the notion that it is an 'idiocy that has lost both memory and meaning'.[26]

Some of these stereotypes do contain a kernel of truth and there is truth in the negative arguments of those cited above. One simply cannot deny the terrible violence these groups carried out against innocent civilians. This study does not ignore or downplay the violent actions and nature of the UVF and the RHC, the killing of innocent Catholics and the sectarian nature of many of their attacks; in particular, those that took place between 1975 and 1977. One need only recall the horrible atrocities, such as the bombing of McGurk's Bar in 1971, where the UVF killed 15 innocent people,[27] the horrific torture killings carried out by the Shankill Butchers[28] and the vicious attack on the Miami Showband in 1975, to name but a few, as evidence of the brutal violence carried out by these organisations.[29]

As Dawn Purvis made clear at the start of this chapter, Unionism, those Protestants, mainly middle to upper class, who want to maintain the Union through legal and constitutional means, also reinforces the marginalisation of Loyalism. For many of these middle- and upper-class Unionists, Loyalists were and still are an embarrassment and not worthy of study or serious consideration because of their involvement in violence. In fact, James McAuley points out that one leading Loyalist thinker, David Ervine, argued that 'loyalism was only defined [by Unionism] when as a result of mounting violence other unionists initiated a process of ideological and political separation from the Protestant working class.'[30]

Some Loyalists consider this ironic. They argue that many of these 'respectable' people allegedly had no problem cooperating with or using Loyalism when it served their purposes. Tom Roberts, a former UVF prisoner and now director of the Ex-Prisoners Interpretive Centre (EPIC), the UVF's ex-prisoners' association, illustrated the resentment many former Loyalists still harbour toward Unionism for their perceived duplicity in the violence and their dismissive and disdainful attitude towards Loyalism. Roberts claims, '[t]here is also a lot of hypocrisy amongst middle-class Unionists who were quite happy for Loyalist paramilitaries to be carrying out violence' and had no problem urging Loyalism to do what it did during the conflict.[31] While one could argue that this is nothing more than idle speculation or a rationalisation by disillusioned former prisoners, the analysis of the UVF's founding in Chapter 1 makes clear that there is validity to both these claims.

Scholarly works, such as Steve Bruce's reinforces the negative image of Loyalism. In fact, he characterises Loyalist political thinking as *The Dismal Vision*.[32] Bruce downplays the political thinking and changes taking place within the UVF leadership in the period under study, dismisses it and relegates it essentially to a side note[33] claiming,

> the actual content of UVF policies ... was of no great significance, because relatively little systematic thought went into formulating those positions and there was little or no consultation with members, most of whom "didn't give a shit about the politics."[34]

He further argues that, 'A number of commentators whose knowledge of the UVF comes only from reading their published literature and their press statements have made the mistake of reading too much into them.'[35] In particular, he singles out Sarah Nelson and her seminal work in *Ulster's Uncertain Defenders*,[36] for criticism, claiming that she gave 'more attention to the political thinking of some UVF leaders than the UVF gave.'[37] Supporting Bruce's contention, one long-time observer of the Northern Ireland conflict once remarked to the author, in a private conversation, 'Loyalism always said the right things. But, always did the wrong things.'[38]

Jennifer Todd contends that Loyalism, by its very nature, was incapable of thinking politically, let alone developing political ideas that would result in a compromise peace. In a 1987 article, Todd argues,

> Ulster Loyalist ideology approximates a self-contained, closed system. The binary structure of thought – purity vs corruption, domination vs humiliation – does not allow for any gradual move towards compromise with or understanding of political opponents ... it follows that there can be no gradual change in Loyalism towards a more moderate or tolerant stance.[39]

Beyond dismissing political Loyalism as unworthy of study, the implication of Bruce's and Todd's writing, like that of O'Donnell's and Farrington's, is that the Provisional IRA (PIRA) was somehow better equipped to develop its political analysis and further ahead of Loyalism politically in this period. While that may be true after the rise of Sinn Féin as a political force in the 1980s, the reality in the 1970s and the 1980s was very different.

While the PIRA did have a tradition into which it could tap, an ideology of re-unification, it had little political thinking outside the *Éire Nua* document that Roy Johnston and Seán Ó Brádaigh worked on in the mid-1960s,[40] and Ruairí Ó Brádaigh and Dáithí Ó Conaill completed in August 1971. This document envisioned a federal Ireland with a decentralised structure and regional parliaments based on the historic four provinces of Ireland. The PIRA Army Council adopted it in 1971,[41] revised and republished it in 1979 (while distancing itself from this document),[42] then completely dropped it by 1981.[43]

In reality, not until the aftermath of the failed 1975 Ceasefire, when Gerry Adams, Martin McGuinness, Danny Morrison and others took control of the IRA, did the IRA begin to engage with political thinking and begin to accept the importance of politics in the Republican struggle.[44] Still the IRA stayed focused on total victory and did not acknowledge publicly that unification, if it came, would come about through politics and negotiation. That came with Gibney's Bodenstown oration in 1992.[45]

Beyond the lack of political thinking, like their counterparts in the Loyalist paramilitaries, many of the PIRA volunteers did not understand nor care about politics. In fact, a 1976 secret government document agreed with this analysis. When assessing the various paramilitary groups it stated, '[o]ne weakness of the Provisional IRA is that they want to get rid of the British and the government of the Republic but have very unclear ideas about what should follow.'[46] Roberts agrees with this analysis. Having had a great deal of contact with Republicans in and out of prison, Roberts argues,

> I know there is a lot of revisionism now in the Provisional movement, but in my view, 1969, [19]70, this was basically a sectarian war here. The Provos will try to tell you different. But, a lot of the nationalists that became involved in that conflict [in] 1969 to [19]70 hadn't a Republican notion in their head.[47]

Rogelio Alonso's 2006 work on the IRA supports Roberts' argument. After conducting interviews with 'seventy activists and former members of the IRA',[48] Alonso concludes that most of them had very hazy ideas about why they were fighting or their understanding of Republicanism.[49] In a telling story, he cites Anthony McIntyre's,[50] a leading Republican thinker, revelation about the level of his political understanding at the time of his arrest:

> An RUC man said to me "why are you a republican?" I said to "unite Ireland?" He said "kid, why do you want to unite Ireland?" I just stopped talking and I realised then... . I didn't know why I wanted a united Ireland.[51]

Beyond the difficulties in their own political thinking and evolution, the Provisional Movement 'wouldn't deal with the Protestant people because they were deluded Irishmen anyway', who would 'waken up some morning and realise they were Irish.'[52] In fact, according to Cusack and McDonald, for Republicans, 'Loyalists don't really exist'; they are nothing more than puppets of Unionism or the British state and are not independent actors.[53] At the same time, many Republicans view Loyalism 'as misguided, poorly led and self-seeking. Indeed it was noted [by Republicans] that anyone who supported the partition of Ireland could not be deemed to have radical politics.'[54] Shirlow, Tonge, McAuley and

McGlynn point out that this attitude continues to persist even today. They argue, 'IRA attitudes towards ... Loyalists, remains based on negative stereotyping'.[55]

The stereotypes of Loyalism served and continue to serve the purpose of reducing it to a two-dimensional caricature. By doing this, the British government, Republicanism, most 'respectable' society, and many writers could, did and do marginalise or ignore what Loyalism tried to do in political terms. Doing so enabled them to justify their attempts to push Loyalism back into the dark corner from whence they believed it came. So, while historians and commentators are justified in acknowledging the shift that eventually took the Provisional IRA towards politics and compromise, they marginalised or ignored and continue to ignore what took place within Loyalism in a much earlier period of the conflict.

Sarah Nelson has speculated as to why both the media and academia ignored the Volunteer Political Party (VPP), the political party the UVF created in 1974, and, by extension, any Loyalist political thinking. She argues, 'this is because they challenge popular centrist and left-wing stereotypes of Protestant Armed groups' and then stated that 'even in the land of the bogs, inconvenient facts do not disappear.'[56]

Dawn Purvis, former leader of the PUP and former Member of the Legislative Assembly, argues,

I think that story has yet to be told. And I get very angry and frustrated when ... people talk about Hume–Adams as the start of the peace process. I think that is wrong. I think there has been a process for many, many years, and it started ... with Gusty Spence and McKee and others ... in Long Kesh. That's where I believe that the roots of the peace process lie. And so that leadership and that inspiration coming from Gusty and, and what those people went through at that time, they were the founders of the peace process. They were the founders of the Good Friday Agreement.[57]

While taking into account all the criticism levelled at Loyalism, in particular the UVF and the RHC, especially Bruce's and Todd's, and even acknowledging some of Bruce's criticisms, this study agrees with Purvis' assertion. The unknown and untold story here is that it was working class loyalism; in particular, those political thinkers in the UVF and the RHC who tried to end the conflict in the 1970s and 1980s. It was these groups and their collaborators outside their organisations who, as early as 1973–74, began to develop political programmes and manifestos for ending the conflict by political means that involved compromise and encompassed all warring factions. They may have done it, as Bruce argues, with 'relatively little systematic thought',[58] and without mass support for their thinking. However, they did do it, and they did it in the early 1970s, much earlier than the Provisional IRA and despite Todd's assertion that they were incapable of doing it.

In this case, these Loyalists led and the PIRA followed. As we know from Gibney's speech, the PIRA had to go through its own long-term process of reassessment before it could compromise with Britain and Loyalism. Looking back at the development of the Peace Process, Dawn Purvis maintains,

That [in the prisons] was the convergence, if you like, of the working classes. Seeing that there was more that brought them together then what there was that divided them. I think there was a divergence of those groups. I think they grew apart. It was only through them converging again. In other words coming together again with Republicanism, that we, we got the peace process and the agreement that we have now.[59]

In essence, Loyalists, or at least the Loyalist leadership within the UVF and the RHC, did not simply react to Sinn Féin's and the IRA's political moves, they anticipated them. In fact, they embraced the politics of compromise many years before Sinn Féin and the IRA engaged with John Hume and accepted the need for political compromise. As Purvis argues, the convergence of Loyalist and Republican politics only took place in the 1990s when the IRA and Sinn Féin accepted that the conflict would end in a political compromise and not in a united Ireland. She further contends that,

In order to bring people together, to build [peace] ... that came from Loyalism. That came from working class communities that were *suffering* the most horrible violence and it was ignored by political leaders.[60]

For these reasons, an incomplete analysis of the conflict endures, one that reduces one side in the conflict to nothing more than, at worst, demons and, at best, two-dimensional stick figures. This leaves us with a skewed understanding of this period, one that ignores a much earlier political process that took place within Loyalism. This may suit political agendas, but it obscures the reality of what Loyalism tried to do politically in the 1970s and 1980s to create the foundation for peace in Northern Ireland. Furthermore, simply accepting the conventional wisdom of the peace process does a disservice to those who risked their lives to transform the conflict in Northern Ireland from a military one to a political one.

To address this incomplete and, at times, biased analysis, this study will build on the work of those authors, who have begun the serious study of Loyalism in all its complexity. While these authors, each in his/her own way examined political developments within Loyalism and how and why they began to develop politically, a full analysis of what the UVF, RHC and their allies in the VPP in 1974 and then the PUP (1977–present) tried to do to end the conflict does not exist. Yes, an analysis exists of what happened in Long Kesh, post-ceasefire developments, and what the UVF and RHC tried to do in the 1980s and afterward. In particular, Graham Spencer's work focuses on the origins and development of Loyalist political thinking in the 1980s and then its contribution to the current peace process. However, no analyst to this date has focused exclusively on the development of politics within the UVF and RHC, what their leaders wrote, what they attempted to do, and why they failed both in the 1970s and the 1980s.

Therefore, this study seeks to remedy this situation by not only studying where the thinking came from, but examining in detail the documents, speeches and manifestos that the RHC, the UVF and their allies published from 1973–87 as they sought a political way forward. This study also makes extensive use of interviews carried out with people who played a central role in the development of this political thinking and tried to move Loyalism towards a compromise peace.

It will end its analysis in 1987 when the PUP, the party that developed out of the UVF and the RHC in 1977, acting as part of the Unionist Task Force (Chapter 7), failed to convince the two main Unionist Parties to adopt voluntary power-sharing in Northern Ireland. With the failure of the Unionist Task Force, even though the PUP, the UVF and the RHC continued to engage with politics and, as Spencer clearly illustrated, make a positive contribution to the peace process, the political initiative shifted to a Republican driven peace process.

This work will also overlap with and act as a supplement – a 'prequel', if you will – to Graham Spencer's *The State of Loyalism in Northern Ireland*. By combining this study of political Loyalism in the period between 1973–87 with Spencer's work on political

Loyalism in the 1980s and 1990s, researchers will for the first time, have a comprehensive analysis of the political evolution of the UVF and the RHC that dates from the earliest days of the conflict to the GFA.

To accomplish this task, Chapters 1–3 rely heavily on synthesis, a number of secondary sources and analysis, and some primary documents and interviews, to understand where the thinking came from and how Loyalism began its journey. In these chapters, the study, as one commentator put it, will plough some 'fairly well-trodden ground'.[61] However, this is necessary because there is no work that brings all of this information and analysis into one study that is accessible to all. At the same time, without a clear understanding of the sources of the 'new' thinking and the various arguments concerning this thinking, then any analysis of the development of the political thinking and actions of the RHC, the UVF and their allies would make no sense.

While traveling this 'well-trodden ground', these chapters will approach their topics in a slightly unorthodox manner, beginning in 1965 in Chapter 1, but then stepping back to do a survey of Northern Ireland's history in Chapter 2. Chapter 1 will begin with a focus on the reconstitution of the UVF in 1965 and the possible role elements of the Unionist Party played in this episode. This will bring the issues of manipulation of the Protestant working class by the Unionist Party and the acquiescence of the Protestant working class in this manipulation to the forefront immediately in this study. It will then deal with the role the UVF played in destabilising Terrence O'Neill's, the Prime Minister of Northern Ireland, moderately reformist government, and the descent into violence by 1969. This chapter will also examine the creation of the RHC and focus on the UVF's reorganisation in this period and why, as a result of the violence, both the UVF and the RHC began to think and act politically outside the traditional lines of Unionism and how that put them on the path to political compromise.

Chapter 2 will then work backwards from Chapter 1 laying out a brief history of how the Unionist Party, which represented the Unionist elite, the landowners and the industrialists, consolidated and maintained its power in Northern Ireland after partition. Through brief case studies, it will show how the Unionist elites maintained their control over working class Protestants through the same process of manipulation and acquiescence that brought the UVF and eventually the RHC into existence in 1965 and 1970, respectively. Finally, using personal testimony, this chapter illustrates how some within the UVF, the RHC and the Protestant working class began to examine their manipulation and acquiescence and how that led to the political awakening within loyalism and its split with traditional Unionism.

Chapter 3 covers ground that is very familiar to all who have studied Loyalism. Using interviews and pulling together secondary-source analysis, this Chapter will also show how Spence succeeded in creating the educated, political cadre in the UVF and RHC within Long Kesh, but failed to get the Provisional IRA to engage in a meaningful way with Loyalism in seeking a way to end the conflict.

Once this foundation is laid then Chapters 4 through 7 proceed with an in-depth and textual analysis of the RHC, UVF, VPP and PUP documents, tracing their political evolution beginning in 1973 and ending in 1987. As mentioned earlier, this was when the leaders of the two main Unionist parties rejected their ideas for 'sharing power', or in their term 'sharing responsibility', in the 1987 Unionist Task Force report, the last significant proposal to emerge from both Unionism and Loyalism before the peace process became associated with Republicans. The interviews, in particular, will play a very significant role throughout these chapters, supplementing the primary documents and some of the secondary analysis.

These chapters not only enrich our knowledge of Loyalism, but also shatter some of what we think we know about Loyalism, what it tried to do and why it failed. What these chapters will demonstrate is how elements of the RHC, UVF and their allies had already realised the conflict had reached a stalemate. They realised that no one could win and that the only way to end the conflict was through the politics of compromise that encompassed all those involved, including the paramilitaries of all sides. Finally, these chapters lay out clearly the sophisticated political thinking developed by these men in terms of finding a political accommodation that would take into account the hopes and desires of everyone in Northern Ireland.

The evidence in these chapters refutes the contention that the IRA always led and the Loyalists followed, while calling into question and challenging a whole set of assumptions and certainties that many take for truth about Loyalism, the nature of the conflict, the peace process and why it took so long to end this conflict. This will force analysts to rethink and reconsider Loyalism's role in the conflict in terms of politics, and that the image of a 'knuckle dragging Neanderthal', the 'dupe of British Imperialism', or those who never had an original political thought; is no longer tenable when talking about all of Loyalism and all Loyalists.

Finally, this study clearly establishes that this was a 'lost opportunity' for not just peace, but also for the Protestant working class community to find its own voice and put forward its own clear vision for a political settlement and the future of Northern Ireland. The political leaders of Loyalism, as represented by the political thinkers in the UVF, the RHC and their supporters, who arose against all odds from the Protestant working class, had pointed the way and tried to lead the way forward to a better life for all in Northern Ireland. However, as this study will also show, they were too far ahead of the IRA, Unionism, and even their own organisations and community in their thinking, and many obstacles, historical circumstances and deliberate roadblocks stood in their way. The result was 20 more years of conflict, death and destruction, as well as the lingering pain, hurt and hatred, the marginalisation of the Protestant working class and the near silencing of its political voice.[62]

# 1

# The Ulster Volunteer Force and O'Neill

In 2007, a Republican mural on the Whiterock Road in Belfast read, 'Collusion is not an Illusion'. The mural displayed a gun with the inscription 'Authorised by MI5' [Military Intelligence – Section Five], and with the words 'APPROVED, On Behalf of her Majesty's Government' stamped on it. The gun hovers over a shrouded body lying on the ground with crosses, marking the many years of the conflict, near the foot of the body. For even greater impact, the mural has a quote attributed to Gusty Spence, one of the first UVF members to be convicted of murder in 1966 as a result of the Malvern Street killing, and the acknowledged icon within Loyalism.[1] This quote is in white letters on a black background that reads, 'An element of the UVF were covertly enlisted by the Ulster government at a fee of 10 shillings a day to promote a sectarian war'. For Republicans, the use of Spence's quote proves beyond doubt that collusion existed amongst the British government, the security forces and the Loyalist paramilitaries during the modern conflict.

Although those who painted this mural intended to prove collusion between the security forces and the Loyalist paramilitaries in the modern era, in particular the 1980s, the quote from Gusty Spence does not fit collusion in the way the artist/s had intended. On one level, it does not fit as this quote seems to be lifted from Roy Garland's biography of Spence and words added to point to British state collusion with Loyalists in sectarian killings, when in fact, in the original quote, Spence was actually talking about the 1935 sectarian riots in Belfast.[2] Beyond this, accepting that these were really Spence's words and they applied to the collusion of the modern era, this mural and the way the artist/s use it actually points to something very different and, in some ways, much more sinister than the collusion to which they are referring. Unintentionally, this mural actually hints at the much talked about, but never proved, relationship between extremist, dissident elements of the ruling Unionist Party in the 1960s and the formation of the UVF in 1965.

When examining this mural as painted, one problem confronts the viewer immediately. After March 1972, the Ulster government no longer existed. In reality, if applied to the modern conflict, what Spence would really be referring to here is the belief that in 1965 elements within the Unionist Party created and used the UVF to start a sectarian war to bring down the government of Terence O'Neill. This is clear from Spence's own words. In separate interviews with Peter Taylor and Roy Garland, Spence claimed that members of the Unionist Party, in an effort to undercut O'Neill, prevented reform in Northern Ireland and, to meet a perceived threat from a new IRA plot, formed or at the least facilitated the formation of the modern UVF.[3] Thus, the message of this mural points to something very different from the 'collusion' meant by the artist.

Although it does not intend to, what this mural does do is point to the elements within Unionism who were willing to start a sectarian war to get rid of O'Neill. They viewed him as weak on the border and prepared to compromise with the enemy, which thus threatened the survival of Ulster. Boulton cites one event in particular that reinforced that belief among some unionists. He argues that,

> The single event which both symbolised O'Neill's revised version of Unionism and highlighted the discontent of traditional Unionists was the visit to Belfast of the prime minister of the Irish Republic, Sean Lemass in January 1965.[4]

This visit led to the famous incident in which the Rev. Ian Paisley and his supporters threw snowballs at Lemass' car.[5] At the time, Paisley, who characterised O'Neill as a bridge, because, as he said, 'A bridge and a traitor both go over to the other side',[6] mobilised protesters 'outside the Stormont parliament with placards declaring, 'No Mass! No Lemass!', 'Down with Lundy's' and 'IRA Murderer Welcomed at Stormont'.[7] These actors then banded together to bring O'Neill down.

## 1965–66: THE UVF AND THE UPV

Talking to Garland about the impact of Lemass' visit in 1965, Spence said,

> As a result there was an uproar in Unionism. Members of O'Neill's own party set up the UVF, a clandestine organization that would commit violent acts to put pressure on the Prime Minister. O'Neill would be removed and someone more amenable to this group's thinking would be put in place.[8]

In another interview with Garland, Spence went further, claiming,

> The U.V.F. was not reconstituted because of a threat from the I.R.A. There might have been – there probably always was an implied threat from the I.R.A. – but I believe it was reconstituted in order to oppose or to be used as a bargaining counter against some of the things which O'Neill had brought out into debate.[9]

While Spence has no doubts about the role that members of the Unionist Party played in creating the UVF and undercutting O'Neill, there is no consensus among those who have studied this period of Northern Ireland's history. However, after examination of the evidence presented below, and set against the backdrop of a unionist fear of a resurgent IRA, rapprochement with the Republic, Unionist Party rivalries, and the fear that O'Neill was too soft on republicanism and nationalism, this study accepts Spence's argument as the one that best explains the creation of the modern UVF.

In his 1973 work on the UVF, David Boulton chronicles the political and social tension extant in this period, tension that he argues Paisley and Lord Carson's son Edward fuelled. However, he does not link this to the conflict within the Unionist Party.[10] The fact that he wrote his book in 1973 may explain why he does not make that claim. At this time, the 'war' was on, and the UVF was just beginning to think politically and trying to break away from 'official' Unionism. However, Boulton does claim that the 'UVF was formed in March (1966) and that the 'leading spirit of the Shankill was thirty-three year old Gusty Spence'.[11]

While Cusack and McDonald claim that, 'Several leading Unionists were clearly fomenting opposition to O'Neill', they argue that there was no one 'pulling the strings' of the UVF.[12] Still, even their work hints at how the UVF was useful to Unionist politicians, citing the fact that a Unionist politician attended the swearing in of Spence and others in Pomeroy.[13]

Meanwhile, Steve Bruce argues that there is no real link between the creation of the UVF and the Unionist Party. He states clearly 'If it [the claim that members of the Unionist Party participated in setting up the UVF] means top party officials or members of the Stormont parliament, then it's unlikely to be true.'[14] Bruce goes further and speculates on the 'likely candidates' from the government and Unionism. In the end, he claims, 'they [the UVF] were essentially a self-recruiting, working class movement'.[15]

Ian Wood writes, 'It is likely that encouragement to men like Gusty Spence came from dissident elements from within the Ulster Unionist Party, though he has never been prepared to name them.'[16] Dawn Purvis contends, 'People sometimes wrongly accuse Gusty of starting the Troubles. Gusty didn't form the UVF in 1966. He was recruited into it ... by Unionist politicians.'[17] In an interview with Henry Sinnerton, Spence claimed that,

> I myself joined the Ulster Volunteer Force because there were certain unionists who reconstituted the UVF ... I was assured that all types of things were going to happen to Northern Ireland. Republicans were going to do this and do that and do the other. Little did I know that I was only a pawn.[18]

Spence elaborated on this in his interviews with Peter Taylor. When questioned about joining the UVF, Spence told Taylor that he 'was approached by two unionist politicians, whom he refused to name, who invited him to join the UVF.'[19] Spence also told Garland that he 'is convinced that some Unionists ... engineered the 'plot' [to overthrow O'Neill] including the formation of the UVF.'[20]

In a 1990 interview Spence told Chris Moore that the 'UVF was not established because of any threat from the IRA', but was 'organised as part of the right-wing unionist opposition to the liberal thinking of Prime Minister O'Neill.'[21] Spence recalled that after his arrest the police kept asking about 'a plot or a coup d'état'.[22] This puzzled Spence as he knew that the only possible coup could come from an 'internal plot within the Unionist Party to get rid of O'Neill.'[23]

The 2002 PUP policy document, *Principles of Loyalism*, clearly states that the founding of the UVF was part of the larger struggle within the Unionist Party. The PUP argues that, 'The UVF was reformed again in 1965 by concerned members of the Ulster Unionist Party (UUP) who opposed the liberalism of Terence O'Neill, then Prime Minister of Northern Ireland.'[24] These 'concerned members' wanted to stop,

> the liberalising policies of the Prime Minister of Northern Ireland, Captain Terence O'Neill. There were elements within the Ulster Unionist Party – indeed within the Government – that wanted to undermine O'Neill and frustrate what they regarded as his programme of appeasement.[25]

Billy Hutchinson, who was very close to Spence, also believes that 'dissident members [of the Unionist Party] sought to undermine the liberal regime of O'Neill',[26] and that they used Spence and others to do their dirty work and then put them into prison to keep them quiet. When asked about whether he knew who those dissident members were, Hutchinson replied, 'Well, it's someone I don't want to name because it actually could be libel.'[27] Nevertheless, he did claim that,

> Spence was used quite a bit by Unionism to actually undermine what was going on. And I think that was evident by the arrests that were made after the Peter Ward murders in [19]66, and the arrest of Gusty and other people from West Belfast ... . So, from that point of view ... people within Unionism weren't happy with what was going on and they used working class people to actually try to overturn O'Neill and they did.[28]

Once in prison and with time to reflect, Spence saw himself caught between the conspirators and O'Neill. Looking back on his arrest and conviction, Spence believes that,

> Terence O'Neill and his government had to show the conspirators that they were the bosses. And whatever minions, and I was a minion, came into their path would be steamrolled, just as simple as that. I was a football between the conspirators and the government.[29]

In 1990, Spence told Chris Moore that he was 'used as a pawn in a political game.'[30] Hutchinson too believes that a conspiracy existed and that elements of the Unionist Party used Spence for their own purposes. Then once Spence was of no more use to them, the Unionist politicians discarded him.

Billy Mitchell, a key thinker and leader in the UVF from the early 1970s and the man who wrote *Principles of Loyalism*, supports both Hutchinson's and Spence's arguments, again without naming anyone. In an interview with Kate Fearon, Mitchell stated,

> The ones who encouraged the formation of the Loyalist paramilitaries didn't officer it. They just said 'we need to defend Ulster' but they left it in the hands of lorry drivers, labourers and brickies.[31]

Ed Moloney and Hugh Jordan may have come closest in pointing out the close connection between the Ulster Unionist Party and the founding of the UVF. Moloney examines a group known as the Ulster Protestant Action (UPA), founded in 1956 in response to the IRA's Border Campaign. He points out that this association was working class in its social makeup and virulently anti-Catholic.[32] It also opposed any compromise with nationalism or Catholicism. As time went on, it attacked the Brookeborough government as too weak on the border and in dealing with the Catholic population. The UPA then began to fight elections against the Unionist Party.[33] However, a split took place within the UPA in 1962 and 'the bulk of the UPA's leadership on the Shankill – McQuade, Bickerstaff, Billy Spence and Billy Elliot – joined the Unionist Party.'[34] This fact is important.

Moloney argues that Billy Spence, Gusty Spence's older brother, now in the Unionist Party and the election agent for Unionist Party Politician Jim Kilfedder, and other former UPA men, created the modern UVF to 'resist O'Neill and the IRA' to 'mislead authorities into thinking that bombings and gun attacks carried out by the UVF were really the IRA's work.'[35] If Moloney is correct, then people like Billy Spence, the UPA men and their allies would be those who could have actively recruited Gusty Spence into the movement. This took place in a period of rising Loyalist violence fomented by Paisley and such 'Loyalist unrest would also be used against O'Neill by conspirators within his own cabinet.'[36] Like Boulton, Moloney claims this occurred in 1966, not 1965.

Hugh Jordan's 2002 work *Milestones in Murder*[37] posits something very similar and provides strong support for both Moloney's thesis and Spence's claim. Like Moloney and Spence, he argues that someone or some groups created the UVF 'as part of the opposition to O'Neill.'[38] Jordan claims that the Royal Ulster Constabulary (RUC) Special Branch believed that those in the Unionist Party who opposed O'Neill were the ones who formed the UVF and recruited men into it.[39] The Special Branch had its suspicions about a number of Unionist politicians who might have been involved in this. Jordan claims that one of those under suspicion was Jim Kilfedder. Accepting Moloney's argument, this would make sense. Jordan believes that the evidence gathered by the Special Branch 'indicated Kilfedder had tutored Spence and others on how to handle police interrogation.'[40] Furthermore, in 1964, men who eventually joined the UVF (at the time they would have been in the UPA) campaigned for Kilfedder. Jordan concludes that the 'links between sections of the Ulster Unionist Party and the emerging paramilitary group, the UVF, were very real indeed.'[41]

In January 2011, Spence's claim of his innocence in the Peter Ward killing on Malvern Street and his story received some validation. On 24 January 2011, The Belfast Telegraph published an article by Brian Rowan, who writes that Spence and his family have called into question his conviction with emergence of evidence supposedly proving his innocence. Rowan writes that within months of Spence's trial in 1966, someone sent a letter to the Home Office 'raising concerns specifically about the Spence guilty verdict'.[42] Spence has always maintained his innocence in the Malvern Street killing and in the article reiterated his claim of innocence stating, 'I never killed that young fella.'[43]

If Spence turns out to be innocent of this murder, then Hutchinson's and Spence's claims of cynical manipulation of Spence and others by dissident elements of the Unionist Party takes on much greater weight. It also conceivably shifts the 'blame' for the first sectarian killing in the modern era onto shadowy figures who, for their own reasons, stoked the fires of a sectarian war.

When examining the testimony of those who were involved in this period and the possible emerging evidence, and Moloney's work, one cannot ignore or dismiss Spence's claims. The Unionist Party elite's role in reorganising the UVF runs throughout the narrative of those in the paramilitaries at that time. Even taking into account their biases, one cannot dismiss their testimony. Like Spence, they believe that elements of official Unionism used them for their own purposes and created the modern sectarian war referenced on the wall in Ballymurphy.

Given the history of the relationship between 'Big House Unionism' and working class Loyalism (see Chapter 2), they would have good reason, as does this study, to believe this. After examining the various arguments, this study argues that the UVF did not simply arise in response to a Republican threat, but was part of the larger battle that was taking place within Unionism – a battle in which Unionism used Spence and the UVF not simply to battle a Republican threat, but as a weapon to bring down O'Neill.

Regardless of its origins, once the UVF reformed it took on its traditional role of defending Ulster against any attempt, either by O'Neill or by the IRA, to undermine the constitution of Northern Ireland. It immediately declared war on the IRA and its splinter groups, claiming, 'Known IRA men will be executed mercilessly and without hesitation'. The UVF also threatened less severe action against anyone 'sheltering and helping them'. Their statement concluded, 'We are heavily armed Protestants dedicated to this cause.'[44]

After this declaration of war, the new UVF carried out the first murder of the modern era when it accidentally killed a 77-year-old Protestant widow in a firebomb attack aimed at a Catholic bar. These men then killed an innocent Catholic on his way home to the Falls Road because they claim to have heard him singing Republican songs.[45] Their third victim was a young Catholic barman, Peter Ward, having a drink in a bar on Malvern Street on the Shankill.[46] He became the target once the UVF unit could not find its intended victim. The government reacted immediately, proscribing the UVF and arresting Spence and two others for the Malvern Street killing. In October 1966, a jury convicted all three of murder and sentenced them to life in prison.[47] Ulster would not hear from the UVF again until 1969. When it did re-emerge, the UVF did not take the fight to the IRA, but instead took the fight to O'Neill.

## 1966–69: CIVIL RIGHTS TO CIVIL WAR

Tom Hayden, former left-wing student leader in the 1960s and former California State Senator, once remarked, 'Rulers first fantasise their devils; then create them'.[48] Nowhere is this truth more evident than in Northern Ireland. In its efforts to undercut O'Neill, elements within mainstream Unionism created the spectre of an imminent armed uprising by a revitalised IRA bent on achieving a united Ireland. This then led to the creation of the UVF in 1965 and sectarian attacks on innocent Catholics. It also portrayed the civil rights movement as a front for the Republican assault on Northern Ireland's constitutional status, which, among other reasons examined below, prevented working class Protestants from joining the movement. This led to both physical and verbal attacks on the civil rights movement, which led to the sectarian violence of 1969, which, in turn, led to the creation of the Provisional IRA. In essence, the Unionist establishment believed that Northern Ireland faced an imminent Republican threat, which did not exist as they imagined it.

While accepting this is how Unionism saw the problem and how it responded to its perception of the threat, Brian Hanley's work, *The Lost Revolution: The Story of the Official IRA and the Workers Party*[49] provides a different view of the civil rights movement and the IRA's role in it. His argument demonstrates that Unionists got the civil rights movement partially correct, but also misread it badly, which caused them to draw the wrong conclusions and take provocative actions.

Hanley argues convincingly that the IRA in the 1960s had developed a 'revolutionary plan' to unite the working class in Northern Ireland. It sought to do this through political, not military, action in order to bring the illegitimate nature of the Unionist state into sharp relief, not just for Catholics but also for the Protestant working class. The IRA envisioned agitating on issues relevant to the working class of both communities with a focus on the injustices suffered by Catholics in the Northern Ireland state. At the same time, the IRA intended to create a mass movement in the Republic of Ireland based around a left-wing analysis and social agenda, and action that focused on employment, housing and worker's rights. Once it formed these mass, working class movements in the north and the south, then and only then would the armed uprising take place to create a 32 county Democratic Socialist Republic of all the people.[50]

In a 1972 speech in Dublin, Liam McMillen, one of the leaders of the then Official IRA (OIRA), explained the history and strategy of the IRA and its relationship with the civil rights movement. He made it clear that, although Republicans did not dominate the Civil Rights Association (CRA), the IRA played a key role in setting up the CRA and later the Northern Ireland Civil Rights Association (NICRA).[51] He also claims that the IRA instructed their members in the movement to create a situation where they could maximise the exposure of the injustices of the state. In particular, he pointed out how, on the civil rights march in Derry/Londonderry in 1968,

> Belfast Republicans had been instructed, in the event of the parade being halted by police cordons, to push leading Nationalist politicians or any other dignitaries who were sure to be at the head of the parade into the police ranks.[52]

On 5 October 1968, during the civil rights march in Derry/Londonderry, the RUC attacked the NICRA march, bloodying a number of prominent politicians in the assault and displaying the brutal reality of the politics and the nature of Unionist rule in Northern Ireland. From this point on, Northern Ireland lurched towards the violent conflict that broke out in August 1969. That same period led to the creation of the violent and, at the time, politically naïve Provisional IRA.

McMillen asserts that, 'It is very probable that had the marchers been permitted to proceed without interference that the CRA would have died a quiet and natural death that day.'[53] However, he also claims that the RUC Special Branch believed that the IRA would use the march to 'set Derry ablaze and create all sorts of havoc'.[54] This belief then led the RUC to overreact to the march and launch the vicious attack on the marchers on 5 October, a day many now date as the first day of the Troubles.

David Ervine supports the analysis of not just of Unionism's reaction to the civil rights movement, but also of the nature of the Northern Ireland state prior to the conflict. In an October 2004 video discussion with a group of University of Pittsburgh students he asked, 'Did stinking polluted politics come before paramilitarism?' He answered his own question saying, 'I think the answer to that is "Yes".'[55] Ervine went on to explain his view of how the failure of Unionism to reform itself led to both the Provisional IRA and the Loyalist paramilitaries:

> When you are a "freedom fighter", a "volunteer", a "terrorist", call it what you will, you have to have somewhere to come from. And in reality, the people, if you like, made the arguments in the seventies, in fact the sixties, about civil rights, was an opportunity for Unionism that Unionism refused to take. And what Unionism did was effectively tell those, who, perhaps, were less inclined to believe that Unionism could be a good partner in government or a good friend in society. They had confirmed for them that Northern Ireland was irreformable, when Unionism refused to give straightforward, legitimate rights to the Catholic population. That meant that someone who was not sure of Unionism's bona fides, had confirmed for them the need to fight against the state, which was irreformable. That was the growth of the ... Provisional IRA struggle. Similarly, the Loyalists, not having any responsibility or control over any of this find themselves being attacked or, the society they come from being attacked, and that gives them somewhere to come from.[56]

Tom Roberts agrees with Ervine's analysis. Roberts argues that, 'The right wing of Unionism prevented O'Neill from moving quickly enough to head off the civil rights movement from ultimately degenerating into violence.'[57] He believes that, with hindsight ... it was the reaction of right wing Unionism preventing O'Neill [from] making reforms quicker that would've headed off the civil rights movement and acceded to, ... with hindsight, were quite reasonable demands, one-man, one-vote, housing.[58]

Roberts continues, claiming that the 'IRA and Republican elements' feeding off the 'reaction of right wing Unionism ... ultimately fed people with the conclusion that you aren't going to be able to reform the Northern Ireland state.'[59] From this analysis, it is clear the IRA really played a much larger role in the civil rights movement than many had previously believed.[60]

In essence, hardline Unionist politicians like Bill Craig, Paisley and others, on the right wing of Unionism, got the civil rights partially right, even though they did not know that at the time. What they got wrong was what the long-term strategic goal of the Republican movement really was and how the IRA sought to achieve that goal.

Unionists examining the civil rights movement through their paranoid and right wing lenses regarded it simply as a Republican plot intended to destroy Northern Ireland and create a united Ireland. They never understood that their perception of the civil rights movement was too simplistic. Thus, they reacted according to their paranoid vision and stoked fears among the Protestant working class that they had to prepare themselves for war against the forces that wanted to bring down their state. Bobby Cosgrove, a trade unionist, former member of the Northern Ireland Labour Party (NILP) and present member of the PUP, remembers, 'We had the fear tactic being put in by the Unionist Party' to the point where some of these politicians believed that, 'even the Northern Ireland Labour Party were Republicans.'[61]

This fear led the state and the ordinary Protestants, egged on by extremist and at times apocalyptic rhetoric emanating from Unionist politicians, to react violently against the civil rights movement. Catholics who now saw the state as irreformable also reacted violently. In essence, the fear mongering and stoking of the sectarian flames by elements within the Unionist Party and people like Ian Paisley led to the violence of August 1969, which produced the conditions that then created the Provisional IRA. In this analysis, Unionism actually created the very 'devil' that it believed already existed.[62]

Despite the rising tensions in Northern Ireland, the UVF essentially lay dormant after the Malvern Street murder, its proscription and the convictions of Spence and his confederates. If elements within the Unionist Party had set up the UVF to undercut the O'Neill administration and replace him with a hardliner, they had failed miserably. O'Neill survived and under British pressure began to implement a programme of reform after the violence of 5 October 1968.

Sill there was one man who 'knew' that O'Neill was a traitor who was prepared to sell out Ulster, and believed it was his job to stop him – Ian Paisley. In 1966, in the face of what he believed was O'Neill's appeasement of Ulster's enemies,[63] Paisley set up the Ulster Constitution Defence Committee (UCDC); Noel Doherty, one of Paisley's disciples set up its paramilitary wing, the Ulster Protestant Volunteers (UPV). The goal of the UCDC was to 'by all lawful methods uphold and maintain the Constitution of Northern Ireland as an integral part of the United Kingdom.'[64]

However, Peter Taylor claims that the UCDC was 'little more than an umbrella for the ... Ulster Protestant Volunteers',[65] and the UPV would serve as the paramilitary wing to protect Ulster's constitutional position. Evidence for Taylor's accusation is the fact that the UPV began working closely with members of the UVF to arm themselves with both guns and bomb-making material in preparation for the coming conflict. In fact, Boulton argues that the UPV actually had the gelignite to give to the UVF.[66] However, before the UPV could carry out any real attacks, the police (RUC) arrested Doherty, who received two years in prison.

An interesting sidelight here that has relevance for later in this study is how Paisley treated Doherty. During the trial, Paisley disowned Doherty and expelled him from the UCDC. Bruce claims that Paisley acted in this manner because Doherty had violated the UCDC constitution, which on the surface is true.[67] Doherty himself believes that Paisley 'shunned him' and essentially left him on his own, ignoring him and ostracising him once the RUC arrested him.[68]

Loyalist paramilitaries from the UDA to the UVF and the RHC had similar experiences with Paisley, whom they eventually came to view as the 'Grand Old Duke of York'.[69] For them, the difference between the Duke of York and Paisley was that Paisley marched them up the hill and then left them there. These men now believe that Paisley and other politicians 'wound up' the people with slogans like 'Ulster will fight!' Then, when people took him literally, he disowned them. This treatment, knowledge and perception would eventually move the political thinkers within Loyalism to chart their own path without Paisley or any Unionist politicians.

By collaborating with elements of the UVF, in particular the Shankill UVF, the UPV intended 'to use explosives to imitate the IRA and hence dramatize the claim that O'Neillism would encourage physical force nationalism.'[70] Following the arrest and conviction of Doherty, that intended plan did not happen. The UVF did not act again until 1969 when it acted in collaboration with the UPV in a series of bombings. However, it did not bomb Republicans, but chose targets that would make it appear that the IRA carried out the attacks, proving that O'Neill and his policies would only lead to a new Republican campaign and a united Ireland.

## 1969: THE END OF O'NEILL

After the civil rights march in Derry/Londonderry in October 1968, O'Neill found himself and Northern Ireland in a 'crisis situation' or at a 'crossroads' as he put it in his famous 'Ulster at the Crossroads' speech of December 1969.[71] Also in December, O'Neill sacked Craig, his hardline cabinet minister who resisted any reforms, providing more fuel for those who believed O'Neill was too soft on nationalism. He then had to meet with British government officials who pushed him for fast and full reforms, while also facing the bellicose rhetoric of Ian Paisley and an Ulster Unionist Party that resisted his reforms.

Hemmed in on all sides, he appealed for calm, restraint and time to implement his reforms. However, marches and demonstrations continued to the end of 1968. Then, on 1 January 1969, a radical student group from Queen's University in Belfast, the People's Democracy, ignored his plea and embarked on a 'long march' from Belfast to Derry/Londonderry. This march ended in violence as off-duty B-Specials, the police auxiliaries, who most Catholics feared and hated, and members of the UPV attacked the marchers. When the injured marchers arrived in Derry/Londonderry and news spread of the attack, serious rioting engulfed the city.[72]

The year got no better for O'Neill. In an attempt to get a mandate for his rule and reforms, he called a general election. However, this backfired as he only defeated Paisley by approximately 1,400 votes: a humiliating result.[73] Even though O'Neill hung on until 28 April, and even passed one-man, one-vote on 23 April, the closeness of the election had weakened him considerably. For the right wing of the Unionist Party and many unionists who wanted rid of O'Neill, one more incident was all that they needed. That incident did not come politically, but rather in bomb attacks carried out by the UPV and UVF in April 1969.

On 30 March 1969, a series of bomb attacks began that lasted through 26 April. Everyone, including the police, believed that the IRA had carried out these bombings. The first attack took place at an electricity substation at Castlereagh, East Belfast. The bombs blacked out much of Belfast and resulted in £500,000 of damage. On 4 April, another bomb went off at a water installation at Dunadry, County Antrim, one of the main water supply lines to Belfast. Then, on the 20, 24 and 26 April three more bomb attacks occurred. In all three attacks, the bombers targeted water pipelines. This was the end. O'Neill resigned two days after the last attack; Sir Arthur Chichester-Clarke replaced him.[74]

Despite the widespread belief that the IRA carried out these attacks, two questions remain, who carried out the attacks and why? These questions and their answers thus bring the discussion of who set up UVF and why they set it up full circle. In reality, these bomb attacks had no other purpose than to remove O'Neill.

The UVF had essentially lain dormant since 1966. It now carried out bomb attacks, aimed not at the IRA, but at O'Neill and his policies of reform and compromise. In fact, Moloney argues that, 'The explosions were the culmination of Billy Spence's strategy of deception which he had devised back in 1966 and three years later it worked with devastating effect.'[75] Even the 1972 Scarman Report into the violence of 1969, concluded that,

> they were the work of Protestant extremists who were anxious to undermine confidence in the government of Captain O'Neill. At the time it was widely thought that the explosions were the work of the IRA, though it is quite clear now that they were not. On 28 April Captain O'Neill resigned and on 1 May was succeeded by Major Chichester Clark.[76]

This evidence clearly supports Spence's claims and those made by the others that the main purpose for creating the UVF was to undercut O'Neill and bring a hardline administration to power. In essence, dissident members of the Unionist Party, hardliners and 'conspirators within his [O'Neill] own cabinet'[77] opposed to concessions and compromise used the UVF to do their dirty work and rid Northern Ireland of O'Neill and 'O'Neillism'.[78]

This change in leadership solved nothing; in fact, it made things much worse. From this point onwards, Northern Ireland moved inexorably towards an armed conflict, which in the end, lasted 25 years and resulted in approximately 3,900 deaths. With no hope of compromise, many on both sides came to believe that violence was the only way to solve Ireland's or Ulster's problems.

## 1970: THE RED HAND COMMANDO

By August 1969, beginning with the 'Battle of the Bogside' and the sectarian rioting in Belfast, the crisis developed into a full-blown conflict. The violence accelerated and became more brutal from 1970 to 1972, when the PIRA launched its armed campaign to unite Ireland and the government and army over-reacted with internment and then the killings on Bloody Sunday.

Initially, the UVF found itself unprepared to strike back against the PIRA in this period. When examining the death tolls for those early years, we see that in 1969, the UVF was responsible for two deaths, one of those a police officer, then none in 1970. However, that changed in 1971 with the rising tide of violence, when the UVF and the RHC, a new Loyalist paramilitary group, killed 17 people. Then in 1972, 35 people died at the hands of the UVF/RHC. In the same period, the PIRA killed 18 people in 1970, 86 in 1971 and 235 in 1972.[79]

As one can see, Loyalist killing was a fraction of that of the PIRA in this period, but as it is clear from above, it did increase in relation to Republican violence. That is evident in tracking the number of killings in 1972. Even though the UVF played a role in the 1966 sectarian murders and in bringing down O'Neill, it played little role in the violence of 1971 and most of 1972, the infamous bombing of McGurk's bar, where the UVF killed 15 innocent people, being a notable and terrible exception. This changed dramatically after Bloody Friday in July 1972 when 22 IRA bombs killed ten people and injured 130 others. Prior to Bloody Friday the UVF and RHC had killed seven people in 1972. Then after this atrocity, the UVF and RHC accelerated their killing dramatically, murdering 28 people in the rest of 1972: mainly innocent Catholics.[80]

So, what had the Republican violence accomplished in this period? The PIRA did get into peace talks with the British government in 1972 that eventually failed. What they did accomplish was to strike fear and terror into the hearts of most Protestants. In 1975, W. H. Van Voris argued that, 'by that time [1972] the Provisional bombs and assassinations had stimulated the Ulster Defence Association' and 'it had begun gliding through darkened streets gunning down

Catholics.'[81] David Ervine words illustrated how some Protestants felt about IRA attacks. He said the IRA always told Protestants, '"We're not really fighting you." Well, we were dying. Our people were dying in fair size numbers, which wasn't bad for people who weren't fighting us.'[82]

Consequently, faced with attacks on their state and local communities, the disbanding of their beloved B-Specials (a force universally loathed by Catholics) and the perceived inability of the state to protect them, ordinary Protestants began to organise local defence associations, such as the Shankill Defence Association, Woodvale Defence Association and others. Many of these associations eventually coalesced into the UDA in the autumn of 1971. The RHC, another self-defence organisation, formed in 1970. Although small in comparison to the UVF and the UDA, the RHC played an important role in the violence and then eventually in trying to develop a plan for peace and power sharing in Northern Ireland.

Most sources date the founding of the RHC to 1972. However, according to one person involved in its founding, a number of men organised the RHC during the fierce violence that took place after a traditional parade by the Orange Order on 27 June 1970.[83] This was the day of the first 'sustained military action by the Provisional IRA', and involved the PIRA's first real action in defending St. Matthew's Catholic Church in the Short Strand.[84] When violence also broke out in Springfield and Ardoyne, a number of men called a meeting and formed what became the Red Hand Commando. The RHC linked up with Shankill Defence Association and John McKeague, who later became the leader of the RHC, and negotiated an alliance with the UVF on 15 July 1972.[85]

As these defence organisations formed in 1970 through 1972, except for the bombings of 1969, the UVF remained largely inactive and disorganised. The relatively few killings it carried out through the late autumn of 1971 illustrate this. The inactivity and the disorganisation also gave those, like Spence, the opportunity to reorganise the UVF and make it not just a disciplined paramilitary organisation, but also one that could develop politically and separately from the Unionist establishment.

## 1972: REORGANISATION OF THE UVF

In 1972, Northern Ireland nearly completed the task of tearing itself apart. In that one year, not counting all the other bombings and shootings, the following events took place: on what everyone now remembers as Bloody Sunday, the British Army shot dead 13 innocent Catholics on 30 January. In response to Bloody Sunday and other factors, Britain suspended the Stormont government and instituted Direct Rule of Northern Ireland from London, bringing an end to, in Spence's words '50 years of misrule'.[86] The PIRA set off a 'no-warning' bomb on 4 March at the Abercorn restaurant in Belfast, killing two and horrifically wounding over 100 people. 16 days later the PIRA killed six more people and wounded 100 others in another 'no-warning' bomb on Lower Donegal Street. The OIRA, the Marxist wing of the IRA that was the rump of the IRA after the PIRA split with them in 1969/1970, bombed the Aldershot base in England in February, killing seven innocent people. On the 25 May, the OIRA then killed a Catholic from the Creggan in Derry/ Londonderry, Ranger Best, who was home on leave from the British Army. On 23 April, 23 explosions took place all over Northern Ireland. However, as stated above, for the Protestant community the worst was yet to come on 'Bloody Friday', 21 July 1972. On that day, the PIRA set off 22 bombs in Belfast, killing ten and injuring 130 people.[87]

While most of this was taking place, Spence was in Crumlin Road Gaol fighting for political status, making contacts with the OIRA, trying to understand how the conflict started and how he ended up in prison. Then on the 1 July 1972, the authorities released him to attend his daughter's wedding. After Spence attended the wedding, the UVF 'abducted' him and he remained a 'captive' for four months. The UVF announced this kidnapping in *Orange Cross,* a Loyalist newspaper that dedicated itself to the welfare of Loyalist prisoners, on 29 July 1972.[88] Roy Garland covers this episode in depth in his book on Spence. For purposes of this study, the focus is on what Spence did and what the ramifications of his work were for the UVF and its eventual political evolution.

Once out of prison and in the hands of the UVF, Spence began the process of reorganising the UVF. He not only sought to restructure it along British military lines, he sought to bring, if not outright political thinking to it, at least thinking on social justice and taking care of the 'needs of the working class people.'[89]

Billy Hutchinson, one of Spence's bodyguards during this period, remembers that one of the things Spence first did was to create an oath that laid out the duties of a volunteer and how the volunteer had to behave as a representative of the UVF.[90] Spence then organised the UVF into companies and battalions across Northern Ireland and had the UVF adopt a uniform of leather jackets and army-style berets.[91] At the same time, he recognised that, if the UVF was to act in violation of the law, many of its members would end up in prison. Therefore, he set out to identify people who would raise money. These individuals would form a welfare organisation that would help take care of 'the families of prisoners and the families of dead volunteers.'[92] Spence envisioned that those working on prisoners' issues would act as non-combatants, and 'liaise between the UVF and families of those either incarcerated or dead volunteers.'[93] Finally, he negotiated an agreement with John McKeague that tied the UVF and RHC together, but allowed each organisation to maintain its own identity and structure.[94]

While reorganising the UVF militarily, Spence attempted to get the UVF to think in different ways. In a statement to *Orange Cross*, he made it clear that he and Loyalism were prepared to negotiate an end to the conflict. He wrote, 'It is our intention to work to secure a lasting and just solution to the morass in which we are now in.'[95]

During his period of 'captivity' Spence also became one of the first Loyalist leaders to question, not the legitimacy of the Northern Ireland state, but the 50 years of Unionist misrule. In an interview filmed while the UVF held him 'captive', Spence accused Unionist politicians of creating the problems not just for Catholics, but also the Protestant working class. He said,

> One has only to look at the Shankill Road, the heart of the empire that lies torn and bleeding. We have known squalor. I was born and reared in it. No one knows better than we do the meaning of slums, the meaning of deprivation, the meaning of suffering for what one believes in, whatever the ideology. In so far as people speak of fifty years of misrule, I wouldn't disagree with that. What I would say is this, that we have suffered every bit as much as the people of the Falls Road, or any other underprivileged quarter – in many cases, more so.[96]

Therefore, he said it was 'time the people, the small people, the have-nots' took control of their own destiny.[97]

Hutchinson, who had close contact with Spence in this period, believes that such political thinking was an integral part of Spence's reorganisation of the UVF. He argues that Spence encouraged those in the UVF to think politically and he mixed in political thinking with his military reorganisation. When questioned about this period Hutchinson remembers that,

He [Spence] also said "soldiers fight wars and politicians fight for the peace". That's what the UVF was. It would bring people to a certain point and the politicians would take over; and the UVF would need to have their own politicians ready.[98]

Spence also enunciated a new concern with social issues and the vision of the UVF working for the 'people'. Hutchinson claims,

In many ways it was a socialist view ... It was about looking after the community. That could mean doing something for the most vulnerable or the elderly ... if the elderly need coal we procured the coal and gave it to them rather than let them freeze. It was a whole new way of looking at society.[99]

This new emphasis on social and political issues often took practical forms. For example, the UVF borrowed the IRA's idea of the 'people's taxis' and set up a taxi service on the Shankill. The UVF claimed that it set up the taxi service because the UVF 'has a public conscience and a duty to the working people.'[100] There was a practical purpose as well, as the UVF could make money from the service. Hutchinson explains the taxi service as,

a service for the people which was being provided by the UVF. And the importance was that it was a proper service but at the same time you could make money but not by actually making it expensive for people, enough so you could make a living but so people could afford to use it.[101]

The UVF leadership and ordinary members of the UVF did not universally accept this thinking, particularly in the midst of the renewed PIRA campaign to unite Ireland. Boulton makes the point that even though Spence opposed sectarian killings and tried to put a stop to them, attacks and killings of innocent Catholics, continued and accelerated, culminating in 1975 when the UVF and RHC carried out approximately 100 killings.[102]

## CONCLUSION

Accepting that prominent Unionist politicians played a role in re-forming the UVF in 1965 makes it much easier to understand why the UVF behaved the way it did until Spence reorganised it in 1972. In 1966, it carried out the first sectarian killings of the modern era, killings that put pressure on O'Neill and highlighted the sectarian tensions that existed in Northern Ireland. Thus, it played a significant role in stoking the fires of a new sectarian war. In 1969, after a month-long bombing campaign in alliance with the UPV, its actions helped bring down the O'Neill government. The fact that it lay virtually dormant until the autumn of 1971 and did not take the lead in defending Loyalist communities in 1969, suggests a leaderless organisation without a focus or purpose. Only in 1972, during Spence's reorganisation of the UVF did a new focus, purpose and set of tactics appear At the same time, a new organisation, the RHC, formed for community self-defence in 1970 and then aligned itself with the UVF during the UVF's reorganisation in 1972.

Beyond understanding how and why the UVF reformed and how the RHC and the UDA came into existence, what is most important, for this study, is the fact that within the UVF and the RHC, working class leadership evolved out of the crisis of the 1966–72 period. This new leadership emerged when, to many ordinary Protestants, the state could no longer protect them nor Northern Ireland's position in the United Kingdom. Eventually, that realisation led them to challenge mainstream Unionism politically, while continuing their violence against the IRA and the Catholic population.

With the coming break with Unionism, the political thinkers within these organisations began to recognise that Unionist politicians did not represent their interests in social and political terms and that they had neglected the Protestant working class as much as they had oppressed the Catholic population. The new leadership that emerged from the RHC and the UVF began to develop its own social and political agenda, its own vision for Northern Ireland – a vision very different from that of the mainstream Unionism.

Therefore, not only did this new cadre of political thinkers in the UVF and the RHC provide leadership in defence of Protestant communities, these Loyalist leaders had begun, as Boulton described it, the 'voyage of self-discovery'.[103] They embarked on a new path that would eventually put them at odds with Unionist elites and would fracture and destroy the alliance that had existed within unionism from the founding of the state. Most importantly, this journey would force them to rethink and re-evaluate the entire history of the Northern Ireland state, the place of working class Protestants in that state and the terrible violence of this period.

# 2
# Manipulation, Acquiescence and Awakening

Unionism as it was and prior to the 1970s was Conservatism. It was Toryism in its raw state. It was the upper class, it was the academics, it was the landowners who controlled unionism. Unionism wasn't about the people. Unionism was about wealth and about control.

Bobby Cosgrove[1]

Oliver Wright, a former British official in Northern Ireland from 1969–70, once portrayed Northern Ireland as it had existed from partition until 1972, as 'a state of tyranny; a minor form of tyranny, not the Stalinist form of tyranny. But that was what the Stormont parliament was about.'[2] While there were no gulags as in the Soviet Union, there was repressive legislation, naked violence and, at the founding of the state, many sectarian killings. In particular, the Belfast Pogroms, between 1920 and 1922, resulted in the deaths of approximately 463 people and the injury of more than 1,100 others, the majority of whom were Catholics.[3] From its inception, it was no Western European social democracy and certainly did not come close to meeting the British standards of justice. Instead, it was a one-party state run in the interests of the ruling Unionist elites who were the landowners, the educated upper classes who were 'born to rule', in essence, those who came from the 'big houses' and 'owned their workers, lock, stock and barrel'.[4] In order to maintain this control and make sure that Catholics could not challenge the state, the Unionist elites enacted restrictive voting laws, as well as putting in place discriminatory housing, and hiring practices. They also gerrymandered voting districts and used the police and the full force of the law against anyone they felt was a threat to their power.

This worked until the 1960s. Then, under the impact of the policies of the post-war British social reforms, the Unionist state found itself, for the first time, facing a challenge from an educated and articulate generation of young Catholics. Educated under the post-war Labour reforms, these young people demanded the creation of a state without discrimination in jobs, housing and voting, and the just and fair application of the law, and policing for all. Essentially, many of these young people and their supporters wanted a state that treated them as British citizens with British rights. In simple terms, this led to the birth of the civil rights movement, which in very rapid fashion led to the violence of 1968–69 and the 25-year armed struggle.

When most people think of Northern Ireland, this short narrative of Catholic oppression is what comes to mind. They would think mainly of how that state, that minor form of tyranny, was able to maintain its control over the minority Catholic population, and how the sectarian and discriminatory nature of the state led to the 'Troubles' in 1969. While that narrative is certainly well-documented, it is not the complete story. In this narrative, the Protestant working class does not come into the conversation, unless it is as a 'dupe' used by Unionism to maintain the state or the British state to do its dirty work.

It is certainly true that the Unionist state could not have done what it did, or maintained itself without either the tacit or the enthusiastic support of the Protestant working class. Unionism had that support, sometimes fanatically one might say, in a cross-class alliance that endured through 1969. Yet, as much as Unionism could count on this support and as much as it feared Republicanism, it feared the potential clash with the Protestant working class just as much if not more and, in particular, it dreaded 'a direct confrontation with that working class'.[5] This led Unionist leaders to take actions to keep their own working class in a subservient position. Their behaviour illustrates this clearly, as we will see during the 1919 Shipyard strike, the 1932 Outdoor Relief Riots and the sectarian riots of 1935. They reacted this way because they feared that if the Protestant working class would begin to identify with their Catholic working class neighbours; this realisation would threaten Unionism's power and control of the state.

Therefore, to preserve their power, the Unionist Party and Unionist establishment had to maintain control over the Protestant working class. At the most fundamental level, they maintained their control by stoking fears among Protestant workers, telling them that if they did not vote for the Unionist Party or if they began to adopt 'socialist' ideas and polices, then they would find themselves in a united Ireland. In circumstances where these tactics did not work, the Unionist Party and elites resorted to encouraging or provoking sectarian violence to maintain their control of Northern Ireland, which in their view was the same as ensuring Northern Ireland's place in the United Kingdom. In essence, they would do whatever it took to maintain a 'Protestant Parliament and a Protestant State'.[6]

In the longer term, this system could only exist without or with minimal contact with the outside world. After World War II, with the British social reforms, the increasing globalisation of communications and the economic slowdown of the 1960s, history did not afford Unionism that luxury. It first faced rising unemployment that affected the Protestant working class in the 1960s. Then came the challenge from a dynamic civil rights movement, and then once the violence broke out, it faced the threat it feared most; a challenge from its own working class.

This was not the first time that Unionism faced a confrontation with its working class. This had already occurred a number of times in Northern Ireland's history. Yet in each case, Unionism had somehow managed to overcome those challenges. What was different in this period was the inability of the state to honour its social contract with the Protestant working class in terms of employment and its perceived inability to protect the border and Protestant working class communities from the violence of the IRA. This eventually led to the breakdown of the consensus that held the cross-class alliance together within the larger unionist community.[7]

When this happened, those who did stand up to Unionism did not challenge the right of Northern Ireland to exist. What they challenged, as Bobby Cosgrove pointed out, was a Unionist state that was, in their eyes, run for the benefit of a few rather than for all the people of Northern Ireland. Once they did this, some within the Protestant working class began their own journey to reimagine and attempt to rebuild Northern Ireland on a new and more inclusive basis.

To understand how this all occurred, it is necessary to examine the nature of the Northern Ireland state prior to 1969 and how the '50 years of misrule' not only led to the civil rights movement, but also hastened the split between Unionism and Loyalism.[8] This chapter will then examine how and why those within Loyalism began to question the way they lived under the Unionist state and what value they had gained from that relationship. Furthermore, understanding their evolving perspective allows us to appreciate how and why they began the journey to develop a working class leadership and a working class response not just to IRA violence, but to the deprivation and degradation they had and continued to suffer under their Protestant parliament.

## 50 YEARS OF MISRULE

For Catholics in Northern Ireland, it was and is axiomatic that Northern Ireland was a failed state and that the 50 years of its existence truly was 50 years of misrule. During those 50 years, Catholics had difficulties in securing housing and employment, and the law ensured that, when they actually had the vote, their vote was meaningless.[9] In cases where the voting rules did not work the way Unionists wanted, they simply changed the voting procedures to make sure that Unionism would remain in control. They did this in 1923 in local elections and then again in 1929 for the national assembly elections.

In the first council elections in Northern Ireland in 1920, opposition parties won control in 24 out of 27 areas;[10] many of those councils pledged allegiance to the 1918 Dáil Éireann, the 1918 national parliament that declared Ireland a republic.[11] Consequently, the Unionist Party, in control of the Northern Ireland Parliament and fearful, as one Unionist minister put it, that 'Unless something is done now, it is only a matter of time, until Derry passes into the hands of the Nationalist and Sinn Féin Parties for all time',[12] worked to ensure that this result would not occur again. The Northern Ireland government, with London's assent, passed a law changing the voting procedures in local elections from proportional representation to 'first past the post', which meant that elections would now be dominated by the most powerful parties.[13] The result was striking. Where the opposition captured all but three councils in 1920, in 1924 the Unionist Party captured all but twelve.[14] Bardon cites the election results in Fermanagh as an example of the devastating impact of this change. He points out that 'Catholics made up 56 per cent of Fermanagh's population, but their representation on local bodies ... fell from 52.5 per cent to 36.75 per cent.'[15]

There was another weapon in Unionism's arsenal that was important in keeping Unionism in control of Northern Ireland – the manner of voting in local elections. Controlling the vote for the local councils was crucial because this was where the real power lay – allocation of housing, jobs and all forms of patronage. The party that dominated the local council determined who had a house and thus who could vote. This worked to the advantage of the Unionist Party, and against both the Protestant and Catholic working class.

One striking example of this was the experience of Austin Currie, an MP at Stormont in the 1960s. He had a vote in the Westminster elections and for parliament in Northern Ireland, but because he and his wife lived with his mother and father, neither could vote in local elections.[16] He points out that in local elections in Northern Ireland,

> the franchise was based on the ratepayer suffrage and the company vote. Ratepayer suffrage meant that, with some exceptions, only those who were owners or tenants of a dwelling (or their spouses) were entitled to vote in local government elections. Thus many adults who were lodgers or still living at their parents' home did not receive a vote. It was estimated that in 1961 over a quarter of the parliamentary electorate were disfranchised at local elections. The company vote resulted in a number of company directors (property owners) being entitled to more than one vote.[17]

He went on to say,

> This was the only way in which the Unionists could remain in control. The allocation of a house was not just the allocation of a house. It was the allocation of two votes. Therefore, in marginal areas, he who controlled the allocation of public authority housing effectively controlled the voting in that area.[18]

To consolidate its power even more, the Unionist Party set about redrawing the electoral boundaries to ensure that even in areas like Derry/Londonderry and Fermanagh, where nationalists outnumbered unionists, Unionists still would still win the elections. The most blatant example of this was in Derry/Londonderry. Michael Farrell points out that in Derry/Londonderry in 1966, the population was '20,102 Catholics and 10,274 Protestants', but because of gerrymandering, the Derry/Londonderry City Council had eight Catholic Councillors and twelve Unionist Councillors.[19] The result was that,

> Nationalists were left in control only of those areas where the Catholic majority was so large that no gerrymander could do away with it ... . No council which became Unionist as a result of it [gerrymandering] was ever re-captured by the Nationalists, and they soon gave up trying.[20]

Even with all these changes, the Unionist Party felt insecure and believed that a threat to its control and, by extension, Northern Ireland, existed by the continued use of proportional representation for the National Assembly. While the Unionist government aimed all of the other changes to the voting system at the nationalist population, ending proportional representation in the vote for the national parliament had one purpose – to target and wipe out any opposition from within unionism, be it independent unionism or the labour tendency within unionism.[21] D. G. Pringle points out the fear that the Unionist Party felt in this period with regard to independent thinking within unionism. He argues,

> Given the strength of the sectarian divide and the size of the Protestant majority, the anti-Partitionist parties did not provide any threat at all to the Unionist majority, but the possibility of the Protestant vote being further split on class issues was a more serious challenge.[22]

Consequently, fearing the development of an opposition emerging in Northern Ireland or a split of the Protestant vote, Craig and the Unionist Party eliminated proportional representation and went to the 'first past the post' system again. In defending this change to the voting procedure, Craig argued that, 'Mr Devlin and his party [Nationalists] are the natural Opposition. Why, then should any Loyalist constituency add strength to it and weaken the influence of my colleagues and myself?'[23] Therefore, Craig wanted 'to secure a straight Unionist/Nationalist – and in practice, Protestant/Catholic – confrontation and to eliminate the Labour and Independent Unionist menace.'[24]

Sam Kyle, head of the NILP, recognised that this change meant that it would 'make it more difficult for minorities to secure representation'.[25] Kyle attacked Craig:

> The Prime Minister says that Nationalists are the natural Opposition. What exactly does he mean if he does not mean his conception of Government is based on the different views held by the sects of the Christian religion?[26]

Joe Devlin, leader of the Nationalist Party agreed with Kyle and accused Craig of perpetuating the 'old party divisions of Protestant and Catholic, Orange and Green'.[27] They were totally correct. In fact, Craig admitted as much in the same debate with Kyle on 25 October 1927. He boldly proclaimed,

> What I want to get in this house and what I believe we will get very much better in this House under the old-fashioned plain and

simple system, are men who are for the Union on the one hand or who are against it and want to go into a Dublin Parliament on the other.[28]

The change to the voting system did just that. After the Unionist Party abolished proportional representation for the 1929 national elections, it could and did make every election about the border and/or their definition of loyalty.[29] The Party had the ability to dominate the elections in a way it could never do under proportional representation.

Under the new voting rules, the Unionist Party, with a smaller percentage of the overall vote, ended up with a greater majority in the parliament. In 1925, the Unionist Party took 55 per cent of the vote and won 32 seats, while the opposition held 20 seats; in 1929 the Unionist Party received 50 per cent of the vote, but got 37 seats reducing the opposition to 15.[30] This left the Unionist Party securely in control of the state. It now had control over both the nationalist population and independent unionists, as well as its own working class.

Beyond making it almost impossible for any opposition to mount a political challenge to the Unionist Party or Protestant dominated state, the Unionist Party passed a law that gave it nearly unlimited power in dealing with any threat, real or perceived. The 'Civil Authorities (Special Powers) Act of 1922', a draconian law, which went into effect on 7 April 1922 and the Northern Ireland Parliament made permanent in 1933, gave the state nearly unlimited power. Its purpose was to keep the nationalist population in its place and make sure that no 'fifth column' ever threatened Unionist power and the Northern Ireland state.

The law was so draconian that George Hanna, at the time an Independent Unionist, noted that only '[o]ne section would have been sufficient' because the law gave the 'Home Secretary ... the power to do whatever he likes, or let somebody else do whatever he likes for him.'[31] The bill allowed for whipping for certain offenses, the death penalty for others and detention without trial; it gave the police great latitude for search and seizure, and the breaking up of public assemblies.[32] In essence, this law gave the government and its agencies dictatorial powers over the entire population of Northern Ireland.

Even before passing this law and prior to partition in 1921, the emerging Unionist government created, with London's blessing and funding, the Ulster Special Constabulary (USC), which included the hated (by Catholics) B-Specials.[33] Carson requested the creation of this loyalist special constabulary during a time of great unrest and fear among unionists as the Irish War of Independence raged and sectarian violence exploded in Belfast.

When the state set up the USC into its three branches (A, B and C), one member of the Unionist Party suggested that 'the old formation of the UVF could be used for the purpose'.[34] Consequently, the USC essentially took in much of the UVF and it became another weapon, along with the Black and Tans and the Royal Irish Constabulary (RIC), in the fight against the IRA.[35] More importantly for the Unionist state, the B-Specials became a vital tool in the maintenance of Unionist dominance and control over the Catholic population throughout Northern Ireland's history.

On 5 April 1922, after partition, the Northern Ireland state set up its own new police force, the Royal Ulster Constabulary (RUC). The government based the RUC on the structure of the old RIC with the remit of taking 'whatever powers you require' and 'with certainty the government would give them [the powers] to the security forces.'[36] With the creation of this force, there were now 'fifty thousand regular and part-time policemen, that is, one policeman for every six families in the region, or put another way, one policeman for every two Catholic families.'[37]

As is clear from the state's actions, the Unionist Party considered Catholics to be 'disloyal citizens' and, as such, believed that Catholics had no right to participate in the life of the state or expect fair treatment from the state. Following from this assumption the Unionist state implemented discriminatory employment policies in the public sector in order to prevent active Catholic participation in the life of Northern Ireland.

In the civil service, those doing the hiring worked to ensure that Catholics did not get jobs and if they did get a job, they could not rise to positions of responsibility. Less than ten per cent of the civil service by 1943 was Catholic and none served in any cabinet or senior position.[38] The state also set up a screening arrangement to weed out 'undesirables', and to ensure that its supporters got jobs and/or benefits while those they considered disloyal got nothing. The doling out of unemployment benefits also operated on this principle.[39] In the tough economic climate of the 1920s and 1930s, these benefits played a significant role in maintaining Unionism, while paradoxically causing Unionism great problems, as was evident in the Outdoor Relief Riots of 1932.

It was no different in the private sector. Most industrial and private sector employment was in Protestant hands, and in most cases, employers would hire only Protestants. Unionist leaders reinforced and encouraged this attitude by openly calling on Protestant employers to hire only Protestants. At a 12 July 1933 celebration, Basil Brooke, Northern Ireland's third Prime Minister said,

> Many in this audience employ Catholics, but I have not one about my place. Catholics are out to destroy Ulster ... . If we in Ulster allow Roman Catholics to work on our farms we are traitors to Ulster ... I would appeal to Loyalists, therefore, wherever possible, to employ good Protestant lads and lassies.[40]

Craig refused to rebuke him and in fact said, 'He spoke entirely on his own ... but there is not one of my colleagues who does not entirely agree with him.'[41]

In heavy industry, Protestants held a disproportionate number of jobs, mainly in the skilled areas, while Catholics, if they could get jobs, tended to work as unskilled labour.[42] In the shipyards, out of 10,000 employees, only 400 were Catholic.[43] 'In the 1920s, the rate of unemployment among Protestants in Northern Ireland was 6.6 per cent while for Catholics it was 17.3 per cent'.[44] Therefore, with the support and encouragement of the state, employers in the private sector actively discriminated against Catholics and made sure that only loyal workers got jobs or benefits. It is no wonder that John Hume, when considering the voting laws, the housing and job discrimination, the draconian Special Powers Law and Unionist domination of the coercive power of the state, asserted that, '[w]ithin what is called the United Kingdom, you had the worst injustices in the whole of Europe.'[45]

By creating a Unionist state only for those they considered loyal to the union, Unionism had also created a Northern Ireland that was indeed a 'cold house for Catholics.'[46] It did this at the cost of basic rights not just for the majority of Catholics, but also a minority of Protestants and at the expense of long-term stability of the state. A system built on disenfranchising at least 30 per cent of the population and a minority of the Protestant population could only survive in isolation by preserving what McKittrick and McVea called the 'static society.'[47] That happened for many years, but by the 1960s, this isolation ended.

In the 1960s, with the rise in unemployment, the emergence of the civil rights movement, the violence that broke out in 1969 and the collapse of Stormont in 1972, some of the staunchest loyalists began to question in whose interest the Unionist Party had ruled and who had enjoyed the benefits of this Unionist state. The questioning came from what seemed like the most unlikely source.

This work cited Gusty Spence's words earlier on how the Protestant working class had suffered at the hands of Unionism. That statement was the most significant attack on what the Unionist state had done not just to the Catholic population, but also to the Protestant working class. Here was Spence, the man who had taken up arms in 1965 to defend 'Ulster' against Republican attacks and subversion, now aware of how this state had not benefitted the Protestant working class and that many Protestants were no better off than their Catholic neighbours. His awareness was not unique. Others would soon follow him.

When the violence broke out in August of 1969 and the Protestants found their state under attack, they did what they had always done. They rallied to the 'flag' and attacked those who they believed wanted to take them into a united Ireland and destroy the constitutional link with Britain by force. Chapter 1 made this clear with its examination of the resurgence of the UVF, the creation of the RHC in 1970 and the formation of the UDA in 1971 to defend Protestant working class communities. What was different this time is that because the state could not protect the Protestant working class communities, a number of people like Spence began to not only organise to 'defend Ulster', but also to question the benefits that the Protestant working class had gained by its allegiance to the Unionist state. This led some to examine their own economic and social situation and begin to question what Unionism had really done for the Protestant working class, a working class that was supposed to be so much better off than the Catholic population.

In discussions about the situation of the Protestant working class, which took place on the Shankill Road in 1994, one of the participants said,

> Republicans have long promoted the notion that the Protestant community was much better off than the Catholic community. This "half-myth" retained its potency because Protestants even believed it themselves. The reality was that whatever privileges the Protestant working class was "granted" were merely "crumbs from the table" – it simply suited certain people to tell us that these 'crumbs' had to be held on at all costs.[48]

Hugh Smyth reflected on his own experience:

We, as Unionists, were made to believe we were first class citizens and we believed it. Catholics were made to believe they were second-class citizens and they believed it. But the truth of the matter was that we were both third class citizens, and nobody gave a damn about us.[49]

Once working class loyalists and Loyalist paramilitaries began to realise their true position, they then began to ask questions about themselves, about their relationship with Unionism and with the Catholic population. In essence, as Nelson said, the situation 'forced them to ask: Suppose some of the things that Catholics say are true? And suppose we have some interests in common, where does that leave our political ideology?'[50] This realisation led to a political awakening of some within the Protestant working class and the paramilitaries and launched them on their political journey.

## RADICALISM AND REACTION

The protestant working class is, through travail, "catching itself on". They know they have been used, for half a century and much more, by the sleek, slick men of the Unionist Party. Now they have turned on that party and murdered it in cold blood.

David Boulton[51]

As discussed in Chapter 1, those involved in the violence of the conflict began to develop and embark on their own path, and, as they did, they began to split away from traditional Unionism.

When they 'caught themselves on' and the split with Unionism did occur, there was no real reason for elements of Loyalism to shift towards reconciliation and compromise, as some within the RHC and the UVF did. In fact, just the opposite was more likely to occur and, in fact, did occur with the founding and development of Ian Paisley's Democratic Unionist Party, (now Northern Ireland's largest party) to which many working class Protestants took their votes. Thus, David Adams, formerly of the Ulster Democratic Party, the party once aligned with the UDA, is correct when he points out that within the unionist community,

there is always room for the voices that are opposed and are moving to the right, but there is very little room for the moderate voice, which tends to get stymied. If you are preaching a harder message, you will always find an audience and an acceptance.[52]

He continues, saying, 'If you are preaching a progressively softer line, you are an outsider.'[53]

However, not all within the Protestant working class went with the Democratic Unionist Party (DUP). Those who began to develop progressive thinking went their own way. They developed a much softer line and came to accept that in the new era, the harder message was no longer relevant. However, true to Adams' words, and as the following chapters will show, once they embarked on the 'softer line', they faced attacks and vilification as outsiders.

Aware here of what the UVF and RHC will do in terms of political thinking and what their documents and proposals posited, two questions present themselves: 'Where did this new thinking come from and how is this tied to the split?' Furthermore, 'How did they move away from the harder message about which Adams spoke?' Given the history of working class acquiescence with Unionism and with the popular image of Loyalists as those who do not think and are nothing more than mindless thugs, it seems inconceivable that new thinking could evolve out of the Protestant working class and, in particular, the paramilitaries. Yet it did, and it led them to break with traditional Unionism. Moreover, the later chapters will illustrate, they developed their own far-reaching, visionary documents that, in the right circumstances, could have ended the conflict much earlier.

In trying to understand where the split came from and how the new thinking came out of that split, interviews revealed that there are as many opinions as there were respondents. These ranged from those who claimed that there was a long tradition of working class radicalism to those who experienced a 'rude awakening' after the outbreak of the conflict.

Roy Garland points out,

> When I asked 'John' about the origins of U.V.F. radicalism he replied that it was always there and was a vital part of protestantism. The basis for a radical rethink was therefore already present in the Protestant 'libertarian tradition.'[54]

In the 1994 discussion on the Shankill Road, one participant agreed with 'John' and claimed that Protestants had a 'radical heritage' that they should be proud of that:

Witness the role and influence of radical Protestants in Ireland: Grattan's parliament; the Volunteer movement; Ulster Tenants Right; Linenhall Library; Athens of the North; Young Ireland (led by sons of the Presbyterian manse ... industrial Ulster was built by radical Protestants (not by right wing sectarian demagogues); birth of historic Republicanism; the Irish language, music and design was all kept alive by Protestant poets, musicians and artists.[55]

William 'Plum' Smith, a former RHC prisoner, agrees that there is long tradition within Protestantism of rebelling and radicalism. Smith argues, 'that's inbuilt within Protestantism that you do protest, and you do challenge.'[56] Citing the history of Protestantism in Ireland, Smith states,

if you look through the history books, you'll see that ... some of those prominent leaders of Republicanism in the past have been Protestants ... . Wolfe Tone, Sir Roger Casement. The United Irishmen were dominated with Protestant thinking and with Protestant leaders.[57]

Smith also accepts that there was a tradition within Protestantism of labour activism, trade union activity and that it should not come as a surprise in the modern era that radical ideas and new thinking came out of the Protestant working class. He claims that there were,

a lot of Protestants involved in trade unions, in different strikes [that] involved ... heavy industry, shipbuilding, and factories, and linen mills. So you had a ... strong tradition of trade unions and trade unionism within the Protestant working class... . And in the first part of the twentieth century ... the Northern Ireland Labour Party was formed. You had a number of Protestants, in fact a majority of Protestants who were in the leadership of it. You had a number of labour councillors who were sitting councillors in Belfast City Council who were representing areas such as the Shankill which ... is the heart of the Empire, the heart of Protestantism, and here right in the heart of Protestantism you've got a Labour candidate.[58]

For Smith and these others, when the split took place and the new thinking began, it 'just didn't come out of space', they were part of 'a long tradition within Protestantism.'[59] Interestingly, Smith also argues that whenever radical leadership developed within the working class and social issues came to the fore,

> there seemed to [be] ... movement to bond ... together ... there always seemed to be the sectarian card was pulled out, the threat of an IRA taking over, or the 32 county [Republic] ... political scaremongering was always thrown out, and in most occasions ... the working class messages that the Protestants were trying to get across would be scuppered.[60]

To a certain extent, the historical record backs up Smith's insights and claims. There is a long labour heritage and a heritage of coming together in solidarity with their Catholic neighbours. However, there is also a terrible sectarian history.[61]

Furthermore, while the Protestant working class sometimes acquiesced in its own oppression and sectarianism, there is also evidence to support Smith's claim that the Unionist state did not hesitate to 'scupper' radical thinking and cross-community action when it emerged out of the Protestant working class. Examples of this are clear in the co-optation of labour in the 1920s, and the splitting of the Protestant and Catholic working classes when they came together in the Outdoor Relief Riots of 1932 and then in the sectarian riots of 1935.

## MANIPULATION AND ACQUIESCENCE

After World War I, with the demobilisation of the armies, and the return home of the soldiers, a great wave of industrial unrest swept across the British Isles. This strike wave affected all the great industrial cities, including Belfast. To pre-empt and prepare for the threat from labour, and even before strikes took place in Belfast, Lord Carson, the founder of the Northern Ireland state, fearing socialism, communism and liberalism in the post-war era, as well as the challenge from labour within unionism, set up the Ulster Unionist Labour Association (UULA) in the hope of controlling Protestant labour.[62]

Patterson and Kaufmann point out that beyond the fears outlined above, Carson also wanted to 'counter the claim that Unionism was a project of the landlord class and the bourgeoisie',[63] so that he could tout the cross-class alliance that supposedly existed within unionism. Edwards maintains that, 'above all the UULA was an elite-driven venture designed to maintain the constitution and preserve unionist unity by providing a controlled outlet for Loyalist-labour interests.'[64] Devlin, in turn, argues that Carson's intention with the UULA was to 'purge the trade union movement of "Bolsheviks" and Republicans.'[65] In other words, the UULA's goal was to make sure that Protestant labour remained loyal to Unionism even at the expense of its own self-interest.

Despite the founding of the UULA and its attempt to control Protestant labour, thousands of skilled workers downed their tools beginning 25 January 1919 in a strike that lasted four weeks.[66] Although the strikers did not gain their demand for a 44-hour week, they had, as Farrell put, it 'given the employers and Unionist leaders a great shock.'[67]

To counter this militancy and challenge to Unionist power, the UULA was important, but at times ineffective;[68] not so Carson's rhetoric. On 12 July 1920, Carson launched an attack on,

These men who come forward posing as the friends of labour care no more about labour than does the man in the moon. Their real object, and the real insidious nature of their propaganda, is that they mislead and bring about disunity amongst our own people; and in the end, before we know where we are, we may find ourselves in the same bondage and slavery as is the rest of Ireland in the South and West.[69]

Devlin argues that, 'Carson was identifying Sinn Féin, Catholicism and Labour as the same intolerable thing, as far as the Orange Order and the Unionist Party were concerned.'[70] In the volatile and violent period of 1920, this speech served to kindle already hot passions.

Inflamed by the IRA killing of the Divisional Commander of the RIC in Cork and encouraged by the Belfast Protestant Association an extremist and sectarian Protestant association of workers, Loyalists attacked and expelled all the Catholic workers from the shipyards.[71] The expulsions spread to other firms and also targeted any Protestant workers the mob considered disloyal. This meant suspected radicals, communists, socialists or those Protestants who tried to protect Catholics.[72] In response to the violence, Carson congratulated the shipyard workers for expelling those 'Papists and Rotten Prods' from the workshops.'[73]

This had its impact. In a period when unemployment was 25 per cent, the expulsions created jobs for Protestant workers and/or prevented more layoffs. Farrell rightly points out that the expulsions put a 'premium on loyalty and cemented the Orange alliance, since

"disloyal" Protestants were likely to be the next to go.'[74] Sarah
Nelson agrees, noting that if a Protestant spoke up and criticised
the established order, 'there was usually a heavy price to pay.'[75]
Stepping out from the pack was dangerous and most Protestant
workers, even if they did not always support the status quo, were
reluctant to challenge it.

To appreciate the strength of this attitude consider that when the
British aligned trade unions stepped in to get the expelled Catholic
and Protestant workers reinstated, the Protestant workers, for the
most part, ignored their unions.[76] The result was the destruction
of a unified labour movement that could have stood for the entire
working class. It is worth quoting Devlin at length here about what
this meant:

> By ignoring the principle of equality in their industrial relationships
> trade unions in Belfast deprived themselves of the opportunities
> to develop the philosophy which proved so essential to the trade
> union movement in Britain in creating an effective political form.
> Sensitivity to the main issues of equality would have driven the
> unions away from the Unionist Government which practiced
> inequalities on such a large scale.[77]

By acquiescing in sectarianism, the unions missed a chance
to stand up to the government and deal with labour issues on
a non-sectarian basis. Yet this is exactly why Unionism had to
undermine working class solidarity. Without the sectarian divisions
it could not preserve its control of the state, which for the Unionist
Party was synonymous with preserving Northern Ireland.

Beyond Unionism's ability to maintain its position through
manipulation, many Protestant workers acquiesced in their own
exploitation. Ramsay McDonald, the first British Labour Prime
Minister, recognised how the Unionist Party maintained control
of the working class and how the working class also accepted its
place. In a 1912 parliamentary speech, McDonald said, 'Whenever
there is an attempt to root out sweating in Belfast the Orange big
drum is beaten.'[78] Once Protestant workers heard the beat of the
drum, the majority of them fell in line. The result was predictable.
Protestant workers, who focused only on the border, would not and
could not resist the redundancies and wage cuts in the hard times
of the 1920s and 1930s. Devlin characterised it this way: 'While
the Protestant worker was in uniform in the streets as an auxiliary

policeman combating IRA activities, his employer was reducing his wages for the same patriotic reason.'[79]

Billy Hutchinson recalls a conversation that he once had with Spence. He tells how Spence believed that 'We acquiesced, because as it was happening to somebody else, we didn't give a damn who [it] was happening to.' According to Hutchinson, Spence believed,

> Working-people weren't consulted by the Unionists. Never. They were only supposed to put their "X" where they were supposed to put their "X", and there was good reason for it in the Protestant psyche. If they didn't put their "X". then "The government will fall, the border will fall, the Jesuits will move in and all hell will break loose." Simplistic? Naïve? A load of crap. But that's what people were told and what people believed.[80]

In other words, the Protestant working class, lacking its own self-confidence, accepted and acted as Unionism expected it to, and, for the most part, rarely questioned the Unionist elites.

One interesting anecdote points out how quiescent and class-collaborationist the Protestant working class became under the constant fear for the border. In 1925, 'after Carson returned from a border commission meeting in 1925, the shipyard workers gave him a gold mounted portion of a foot rule-the inch he had not surrendered.'[81] This took place in the very same year the shipyard workers' wages went from 87 shillings for 47-hour workweek to 47 shillings for the same work and unemployment was at approximately 24 per cent.[82] As Farrell sarcastically points out, 'Carson had no further need to worry about the Labour menace.'[83]

The Outdoor Relief Riots of 1932, when Catholics and Protestant workers came together in a strike during the Great Depression and their aftermath illustrate the manipulation and acquiescence of the Protestant working class. This event and its final outcome showed how effectively Unionism controlled the state, how the working class Loyalists, to a certain extent, had adapted to that state, and how cynically Unionism could act to ensure nothing would threaten the Northern Ireland state and Unionist power. Due to its complexity, it is beyond the scope of this project to do a detailed analysis of this episode, but it is necessary to briefly address this event and the sectarian riots of 1935 to illustrate the Unionist manipulation and acquiescence of Protestant workers.

In the depths of the Great Depression and faced with the heartlessness of the Poor Law Guardians, who saw unemployment as God's punishment and/or the fault of the unemployed themselves, Catholic and Protestant workers banded together in this legendary strike.[84] These workers struck on 3 October 1932 for increased relief payments and marched together to the tune of 'Yes. We Have No Bananas', the only song both Catholic and Protestant bands knew how to play together.[85] The strike lasted two weeks and succeeded in winning increased payments and better treatment for both Catholic and Protestant workers and the unemployed.[86] Some observers believed that this was the beginning of the cross-sectarian working class alliance. However, a long-term alliance across the sectarian divide did not result.

As Plum Smith has already pointed out, the workers faced a government prepared to divide and conquer. In dealing with the strikers, the government gave orders to fire on Catholics on the Falls Road and to use batons on the Shankill Road. As a result, the police shot two people dead on the Falls Road, one of whom was a Protestant from the Shankill Road.[87] Devlin explains that the reason the police did this was 'to divide the workers into different religious camps.'[88] In other words, even in dealing with riots, Unionism did it on a sectarian basis to maintain and exacerbate divisions within the working class.

In the aftermath of the Outdoor Relief Riots, working class Protestants, suffering just as badly as their Catholic neighbours, did not immediately respond to sectarian provocations. However, the Unionist Party would not let this last long. There is no doubt that among many in the working class sectarian feelings were strong and many Protestants viewed Catholics with distrust and fear. Therefore, the Unionist establishment made sure this solidarity would not last by playing on and manipulating those sectarian fears and feelings.

In 1931, even before the Outdoor Relief Riots, elements of the Unionist Party participated in the setting up of the Ulster Protestant League (UPL), an extremist sectarian, religious-political organisation.[89] In the midst of the Great Depression and the terrible suffering by all workers, this group agitated to prevent the hiring of Catholic workers by Protestant employers, and it railed against and warned about the dangers of communism and Sinn Féin, often in the same breath.[90] While the IRA and many nationalists still harboured dreams of unification, the concern for many in this period was economic. Consequently, the UPL and others stoked the sectarian fires in an attempt to make the battle over limited resources into one between the two communities and thereby keep the working classes from unifying. In fact, Graham Walker argues that, 'The activities of the UPL lay behind the severe sectarian violence of the summer of 1935 in Belfast, in which Loyalist mobs fought the police as well as Catholics.'[91]

Politicians inflamed the Protestant population with incendiary speeches aimed at creating fear among Protestants. In particular, the speeches by Craig and Sir Basil Brooke, Northern Ireland's third Prime Minister, referenced earlier in this study that called on employers to hire only Protestant workers, inflamed already high tensions. Craig revitalised the UULA in order to keep Protestant workers loyal and along with agitation of the UPL ensured that the working class did not achieve the solidarity that it had in 1932. These actions were successful.[92] After two years of rising tensions and violence, Belfast exploded in sectarian violence on 12 July 1935 on a scale unseen since 1922. The rioting lasted three weeks and resulted in 13 deaths, hundreds more injured or wounded and at least 500 Catholic families driven from their homes. The riots and repression destroyed any hope of a cross-sectarian alliance within the working classes.[93]

Some argue that beyond the extremist political agitation, actors within the Unionist Party made sure that the 1935 riots occurred. As mentioned earlier, Spence told Garland,

People do not wish to know that their government hired gunmen at ten bob a day to shoot Catholics and to ignite sectarianism in order to break the fleeting unity between Prods and Taigs. The Orange Order played a part in this because they insisted on marching along York Street.[94]

Bobby Cosgrove agrees with this and also tells a story that he heard many years earlier about this period:

This gentleman was involved in the 1920s and he was a gunman and he also worked for the mafia in New York City. He worked for the mobs in the 1930s. He came back to Belfast ... . me and another lad, who I suppose was a writer ... had a conversation over a couple of pints, a brilliant conversation getting, you know, his past from him ... and he's telling us that [his] biggest regret ... the only regret that he had. He didn't have regrets with what he done in the 1920s. He didn't have regrets with that. But he had regrets during the 1935 Outdoor Relief. He was paid a hundred pounds to start a riot in Loyalist areas against the Catholics.[95]

Spence and Cosgrove, as well as many others have no doubt about what was behind this. Cosgrove states clearly that,

> Divide and conquer being the name of the game. And it was the Unionist government and Stormont that paid him. And I know that to be genuine and the same thing I would say ... they never changed their attitude ... it never changed. It was all about control ... As long as they were in control.[96]

Although there is no way of verifying Cosgrove's account, one cannot discount this story because the history of the Unionist establishment provides ample evidence of the 'divide and conquer' strategy. As we shall see, Chapter 5's analysis of the smear campaign launched against the VPP, the UVF and the RHC, provides evidence that gives weight to Cosgrove's story. That chapter makes clear to what lengths the Unionist state, sometimes in alliance with elements of the British establishment, would go to crush any threat that came from within its own community. Furthermore, this evidence supports the contention that Unionism feared political loyalism more than it did Republicanism.

## THE AWAKENING AND THE SPLIT

When asked if he and those around him had any thoughts about 50 years of 'Unionist misrule' before Spence made his comments, Hutchinson replied,

> I think not all of us but some of us [did have those thoughts]. I was very young at the time and I suppose I was very lucky to be brought up in a socialist household. My father was a socialist and my mother was a Unionist ... . My father was always really down on Unionist politicians and used similar language to Gusty ... that the city hall was petty larceny and Stormont was grand larceny and the only people who suffered was the working classes. The first person I heard saying "You can't eat a flag" was my father, and that was his argument.[97]

In another context, Hutchinson asserted that,

> You couldn't slide a piece of paper between the differences between Catholic poverty and Protestant poverty. Both lived in poverty, except one side didn't recognise it because they were

judging themselves by what Catholics had. Working class Prods may have had jobs, but they were paid a pittance and endured appalling conditions. My father used to put wallpaper on with nails because the walls were so damp. Since Catholics were a bit worse off, Protestants accepted their lot.[98]

When asked when the split took place between working class Loyalism and traditional Unionism, Hutchinson said,

I was coming at this feeling that we'd been betrayed by Unionism. They hadn't protected the community when we were being attacked by the IRA, that they hadn't taken the right tactics against them. So from that point of view when Gusty was saying that sort of stuff, it was resonating with me, you know in terms of what was happening to people on the Shankill Road. You could see the poverty, you could touch it, it was palpable. I often talk about my childhood, but I had a good, enriched childhood, but it was in poverty and my grandparents lived in poverty and my mother and father weren't that much better off, maybe a bit because they both worked. [99]

For Hutchinson, the break came when he realised that the state could not protect the Protestant people. That realisation and his father's influence led him to think about how else Unionism had let the Protestant people down. Hugh Smyth agrees: 'Here I am a so-called privileged Protestant, who was living nine in a house, two bedrooms, and I'm saying, 'Well, what have I got?' that makes me privileged ... . look, we're being taken on here, we're all third class citizens here.'[100] Jim McDonald shares this perspective:

I mean I lived in a house in Ohio Street with an outside toilet. I'm not talking about fifty years ago like, I'm talking about when the troubles was [sic] on. I had to go out to an outside toilet with an umbrella up when it was raining. When the rain was running down all over the place. I mean I was one of the chosen race.[101]

In a private meeting with a former UVF prisoner, we were examining photographs from the 1912–14 period of this person's hometown. There were photographs of young people shoeless and obviously very poor from the Protestant community. He looked up and sarcastically remarked, 'Right. The ascendancy.'[102]

In her study, Nelson cites the words of a Shankill resident, who came to the realisation that the 'politicians didn't give a damn about us ... We used to think we did better than the RCs [Roman Catholics]. I realised the civil rights people had been right about us being conned for so long.'[103]

In Peter Taylor's interviews with Billy Mitchell and Gregory Campbell, they both discussed the level of poverty that they had experienced. Campbell told Taylor, 'We had two small rooms downstairs, two bedrooms upstairs, no running water and the old outside toilet.[104] Mitchell recalls,

> You went to the toilet in a bucket and emptied the crap in your pit. It was hard going. The fresh water was about two miles away. It had to be carried in buckets and mother had to go to the well to draw the water. And there was no hot water. Your bath was one of those galvanised things that was filled with boiling kettles. That was the way we were brought up.[105]

The reality of life in Northern Ireland for most working class Protestants was similar to what Hutchinson, Campbell and Mitchell had experienced. True, Protestants had the access to the jobs that Catholics did not, but they lived in conditions almost similar to their Catholic counterparts. As Taylor points out, 'most of the Protestant working class was equally impoverished in terms of social conditions.'[106]

Ron Weiner's work on the Shankill Road supports this argument. He cites the housing issues in Belfast and one particular case on the Shankill Road. Weiner mentions that slum clearance schemes began before World War I on the Shankill, the Falls and York Street, yet in 1974, an elderly resident on the Shankill was still living in her house that was condemned some 60 years earlier.[107] Hugh Smyth, PUP representative on the Shankill, recalls something very similar, claiming that 'we lived in housing that should have been demolished and rebuilt 40 years before it eventually was ... horrible conditions.'[108]

> For Smyth and others, their initial awareness about their conditions was almost like a conversion. There was a snap and all of a sudden your eyes had been opened. It's as if you're lying unconscious and all of a sudden you awake and you see exactly what's been going on around you ... it just was one of them rude awakenings that one person said, "Hold on there." You see, for

all too long, nobody ever questioned their political masters – that was the unseemly thing to do. "How dare you question me?" So when I and people like me questioned it, then other areas ... places not only in Belfast ... they all equally started to question – "Hold on, Hugh Smyth's right." "Glenny Barr's right." "What is going on here? What are these people doing for us? Where is this first class citizen that I am supposed to be? What benefit has it brought to me?" It's really a matter of people opening their eyes.[109]

Coming to this realisation also led Smyth and others to question how Unionism had treated the Protestant working class, where it was going and what the Protestant working class needed to do to get out of the situation in which it found itself. According to Smyth,

When the troubles started we looked around us and there was no one to help. And ... where was our politicians? They run [sic] away and left us ... And in many ways, people started to question – hold on a minute, "What are we doing? What are we fighting for? What is going on here?" People not only like myself, but all over started to question –"Why am I a Unionist?" Not so much from the constitutional point of view, but "Why am I voting for that donkey?" So we actually started to question ... and we started to look around and say well, "I feel we can do a better job than that. There's Mr X, Mr Y and Mr Z, he'll do a better job than what they have." So we tried to encourage that.[110]

However, as Smyth points out, many Protestants faced the same obstacles as had those in the 1920s and 1930s, and those who came later, when they stepped out of line and began to question Unionism. Hugh Smyth even noted that this had happened to the original PUP in 1938. The original PUP also concerned itself with socio-economic issues. It lost the 1938 elections because that election turned on the issue of the border in the wake of the DeValera Constitution of Eire that laid claim to Northern Ireland. The Party then folded.

Besides the issue of the border, Smyth also argues that, 'What happened to those boys was that they were branded "communists" and "socialists."'[111] Like the first PUP, Smyth would also find himself and people like him branded as 'socialists, communists'; such charges 'scared the people off voting for you.' Like those before him and those who came later, those within unionism who wanted to focus on class issues could not make the inroads that they had hoped. As Smyth said, 'we deserved better.'[112]

Bobby Cosgrove recounted his moment of the awareness of the muddled nature of the Protestant working class' allegiance to the state. This moment led him to make the break with Unionism:

There was a couple of events that happened that changed my way of thinking. In the late [19]60s, I worked for the old Belfast City Council, closing up, building up, blocking up derelict houses for the redevelopment that was taking place in the city. And one of these sites was down around the area of Donegal Pass in the city and the other was the York Street area. In the Donegal Pass area, staunchly Loyalist area, there was a great deal of poverty even in the [19]60s. Regardless of what people thought, Protestant working class didn't have a great style of life. Well one of the things that really got me going one day was coming up around the 11th of July. And we were just getting ready for the holidays, finishing off a couple of houses and ... there was a wee family and I used to bring extra lunch with me and feed them because they were never fed. Well ... up the street comes a mother, father and four children. It was the 11th of July, going into the 12th holidays, they had just got their benefit money and they had two armfuls of drink and an arm with decorations, Union flags, Union decorations, loyalist LP records, but not one piece of grub. And I says when I saw it, you know, what's happening when we have a society where people ... where we have a society where people put in front of them their children, their cause.[113]

After this experience, Cosgrove joined the NILP.

Speaking of his political awakening to Unionism, Winston 'Winkie' Rea, a member of the RHC and Spence's son-in-law, tells an interesting story about the working class and paramilitary relationship with Unionism:

I remember ... there was a rally in Belfast in 1970 and there's actually a photograph at Stormont where I'm in the photograph. On that particular day, I was given the duty of being a bodyguard to a very prominent politician in Northern Ireland, a Mr Bill Craig.[114] And it was my duty that day, along with another big fella, from Bangor, County Down in Northern Ireland, and he was the other bodyguard. On that particular day, both of us were armed, and our job was to protect Bill Craig. But, after the rally, John McKeague[115] came to us, and he says "Listen, we're all going back to Bill Craig's house", to get tea and sandwiches, etc. So, when the rally ended we all headed back to Bill Craig's house, which was a rather large house compared to the house where I lived in, in West Belfast. And, the guy from Bangor and myself thought we were going in here to get tea and sandwiches, when in actual fact, we were guided to a garden shed, where we were never given a glass of water.[116]

Liz Rea, Winkie Rea's wife and Spence's daughter, in a separate interview, remembers this incident vividly:

Winkie has, I think he has, a photograph, actually taken years ago of him and a few other ones beside Bill Craig up at Stormont, actually being bodyguard for Bill Craig. And then when they got arrested Bill Craig denied he ever knew them and he's got a photograph to prove that he was doing one of the bodyguards.[117]

She recalls the same thing happening to her father Gusty in his relations with Ian Paisley:

You know, same was with Ian Paisley where my father was concerned. He denied ... Gusty Spence, "Who's Gusty Spence?" But bear in mind he gave my mother a ride home from hospital not very long before my father got arrested. But sure, Ian Paisley didn't know Gusty Spence.[118]

Still, even with his and Spence's experience, the full meaning or impact of these events did not come to Winkie Rea right away. Reflecting on the incident with Craig, Rea said, 'I didn't really think much of it then. But I did reflect on it in jail. I said to myself, "Don't ever let people treat you like that again".' True, he had experienced the hypocrisy, but not until he went to prison did he begin to reflect on this. Once he did, he,

came to a position, where I was looking at why Protestants disliked Catholics so much and why Catholics disliked Protestants so much. And I started to think, before I went into jail, to compare the conditions which I lived in which were the same conditions the people in the Falls lived in. And again, when you're asking yourself these questions and answering them in a very truthful manner, there was no bloody difference. So, I couldn't understand why Irishman must fight Irishman.[119]

Tom Roberts had a similar experience. When answering a question about when he began to reconsider the relationship with Unionism, Roberts replied,

It was probably when the conflict began that I slowly developed an interest in politics and how we had ultimately arrived at the situation where we were involved in violent conflict. You know, it provokes you to look at the reasons why and you know, I came to realise that the Unionist Party didn't do us any favours as working class Protestants and unionists. We were led to believe that they were looking after our interest, when in reality we were no better off than our nationalist counter-parts and in many cases worse off.[120]

Asked when his thinking began to evolve, Roberts answered,

Probably during my involvement with the UVF, during the seventies. But, probably when I went to prison and had a lot more time to really [consider] the theories behind the politics that went on here. You know, it sort of reinforced in my mind ... it was a ruling class, to preserve the sectarian edge in politics here, simply to preserve their own position.[121]

In essence, Roberts and others cited above began to question the working class relationship with Unionism, when they came to understand how Unionism maintained its political position and power.

As significant as this breakthrough was for these individuals and others in the working class, one of the key events that set loyalism free to find its own political path was the proroguing of the Stormont government in March 1972. Although this sparked outrage, demonstrations and strikes among all Unionists and Loyalists, it also provided an opportunity for people, in particular politically aware Loyalists, to begin to reimagine Northern Ireland. In fact, Roy Garland writes,

Gusty links this [political analysis] to the demise of Stormont which, he argues, set working-class Protestants free from the old ideological constraints. In the end the consensus seemed to favour conciliation, and a form of democratic socialism which retained the link with the U.K.[122]

Hutchinson agrees: 'Direct Rule was probably one of the best things that ever happened to Loyalists. It broke the chain of always having to accept whatever the ruling Protestant Ascendancy dished out.'[123]

Sarah Nelson's work supports this argument. She claims that the 'most visible effects of Direct Rule was that it stirred a new class consciousness, both among members of the Protestant paramilitary and workers' groups, and among residents of loyalist areas.'[124] This opened up the space to discuss issues that people always feared to talk about and created an 'irrevocable split with traditional unionism'.[125] Nelson argues that,

> Six months before direct rule, anyone who whispered certain phrases was liable to be branded socialistic or republican by their neighbours. After Stormont was suspended the same phrases became clichés, and any UDA or LAW [Loyalist Association of Workers] man worth his salt felt he had to sprinkle them liberally through his conversation. They included "'fifty years of misrule", "fur coat brigade", "we'll never be conned by the Unionists again", "from now on working people will have a say" and "they never did anything about our bad houses and unemployment." This new bluntness went along with a willingness to take independent paramilitary and community action.[126]

## CONCLUSION

What is clear from this analysis and the memories, and reflections of those interviewed is that radical thinking and the split with Unionism had long-term roots and did not come from 'out of the blue'. The real break began to take place with the unemployment of the 1960s, Unionism's inability to protect the Protestant working class from the IRA, and probably most importantly, the collapse of Stormont. After these Loyalists began to question what else the state could not or would not do, they also began to realise that Unionism had used and manipulated them into believing they were first class citizens, when in reality they were no better off than the Catholics whom they were fighting. Some, in fact a minority, within the Protestant working class and the paramilitaries had come to realise that some of the things that Catholics said were actually true and they had some interests in common. This forced them to rethink their political ideology and embark on a journey to develop proposals that would never allow Northern Ireland to suffer the 'stinking, polluted politics' that had led to the violence of this period. This would then lead some within Loyalism to begin the journey that was, to paraphrase Boulton, 'the light in the darkness' of this period.

As Winkie Rea, and Tom Roberts and many others found, that path began, ironically, in the prisons of Crumlin Road and Long Kesh. It would culminate in the Loyalist blueprint for a new, inclusive government found in the initial *Sharing Responsibility* document in 1977, and the role these men would eventually play in bringing peace to Northern Ireland.

# 3
# The Prison Experience and Loyalist Politics

While republicans in Long Kesh discussed and analysed (and Loyalist paramilitaries did body building) unionist politicians wanted to return to Stormont.

Patrick Murphy[1]

Although aiming his criticism at Unionism in 2003, Patrick Murphy, put into words what many people already believed about Loyalists and how they spent their time in prison.[2] Murphy, like Todd, dismisses the impact prison had on individual Loyalists and Loyalism, while reinforcing the stereotype of Loyalism as unthinking, unable to grow politically while in prison and unprepared to challenge Unionism once out of prison. Recently, Anthony McIntyre, a former PIRA life-prisoner, now a Ph.D. and commentator on Northern Ireland, disputed this stereotype from the Republican side, arguing that not all Republicans developed politically while in prison. He claims that,

> The many books on the Republican wings did little more than decorate the shelving they occupied seems to have escaped notice in the hype of intellectual excitement generated by the "discovery" of an extensive library. And the pornography that was widely available, if not officially read, on republican wings ... That repository of cruder literature was not the one that the republican jail leadership wanted to put on public display.[3]

The 2010 book *Abandoning Historical Conflict?* also challenges Murphy's assertion regarding Loyalist political development. In the chapter entitled 'Imprisonment, ideological development and change',[4] the authors subjected this claim to an in-depth analysis through interviews with former prisoners and found Murphy's thesis wanting in relation to the UVF and to a certain extent the UDA.[5] This should not surprise anyone who has read the UVF journal *Combat* in the 1970s, the RHC journal *Loyalist News*,[6] and the Loyalist prisoner newspaper *Orange Cross*. At the same time, Colin Crawford's 1999 work *Defenders or Criminals?: Loyalist Prisoners and Criminalisation*, along with Henry Sinnerton's *David Ervine: Unchartered Waters*, Graham Spencer's *The State of Loyalism in Northern Ireland*, Roy Garland's *Gusty Spence*, Peter Taylor's *Loyalists: War and Peace in Northern Ireland* and *Abandoning Historical Conflict?* by Tonge, Shirlow and Catherine McGlynn, all have called this stereotype of Loyalism into question. Their work, along with Marion Green's 1998 booklet, *The Prison Experience – A Loyalist Perspective*,[7] which relied heavily on in-depth interviews with ex-prisoners and their families, provides a very different image of Loyalists in prison.

Rejecting the accepted wisdom that all Loyalists wasted their time in prison, this chapter will demonstrate conclusively that many members of the UVF and the RHC did indeed educate themselves and move towards politics and the politics of compromise while in prison. Furthermore, the RHC and the UVF developed a political cadre that eventually secured the Loyalist ceasefire in 1994 and provided many of the political ideas that have helped transform the conflict in Northern Ireland.

## THE LONG KESH UNIVERSITY[8]

In a private conversation in 2009, a friend in Belfast spoke of her daughter's battle with one particular teacher as she completed her 'A' level in History. The two had a very strong disagreement about the interpretation of a particular point of history. When her instructor asked where she got such ideas, her daughter replied, 'From my father.' The teacher then asked her where her father got his degree. She responded: 'The University of Lisburn.' At first, the teacher did not understand this reference and then he realised she was referring to her father's time in Long Kesh.

This anecdote demonstrates how Long Kesh has entered the popular mind as a 'university', where many men studied, learned, and developed their political skills and their political thinking. Of course, it was not a university in the traditional sense, but to those who were there, it was every bit as important as a university. For the prisoners who availed themselves of the opportunities in Long Kesh, their education prepared them for the political arena that many would enter when their terms ended. However, many from the British and Unionist establishments, while acknowledging that Long Kesh was a 'university', believed it was 'a school of subversion', a 'University of Terror'.[9] Regardless of how the establishment viewed Long Kesh in the 1970s, to the prisoners on both sides it was a 'university' where they studied many subjects including politics and history.

The common perception, as illustrated in the opening quote of this chapter, is that Republicans 'always used their time in prison well', educating themselves and developing political programmes.[10] Republicans, for the most part, made the most of their time while there by educating themselves and turning Long Kesh into another front in the war against the British state.[11] In particular, it was in Cage 11 where Gerry Adams developed the 'Long War' strategy.[12] However, except for the works cited above, historians and scholars have ignored or given little attention to the political development of Loyalism within Crumlin Road Gaol and Long Kesh.[13] Nonetheless, the prison experience was critical to the development of working class Loyalist politics and the cadre who eventually brought Loyalism to the ceasefires of 1994 and into the talks that led to the GFA.

## GUSTY SPENCE

Any study of the impact of the prison experience on Loyalism must begin with Gusty Spence. Without any doubt, Spence was central to the political reassessment that took place among the UVF and the RHC prisoners in Long Kesh. He and the work he did in Long Kesh to foster political thinking among the UVF and RHC prisoners was crucial to the creation of the cadre of Loyalist political thinkers and actors who came out of Long Kesh and brought Loyalism on to the political path and towards the ceasefires.

Before he died, I had contacted Spence through mutual friends to see if an interview would be possible. Spence declined my request, but did explain his reasons for doing so. Consequently, when dealing with Spence, this chapter will depend heavily on Henry Sinnerton's and Roy Garland's work on Spence and his impact on Loyalist political development, as well as Garland's work on the UVF, *UVF: Negotiating History*. The extensive interviews each conducted with Spence, David Ervine, and Billy Hutchinson among others will help demonstrate how Spence sparked and developed the political thinking of individuals within both the UVF and RHC.

To create a richer narrative of this period, this chapter will also utilise the primary documents from the Loyalist press, *Orange Cross*, the Loyalist prisoners support newspaper, the RHC's *Loyalist News*, and the UVF journal *Combat* as well as the personal interviews conducted by the author with those who were in Long Kesh under

Spence. From these sources, this study argues that there would not have been a real peace process from the Loyalist side nor would the UVF and the RHC have developed their political thinking without Gusty Spence.

All the extant work on the development of politics within Loyalism particularly that on the UVF and the RHC, concurs with this assessment. Peter Taylor argues,

> Spence more than any other single person sowed in the hard soil of Long Kesh the political ideas that were to flourish many years later in the form of the UVF's new political party, the Progressive Unionist Party (PUP).[14]

Eleven years later, the authors of the 2010 study *Abandoning Historical Conflict?* claim that,

> For those associated with the UVF the process was directly influenced by the personality and political perspective of Gusty Spence, in his role as Officer Commanding within the prison structure, where he called for a "universal ceasefire" and argued that "Loyalist and Republican must sit down together."[15]

In the interviews conducted for this work, all, including two Republicans, credit Spence with beginning the Loyalist journey of exploration. Billy Hutchinson puts it succinctly when he claims, 'The Loyalist evolution began when Gusty began imparting what he had learned to the men who were coming in.'[16] Dawn Purvis concurs:

> He [Spence] began that critical self-analysis, reading books examining actions, listening to politicians and then in Long Kesh, that engagement with Official IRA and others, was all that critical analysis and engagement and debate and discussion about the nature of the causes of the conflict. The politicians seeking to divide working class people, to manipulate working class people, to promote sectarianism in order to preserve power. You know, looking at the civil rights movement, how it came about, which were British citizens asking for British rights in this part of the United Kingdom, and all that. And I think that is where Gusty got his ideas from, because people talk about raising the consciousness of the working class and I think that's what happened to Gusty.[17]

Tony Catney, a former Provisional IRA prisoner remembers,

There was talk of, in Long Kesh, of how Gusty Spence used to come to the wire during their [PIRA] football matches to learn Irish. You know, and that was something for a Loyalist, "What are they doing there learning Irish?" And Gusty Spence was very open about what he was doing. And what he was doing was he wanted an insight into Irish Republicanism. He wanted to know how Irish Republicans thought. And, I would say, adopted the maxim of "keep your friends close, and your enemies closer still". But somewhere in that, "keeping your enemies closer still" means that you're also exposing yourself to their views.[18]

Billy Hutchinson remembers that, 'for people like David Ervine, Eddie Kinner, Billy Mitchell and me, Gusty was a provocateur, challenging us to assess what was going on.'[19] Hutchinson experienced this first hand on his first meeting with Spence in Long Kesh. Even though Hutchinson knew Spence well, Spence still attempted to 'provoke' him by questioning him in the way he questioned all new prisoners:

"Why are you here?" asked Gusty
"I pleaded guilty", I told him.
"No. Why are you here?" he continued.
"I was defending my country."
"No, no, no, no, no! What circumstances in your life brought you a life sentence?"[20]

Hutchinson continues, 'Gusty felt we needed to understand why we were fighting and to whom we were loyal before we could grasp what we were fighting for and how.'[21] According to Hutchinson, Spence had a simple message:

Question, question, question. Challenge, challenge, challenge. Understand, understand, understand. Always assess. Always analyse. Always question. Never accept anything without knowing why and trying to truly understand what the situation really is.[22]

Hutchinson also pointed out that 'Gusty also taught us that negotiation was the most important thing. You always refrain from violence.'[23] All of this had specific goal of preparing these men for politics. As he got them to question everything and begin to understand history and politics and the art of negotiating, Hutchinson argues that Spence challenged them by asking, 'When the war is over, are you just going to hand it [power] back to those shit bags who put you in prison in the first place?'[24]

However before he could provoke his own men into evaluating why they were in prison, Spence had to go through his own process of 'enlightenment'. Spence landed in prison in 1966 for the killing of Peter Ward and until 1972, he continued to believe in the use of violence to 'defend Ulster' and the constitutional link with Britain. In fact when Spence was 'on the run' in 1972, he gave this famous interview to the BBC:

> Interviewer: "You've got guns?"
> Spence: "Yes."
> Interviewer: "And you are prepared to use them?"
> Spence: "True."
> Interviewer: "And you have used them?"
> Spence: "Yes."
> Interviewer: "When?"
> Spence: "On various occasions."
> Interviewer: "Against?"
> Spence: "Against anyone who would usurp the constitution of Ulster."[25]

Once back in prison, Spence continued to study and question why he was in prison and why he believed Loyalists needed to fight 'For God and Ulster'. In an interview with Garland, Spence provided a telling insight into what began his questioning of the armed struggle:

> As I walked round, feeling lonely in the bleak night I saw a lone figure from the Republican hut, less than 100 yards from our hut, and the Loyalist compound. He stopped at the wire and said, "Is that you Gusty?" I didn't recognise him but replied, "Is that you Paddy?" He says, "What the fuck are we doing here Gusty?" I says, "To be honest with you, I don't know, I'm questioning that now and I've been questioning it for some time."[26]

Billy Hutchinson is also convinced that Spence's new perspective came about in the prisons when, as Hutchinson put it, 'he had been forced to ferret out those historical and political facts which led him to ... serving a life sentence with a minimum of twenty years.'[27]

Through the reflection and the process of self-education, Spence came to realise the futility of violence. *Combat* echoed his realisation in a 1975 article entitled 'The Futility of Violence'. Although there is no by-line for the writer, the sentiments in the article reflect Spence's and the political thinking that had taken hold among some elements of the UVF and the RHC in this period. It is worth quoting at length:

> In seeking to conduct our political and religious battles primarily by violent means we have been defeating ourselves internally. Political and sectarian violence (and for that matter, institution-alised violence) is wholly inconsistent with the goals of freedom in society, the value of human life and the dignity of the individual. In seeking to make our Province safe for democracy, we are, at the same time surrendering those things which make democracy worthwhile. As Albert Einstein once said, "I am convinced that degeneracy follows every autocratic system of violence; for violence inevitably attracts moral inferiors." How true this statement is today in Ulster. Violence is an ugly mob madness that crucifies the truth-tellers, chokes the artistes and sidetracks reforms. In the midst of the pounding clatter of the bombs and firearms, can we not take time to consider that violence is not the mid-wife of freedom-but its assassin? Surely the time has come for all patriots to make a declaration of intent to forsake the gun (at least for a spell) in favour of dialogue.[28]

Armed with this analysis and now, in Roy Garland's words, an 'enlightened Ulsterman',[29] Spence explicitly rejected sectarianism, called for an end to the war and for negotiations among the armed groups. He argued, even in the early 1970s, that no side could win the war and that Loyalists and Republicans would eventually have to sit down together to hammer out the future of Northern Ireland.

The question then for Spence was what to do with this new knowledge and awareness and how to prepare Loyalism for a time when the conflict ended and Loyalism would have to represent itself in the political arena rather than turning power back to the politicians. To do this, he had to develop the environment and then the cadre who could carry out that task.

## SPENCE UNIVERSITY

Before his death, David Ervine often repeated the story of his first encounter with Spence in Long Kesh. In a personal discussion for this research, he related the story in almost the same terms as those he used when Peter Taylor interviewed him in the 1990s, and it was nearly identical to Hutchinson's experience. Taylor provided the following account:

> "Why are you here?" Ervine was affronted. I said, "Possession of explosives," and he [Spence] says, "No, no, no, no, no. Why are you here?" I thought, "Arrogant bastard – for defending my people!" But, it was a question that caused me some concern because I don't know that I thought very long about why I was doing what I was doing and why I subsequently ended up in gaol.[30]

In an interview with Taylor for his book and documentary, Spence explained his reasons for doing this:

> What I wanted to do was to provoke them into thinking about why they were there. Not defence. Defence was only the manifestation of why they were there. I wanted to know the reasons why they were there.[31]

Ervine recounted how 'We were provoked, tortured almost, by Spence.'[32] He remembers that Spence challenged him and the rest of the prisoners about power-sharing, and the 'politics of the fishbowl', meaning that by bringing their enemies into government, they could then keep an eye on them and vice versa, which at the time Ervine, like many others was not ready to consider.[33] Nevertheless, this provocation had its purpose and its result. Reflecting on this encounter Ervine recalled that,

> Gusty unlocked the door, pushed it slightly ajar and gave me the offer to walk through it or not as was my choice. I think that was as good for me as anything that ever happened in my life. I don't advocate prison for reflection but it is certainly the place to do it.[34]

Hutchinson declares,

> We weren't forced to pick up the gauntlet that Gusty threw down. It wasn't an "in your face" political philosophy which had to be followed simply because Gusty was the CO [Commanding Officer]. He opened the door and invited us in; but we had to make the decision and take that step.[35]

Not all took the challenge and followed Spence on his journey. Nevertheless, many did follow him and they eventually became the leaders and activists in the PUP, the ceasefires and the talks that led to the GFA.

Spence knew that challenging the individual volunteers as they came into Long Kesh was one thing, but creating the environment and providing the opportunities for them to follow him on Loyalism's journey was a completely different task. The first job Spence and the UVF/RHC leadership faced once inside Long Kesh was to minimise conflict inside their own compounds, to establish discipline, to make sure the prisoners saw themselves as soldiers and to prevent men from descending into despair. The goal was to prepare a situation where 'people didn't have idle hands' and they could use their 'time constructively'.[36]

He also challenged them to think of themselves as 'political' prisoners and as 'prisoners of war', and he held them to a higher standard than he would ordinary prisoners.[37] Plum Smith, the first education officer in Long Kesh agrees with Spence and states that the prisoners were,

> going to wear our own clothes because we're not criminals. We're not going to wear the prison clothes. We're not going to chop wood. We're not going to do the jobs that you tell us what to do because the jobs ... are menial jobs that we don't even do outside. So we're not going to do them inside.[38]

Therefore, if the prisoners would not adhere to the prison regime then the Officers Commanding (OCs) would have to establish a regime in line with how the prisoners viewed themselves.

Spence also realised early on that the prisoners needed a structured environment to get through the day or they would sink into depression and/or despair.[39] To prevent this from happening, Ervine reports that 'Spence had a lot of things in place that were about keeping you occupied and giving you a concept of pride', and that included keeping the compounds and barracks spotless.[40] Therefore, upon arrival in Long Kesh in December 1972, Spence set about establishing a routine. One former prisoner said, 'Gusty made up a rota of duties which were shared', and which kept the prisoners occupied.[41] This routine involved reveille, muster parade, cleaning details, fitness and education. At the same time, the UVF created a command structure for the entire camp with an OC in each compound and based on British Army lines. They set up standing orders, which laid out the entire day for the men and regulated all activities throughout the day.[42] As one former prisoner put it, if 'you didn't structure your day then you would lie in bed and vegetate.'[43]

As Green, Sinnerton and Garland have pointed out; education eventually became a very important part of life also in the UVF/RHC compounds in Long Kesh. This education could take on different forms. Initially, 'handicrafts were introduced to the compounds in order to occupy the men's minds', and many prisoners took to them and engaged in leather craft, toy making and glass picture making, among other handicrafts.[44] One former prisoner explained what this regime meant to him:

> I revelled in the drill and classes, partook of all the educational studies and lectures and wanted to learn all the new skills that were on offer. The ones we called "the older hands", meaning those who had been in the Crum in the sixties, were teaching handicrafts and it was amazing to see what skills they had developed.[45]

Beyond keeping the prisoners occupied, the education programmes helped many of the illiterate younger prisoners learn how to read and write. This was very important for these individuals personally, as this helped them maintain communication with their families and friends on the outside.[46] It was also very important for another reason. According to Smith, once 'they got an education, they were able to write letters, they were able to do something ... and then we put the rest onto that'.[47] In essence, once the UVF and RHC got education programmes started in the prison, the next step for the prisoners was to demand formal lectures and access to 'O' and 'A' levels then to Open University classes, which they eventually got by 1979.[48]

To supplement the formal education, Spence also organised seminars and brought speakers into the compounds to lecture on various topics.[49] Mini-Oxford debates took place as the prisoners found themselves debating issues like sectarianism, the nature of the Protestant working class, their own lack of opportunity and power sharing.[50] They even debated the thesis that the PIRA might be right in its fight for a united Ireland.[51] Garland asked Spence, 'You were really questioning the basis of society, the whole structure of society?' Spence replied,

> It's true, that's what Long Kesh was all about. It was about investigating our backgrounds, our attitudes to life and everything

else. The way people have been manipulated or told that they were "The people".[52]

Hutchinson agrees with this. He remembers his time in Long Kesh as a period where,

> we were learning valuable lessons, the first of which was to question: Who are these political leaders? What have they done for our country? The second lesson was to analyse: How have they led our country? Their record was abysmal, to say the least. The third lesson was to challenge. There had to be a new leadership because the old leadership had failed. And from where was the new leadership to come? From our perspective, it had to come from us.[53]

In these seminars, discussion and debates, nothing was off-limits. The prisoners learned to think for themselves, critically analyse, develop their confidence and their own ideas, and subject those ideas to debate and discussion. As a result, these men began to question everything. They now,

> wanted to know, "what is in it for us, we don't want to go back to the same old things again, we want something new, we want something better?" We were saying we want something new, not only for the Prods, we want something new for everyone whereby everyone would have had some form of input into society, where they could be listened to.[54]

Through the formal and informal learning that took place in these seminars, a young, politically aware cadre developed that would begin the development of the new Loyalist political thinking. This thinking eventually manifested itself in the Volunteer Political Party in 1974, the development and writing of the first iteration of *Sharing Responsibility* in 1977, and, eventually, in the founding of the PUP in 1979.

One last point needs to be made here. As is evident from the opening of this chapter, the common perception of Loyalism and Loyalists is that they were somehow 'stupid' or that they wasted their time in prison. In fact, one former UVF prisoner resents people saying, 'You went to jail and you got educated' because for him 'that presupposes you were stupid before you went or you didn't bother'.[55] Based on the evidence presented here, clearly, the supposition that Loyalists were stupid or 'didn't bother' is a gross oversimplification of the Loyalist prison experience. If there is any doubt after the above analysis then the article in *Combat* in 1979 entitled 'Priorities in Prison Education' should erase that.

Billy Mitchell, the 'Educations Officer' at the time, wrote that 90.78 per cent of special category status UVF/RHC prisoners were involved in some form of education and/or training. In fact, out of 141 UVF/RHC special category (politically motivated), there were 69 prisoners engaged in 'O' level education, 19 in 'A' levels, two in correspondence courses, seven in Open University courses, twelve in Higher Level private study and 59 in private study at other levels.[56] Overall, 121 UVF/RHC prisoners participated in some form of academic education at this time. 137 of these prisoners also participated in handicrafts classes. Billy Hutchinson's recent work showed that 'from both the Compound and H-Block systems, 24 Loyalists worked towards or graduated with degrees'.[57] These statistics alone, as well as what came out of the UVF/RHC compounds in terms of politics and political thinkers, prove that Loyalism did avail itself of opportunities for education and did not simply focus on 'body building'.

Seeing what Spence accomplished in terms of education and his own special regime in the UVF/RHC compounds, one must accept Sinnerton's analysis that,

Gusty Spence's tough regime and persuasive philosophy of self-help ... permitted men to take a long hard look at themselves; afforded through education, political and formal, a measure of control over the future direction of their lives; gave them the confidence to see opportunities when released back into their communities; promoted a sense of initiative which enabled men to capitalise on opportunity.[58]

These traits would serve them well inside and outside of prison when they began to develop their own political programme.

## ENGAGEMENT

Even before the UVF/RHC began its foray into education and politics inside Long Kesh, it had engaged with both the OIRA and PIRA in the early 1970s.[59] Later, in response to attacks on it from within its own organisation and community, the UVF later vehemently denied these meetings ever took place. However, these meetings between the OIRA and the UVF did take place outside the prisons where they discussed areas of common interest.[60] Inside both Long Kesh and Crumlin Road Gaol, Spence had regular contact with both P. J. Monaghan of the OIRA and Billy McKee of the PIRA where they worked together to achieve political status in Crumlin Road and to develop the 'no-conflict policy' for the prisoners of Long Kesh.[61] In fact, relationships had developed to such a level between the OIRA and the UVF that Spence could send a letter of condolence to Joe McCann's (OIRA) widow, after the British Army shot McCann dead in 1972.

This letter illustrated how far Spence had already moved by 1972 and reportedly 'electrified' the crowd at McCann's funeral when news of its existence spread.[62] Spence saluted McCann, the enemy, as 'an honourable and brave soldier' and offered McCann's widow his 'deepest and profoundest sympathy on the tragic death of your beloved husband, Joe'.[63]

Spence was able to do this because he and the UVF had begun to engage with the OIRA inside the prisons and, as we know outside the prisons as well. This happened for two reasons in particular. In the first instance, the OIRA actively sought out contact with the UVF in 1971 and 1972 when they began to enter the prisons.[64] This fit with the OIRA policy of making contact with the UVF and building working class links across the sectarian divide.[65] Secondly, in one of the ironies of this conflict, the UVF and the OIRA shared the third floor of 'A' wing in Crumlin Road, as the Provisionals did not want to share their wing with the OIRA because of their rivalry. Here, the UVF and OIRA prisoners spent a great deal of time in discussions, debate and learning each other's positions.[66] This pattern of contact reasserted itself in Long Kesh where the UVF/RHC prisoners took classes with the OIRA prisoners, while the PIRA prisoners kept to their own classrooms.

This mingling of historic enemies was crucial for many within the UVF. Looking back at this period Billy Hutchinson states that,

We learned quite a lot from republicans, no question about that. We learned politics. The whole time I was studying in Long Kesh, whether it was for O levels or A levels or OU [Open University], I always had republicans in my class, particularly the Official IRA ... We watched them, we listened to them, we analysed what they did. And we said: "That's how we need to be if we are going to survive. We need to make our arguments."[67]

While the UVF and the OIRA maintained contact and shared ideas, the PIRA did not really integrate with Loyalists. As a result, the UVF perceived them, unlike the OIRA, as sectarian and without any political programme other than a United Ireland. In fact, Ervine pointed out that when he engaged with one PIRA volunteer at the wire in Long Kesh, he was shocked at the simplicity of his thinking. Ervine related the following story 'I said to him "Well, where's your victory?" And his reply was shocking in its simplicity: "Our victory is every day we can hold the might of the British Army."'[68] For Ervine, this was a tragic answer as it meant that for the PIRA, the 'war was the cause'.[69]

Their attitude towards Loyalists and Loyalism was also a problem. In line with evidence presented earlier in this study about Republican attitudes and expanded on in Chapter 5, the PIRA maintained the attitude that once they got a united Ireland, then Loyalists would wake up and realise they were Irish. Therefore, they did not need to engage with them in the way the OIRA did.

## THE CAMP COUNCIL

There are all types of Political Prisoners housed in the Camp and the miracle of the matter is that there is a great absence of factional tension. Men of common sense know that all are Prisoners and have resolved that Sectarianism must not be allowed to rear its head in Long Kesh … the unanimity which exists might travel further afield.

Joint Camp PROS (Public Relations Officers)[70]

One of the more fascinating and least understood episodes of the conflict was the development and actions of the Camp Council of Long Kesh. Garland wrote briefly about the camp council in his work on Spence, but focused mainly on the Downtown Office Scheme for the resettlement of prisoners. Only Colin Crawford, a former prisons officer, wrote an in-depth study of the camp council in his Master's thesis entitled *Long Kesh: An Alternative Perspective*[71] and in his book based on that work entitled *Defenders or Criminals? Loyalist Prisoners and Criminalisation.*[72] However, the camp council is crucial to understanding the political evolution of the UVF/RHC and in the development of their ideas for the future of Northern Ireland. Even more importantly, studying the camp council and its eventual failure helps to explain why no matter what the UVF and the RHC did, their ideas failed to reach the PIRA and the larger society.

When writing about the camp council and its failure, Crawford calls the failure of the camp council a 'bitter disappointment of an opportunity missed'.[73] This is an important insight and is central for this study. Viewed in retrospect, this was a 'lost opportunity' for its failure meant that the lessons the paramilitary leaders had learned in prison could not travel further afield as an example to the larger society.

Among the various paramilitary groups, the commandants of each group instituted the 'no-conflict' policy in 1972 in Crumlin Road Gaol and then in Long Kesh in 1973. This policy evolved from the understanding that had developed among the OCs of the different paramilitary groups. They realised that they had to learn to 'share the space' inside the prisons and that, while in prison, they both had the same enemy – the prison system itself.

The policy initially came about in Crumlin Road Gaol in response to fights there. In Long Kesh there were also areas where the prisoners had contact with each other. This too led to fights and many problems among the paramilitary groups. Consequently, the OCs put the same 'no conflict' policy into effect inside Long Kesh. Plum Smith, the first Loyalist internee in Long Kesh explains what happened. He claims that the,

> no conflict policy ... was set up in Long Kesh because of conflict. Because what had happened was, going down to visits etc. you were bumping into people who'd maybe killed a relative of yours ... so we introduced it then ... about [19]73 in the camp but it had already been operating in the prison for years.[74]

What occurred here was that the OC's of the various organisations collaborated and worked together around interests common to all prisoners. This collaboration would take on a new form in 1974 with the creation of the camp council.

Crawford argues that the camp council formed in March 1974 in response to changes to the visitation area after a PIRA remand (prisoner awaiting trial) prisoner escaped.[75] Billy Hutchinson agrees and expands on this by arguing that the camp council would never have formed without Spence, and claims, 'The whole Camp Council idea came out of meetings between Gusty Spence, Francy Card, and Billy McKee'.[76] Winkie Rea, an RHC prisoner at the time agrees claiming, 'It [Camp Council of Long Kesh] was the brainchild of

Gusty Spence. He was the driving force behind it.'[77] Ervine concurs saying that the,

> Camp Council in which every faction [was] all pulled together by Spence to [engage in] dialogue about the conditions in the jail, to challenge the jail regime about our conditions and circumstances.[78]

Ervine also argued that the real reason behind Spence's push for the camp council was to bring together the warring factions to talk politics.[79]

Under Spence's influence, the camp council successfully worked to overturn the new visitation rules. The Council instructed all Special Category prisoners to go on a 'visitation strike' and refuse to request or accept visitations for 14 weeks until the prison authorities changed the visitations procedure.[80] Over the next seven months the prisoners, under direction of the camp council also collaborated in a 'food strike (August–September 1974). In this strike, all the 'Loyalist and Republican paramilitary groups draped sheets and pillowcases over the perimeter fences and commenced throwing prison food rations over the fencing onto the road outside'.[81] The prisoners themselves set up a clothes line and dubbed it the 'Ho Chi Minh trail' that allowed all the prisoners to share their food during the strike.[82]

The climax to this collaboration would have been one of the most unique alliances in the history of the conflict in Northern Ireland. In the face of continuing provocations and beatings by prison guards, the camp council agreed to retaliate in a joint action within Long Kesh. Spence told Garland that,

> The commanding officers agreed that if the security forces came in to beat people without justification (that qualification was very important), the camp would rise and anything standing would be burned to ashes. The Camp Council comprising the UDA, UVF, INLA [Irish National Liberation Army], Provos, Officials including detainees, agreed on that. The camp would be burned, but there had to be real justification.[83]

However, after an incident involving an attack on a prison officer, the situation deteriorated and the PIRA made the unilateral decision to burn the camp. The OIRA joined with Provos, while the UVF brought all of its prisoners into Compounds 14 and 19 for defensive purposes. They had also taken medicines and medical supplies from the camp hospital as a precaution.[84]

During the battle in the camp between the Republicans and the authorities, Loyalists rescued and provided first aid to wounded Republicans.[85] Then when it became clear that the army and security forces would overwhelm the Republicans, Jimmy Craig (UDA OC), Spence and John McKeague (RHC) acted as intermediaries to stop the fighting.[86] Spence, in particular, negotiated the end of the pitched battle, although the army did not live up to its end of the agreement and carried out vicious attacks on the Republican prisoners, a fact which appalled and sickened him.[87]

These episodes and instances of collaboration are important to this study because they indicate the beginnings of an understanding between enemies, the beginning of learning how to work together without giving up one's political beliefs and, more importantly, and this is a key insight, learning how to share the space in which they lived.[88] We see those who carried out the war on the outside learning how to cooperate, albeit on a very fundamental level of common interests, such as food and visitation, living conditions, and compassionate parole.[89]

The prisoners and the camp council began to transform the conflict in the prisons, while at the same time learning how to share their contested space and engage in dialogue. In essence, as the camp council put it, 'Men of common sense know that all are Prisoners and have resolved that Sectarianism must not be allowed to rear its head in Long Kesh.'[90] It is clear that those who learned how to work together inside Long Kesh believed that their experience could serve as an example for the larger society. However, the chances for cooperation inside the camp diminished after the fire. The hope that the camp council could play a role in ending the conflict also disappeared.

Having said this, there is some argument as to why the camp council failed to develop and have an impact on the larger conflict. Spence himself told Garland that the cooperation that began to develop in the prisons came from the prisoners themselves and, especially after 1975, the government 'played no part in making the peace except to accommodate a series of face-to-face meetings.'[91] Consequently, even though the prisoners had learned to work together without compromising principles, they had no active support from those who had the power to facilitate discussions that could lead to peace.

In 1975, talks did take place among the various members of the camp council, and with Stanley Orme, the British Minister of State, in the hope of reaching a political accommodation. However, Crawford argues that the 'high handed' manner that the British handled these talks led to their collapse. Crawford claims, 'In the end it was British attitudes and British demands which ensured the termination of the talks and the potential to develop any peace process.'[92] He is even more vehement when discussing the impact of British policies.

Crawford blames the introduction of criminalisation for destroying the camp council, calling it 'a calculated act of provocation against the paramilitaries.'[93] He argues that the British did not just miss an opportunity 'to establish a peace forum between the paramilitary groups, they destroyed it.'[94] Bobby Cosgrove supports Crawford's analysis. Cosgrove, who had contacts with the UVF at the time and with the Volunteer Political Party, argues, 'the British government blew it.'[95]

Plum Smith does not believe that British actions brought on the collapse of the camp council. He points out that, 'After the fire what you had was Republicans all in one section of the camp and Loyalists in the other section. So you had a complete split. And then the camp council was split geographically.'[96] In essence, after the fire, the prisoners and the camp council did not have the same ability to meet and carry out discussions.

Marion Green also argues that segregation damaged cooperation as the prisoners were now isolated from each other. Not only did this damage the official cooperation, this action destroyed budding personal relationships. Green quotes one UVF prisoner, who before the fire 'had been learning Irish language from some of the Republican prisoners.' After the fire, he said, 'that was my Irish lessons hit on the head as we no longer had any contact.'[97] Other respondents on this question agreed that the fire and resultant segregation negatively affected the cooperation that had begun in Long Kesh.

While Billy Hutchinson agrees with Smith, he also argues that the PIRA's reluctance to continue with the camp council, criminalisation and the fire undercut the camp council and made it much more difficult for the council to function, to represent the interests of the prisoners, and continue the process of collaboration and early conflict transformation.[98] Ervine agrees. He argues that, 'The Provos ran away from it eventually because the idea was that you would then extrapolate from these contacts to the outside, and the Provos ran away from that.'[99]

Tony Catney, a former PIRA prisoner, also discussed the reticence among the Provisional leadership to continue with the camp council. He contends that the Republican leadership in Long Kesh pulled back from the council because the outside IRA leadership believed it was no longer in the interests of Republicans to collaborate with Loyalists. He claims that the Republican leadership believed that the British were going to disengage from Northern Ireland and so they collaborated in the talks. He claims that Adams argued against this analysis and that Adams' thinking was correct. However, it meant that the Provisional movement saw no need to work with Loyalism, as it would have to continue the struggle against the British state.[100]

A former OIRA prisoner, Harry Donaghy, agrees with Crawford on the failure of the camp council and the ramifications of that failure. He argues that 'the whole question of special category status was coming into sharp relief' and this 'brought severe pressure on the concept of the camp councils.'[101] With criminalisation came the blanket protests, then the dirty protests' and finally the hunger strikes and, as Donaghy put it, 'the opportunities or the circumstances just didn't exist for those types of engagements.'[102] Catney supports Donaghy's argument and claims that,

> it was clear that the prison administration were not happy with the way that the camp council idea was starting to take on a greater and greater role ... inside the prison. Now some of that may have been because it was seen as too subversive, some of it may have been because the NIO [Northern Ireland Office][103] briefings were already informing them that the withdrawal of status would mean a whole new prison regime.[104]

This final reason is important. As long as the prisoners retained their special category status, they had the opportunity to educate themselves, work together, collaborate, and find common ground. However, once criminalisation took effect, the jails became just another front in the conflict between Republicans and the British state. This contrasted sharply with what the prisons had become before criminalisation, an area for finding common ground, learning to share space, and where the battle was between the prisoners and the prison administration.

Obviously, there is no clear consensus on why the camp council failed, but all these opinions and analysis have validity and taken together are crucial to understanding why the cooperation failed to transform the conflict and eventually to understanding why Spence's project failed. It also helps explain why the Loyalist political project failed. Regardless, what the camp council did do was to provide a crucial meeting place where Loyalists and Republicans could work on issues that were common to both groups, and to begin to seek a way to live in peace and then export their experience outside the prisons. Nowhere was this hope and desire better illustrated than the 'Downtown Office' scheme, a prison resettlement scheme, which could have served to advance the prospects of peace if it had received the chance to work.

## THE DOWNTOWN OFFICE SCHEME

Although the fire crippled the camp council, the council continued to function until the government completely closed the Special Category compounds and moved all those prisoners into the H-Blocks in the late 1980s. Yet in the aftermath of the fire, cooperation among the leaders of the paramilitary groups not only continued but, in some ways, deepened. As Smith points out the authorities needed the council on a practical level as it suited them in helping them run the prison:

> The camp council suited them in that it stopped any friction. It could stop attacks on prison officers. It could also have an influence in prison officers not being drawn on the outside. There were issues there that would suit the British government, suit the prison regime.[105]

But it also evolved and began to work towards exporting the cooperation and dialogue that was taking place in the prisons into the larger society outside, and reflected the camp council's desire to replicate their experience outside Long Kesh.[106]

The most significant initiative to come out of the camp council surfaced in 1975 with the 'Downtown Office' scheme, a central 'downtown office' (in Belfast) that would be 'used as a base where the representatives of the various Prisoners' Welfare bodies could meet, discuss and work for the common welfare of all prisoners.'[107] This initiative developed out of two position papers, the PIRA document, 'Outline Scheme for Resettlement', and the UVF document, 'Proposals for Re-Settlement Programme for Special Category Prisoners', which *Combat* eventually published in October 1975.[108]

The PIRA proposed a central office in Belfast where all prisoners and their families could get the help needed to reintegrate into their communities once they left prison.[109] The UVF proposal focused on alleviating 'the unwarranted hardships of Special Category Prisoners and their families.'[110] In its proposals, the UVF laid out a detailed analysis of the economic problems faced by the prisoners and their families. The UVF proposal also focused on helping released prisoners to reintegrate into society and helping them and their families deal with the social services.[111] As Crawford points out, the respective groups presented these two documents to the camp council, which then developed an agreed document for submission to the NIO. The main thrust of the document focused on the needs and concerns of all prisoners and envisioned an office in which all concerned with prisoner issues could come together and collaborate to best represent the interests of the prisoners and their families.

Beyond the remarkable collaboration that led to the Downtown Office scheme, something much larger was at work here. If the Downtown Office became reality, the Office itself would have facilitated cooperation and dialogue among the representatives of the paramilitary groups in the office while they worked together on issues of common interest to all prisoners and groups. Crawford argues that the leaders of the paramilitary groups wanted to 'transpose the process they had been engaged in [in prison] to the wider community.'[112] Spence's own words support Crawford:

> The paramilitary representatives attempted to "export" the cooperation to the outside world through the medium of a "downtown" office in Belfast wherein welfare groups interested in paramilitary prisoners could meet and maximise their welfare efforts on behalf of those people in whom they had an interest. Heaven only knows where such cooperation could have led Northern Ireland.[113]

Spence also envisioned lecturers from Queen's University leading discussions and giving lectures. He hoped that these discussions and lectures could develop a process that would lead to dialogue, which could then eventually lead to the same understanding that had taken place in Long Kesh.

Nonetheless, it is still difficult to get at a full understanding of the hopes and the intentions behind the Downtown Office scheme, not only because it failed but also for reasons that are more mundane. In the interviews conducted for this work, the respondents had vague recollections of the Downtown Office scheme or its purpose. One can then assume that the moves taking place at the leadership level did not always involve the ordinary volunteers. Another difficulty is that most of the principals involved in this initiative are dead. Therefore, we must rely on what those who have some knowledge of the Downtown Office, as well as the writings of Garland, Green, and Crawford and their analysis of it.

What is clear from the accessible material is that the camp council had a vision. Beyond taking care of the concerns of the prisoners, this vision was to use the Downtown Office, as a vehicle for 'dialogue and exchanges of views between the paramilitaries.'[114] What it would have done or at least some hoped it would do, was to recreate 'the Camp Council in a larger form' and would have acted, initially, under the supervision of the Camp Council.[115] The goal was to facilitate dialogue, create relationships, and develop an understanding of the common ground that existed among the warring communities in the hope of transforming the conflict from a military one in to a political one.

Viewed in retrospect, this was a noble aim, an initiative that 'was the stuff of history',[116] which should have received the support of the government, the political parties, and all who sought to find a way to end the conflict. However, that was far from the case. The Downtown Office scheme encountered resistance from its inception and collapsed almost immediately.

Colin Crawford argues that when word leaked out about this cooperation, the initiative sparked a very strong reaction within official circles. The idea was radical enough in this period that, when it became public, the traditional parties and governmental organisations felt threated by it. Both Unionism and traditional nationalism attacked it in extremely vitriolic terms saying that allowing this cooperation to take place was nothing more than 'giving status and dignity to murderers.' The 'respectable' political parties, individual politicians on all sides, and many commentators attacked the cooperation and the very idea of negotiating with those they considered nothing more than common 'criminals'.[117]

Crawford cites the negative response by the DUP, representatives of the Dublin government, and the Official Unionist Party (OUP) to the reports of paramilitary cooperation.[118] He points out that instead of utilising this initiative as a way to end the conflict, they wanted no compromise or talks with or between any paramilitary groups; they saw victory as the only option in the war against the IRA and terrorism. Harry West of the OUP explicitly stated, 'We are not going to have two sorts of gunmen running the country.'[119]

Why was there such a negative response to an initiative that could have ended this conflict? On one level, many people, including politicians, could not stomach anything that came from those who had committed crimes, including murder. On another level, Crawford believes that something more sinister may have been at work. As we know, the Protestant community viewed Loyalists as criminals undeserving of any recognition. Loyalists had their place and it was not as politicians or practitioners of conflict transformation. Related to this was Crawford's interpretation of why the Downtown Office failed. He argues,

> A political initiative by the paramilitaries would have represented a formidable threat to the political establishment for two reasons. First, a paramilitary leadership by its nature is a working class-leadership, which would have presented a challenge to elite and privileged groups on both sides. Second, and more importantly, a paramilitary controlled downtown office would have represented the beginnings of a cross-community alliance which, if developed, could have challenged the whole social structure of Northern Ireland.[120]

Although, this may be true, there were limits as to how far the paramilitary organisations on the outside would allow the cooperation to develop. This is clear by the negative response to the Downtown Office scheme by the Provisional IRA, even though David Morley, the PIRA OC, helped develop the idea. There is no doubt that the PIRA on the outside of the prisons walked away from the Downtown Office proposal.

Catney believes the IRA had participated in the Camp Council and the Downtown Office scheme because,

> a lot of Republicans, and particularly a lot of leadership ... believed that the economic downturn, and the closure of major British concerns was an indication of their preparation for withdrawal. A lot of people had gotten that into their head that like, "this is it" and "what we need to do now is position ourselves for the Brits pulling out."[121]

As with the Camp Council, he believes that when the IRA leadership realised that it really was an economic downturn and not preparation for British disengagement, the IRA no longer saw any purpose for working within these structures.

Catney's view dovetails with what Spence told Garland. Spence believed that Morley had to pull back from support of his own proposals because of resistance inside Long Kesh and more importantly from the hardliners in the Army Council.[122] Peter Shirlow and Kieran McEvoy provide an answer as to why the IRA walked away from the 'downtown scheme':

> The ideology of a 'downtown centre' conflicted ... with Republican ideology and their determination to view the conflict as a war with the British state and not with Loyalism. Endorsing the concept of a centre would have meant lending credence to the ... claim that the conflict was essentially internal and between Loyalists and Republicans.[123]

The Camp Council and especially the Downtown Office represented close cooperation among the paramilitary groups and, at the same time, called the IRA narrative of the conflict into question. Consequently, the IRA hardliners wanted nothing to do with either scheme.

Shirlow and McEvoy also argue that, 'In the end, the British government's decision to end Special Category Status and to introduce 'criminalisation'[124] in 1976 led to the abandonment of the 'downtown centre' idea'.[125] Billy Hutchinson concurs, arguing that the 'government destroyed all that [Downtown Office and its by-products] by scuppering plans for the downtown outreach and then, by announcing the end of Special Category Status.'[126] This, despite the fact that just one year earlier, the British government, had legalised the UVF and Sinn Féin to try to bring them into politics.

Both Crawford's and Donaghy's comments above lend powerful support to this argument. The continued progress of the camp council and the Downtown Office proposal required that the cooperation and solidarity that developed inside Long Kesh had to continue. However, as Donaghy points out, criminalisation turned the prisons into part of the overall conflict pitting Republicans against the state, instead of an area where the paramilitaries could work together away from the bullets and the bombs.

While one part of the government looked to move the paramilitaries away from armed conflict, for its own ends, another part of the government, with the introduction of 'criminalisation', undermined what could have been a nascent peace process. After March 1976, the government no longer gave 'political status' to any prisoner, regardless of motivation. Instead, from that point on, those convicted found themselves treated and punished as common criminals. This, for all new prisoners, ended what one ex-prisoner had called 'humane confinement' under special category status: humane confinement that had enabled dialogue among the paramilitary groups. But, because of the new policy of criminalisation,

> Instead of fostering this initiative, [the cooperation] the government committed itself to criminalising the political prisoners in Northern Ireland, in a calculated act of provocation against the paramilitaries.[127]

As we shall see, criminalisation led to the Dirty Protest, the 1981 Hunger Strikes and the rise of Sinn Féin. It also, as David Ervine once said 'set the peace process back 20 years.'[128]

## CONCLUSION

In 2002, Billy Mitchell wrote, 'The foundations for the transition from armed responses to the Republican campaign to a political response were laid within the cages of Long Kesh.'[129] Billy Hutchinson agrees: 'The peace process began with the camp council in Long Kesh.'[130] He points out that,

> It was the beginning of a process where people were actually talking to each other, recognising each other, and for me, that was the beginning of the peace process, because it was the first time that the organisations, every organisation was talking to each other around a table.[131]

This study agrees with this analysis and argues that this cooperation, dialogue and initiatives came about in large part because of Gusty Spence. Spence's work, along with some within the OIRA, brought the OIRA and the UVF/RHC men together in classes and in building relationships. He brought together disparate factions, including PIRA, while also developing the cooperation that culminated in the camp council and the Downtown Office scheme. This cooperation and these relationships would prove invaluable 20 years later in the peace process.

Another significant factor in the evolution of Loyalist politics was the profound influence Spence had on the cadre of UVF prisoners in this period both in their formal and informal education, and in socialisation into prison life. Urged on by Spence, these men called into question everything they believed they knew. They questioned everything from their politics to what they thought caused the current conflict. This was some but not all UVF and RHC volunteers. Still, this was a significant accomplishment. Those who did develop politically helped to develop the Downtown Office proposal. They were also the ones who came to realise that the force of their arguments was stronger than the power of their guns and that the military conflict in Northern Ireland would only end once all sides embraced dialogue and compromise.

While this chapter has analysed what happened in the prisons that facilitated the political thinking of Loyalists and the common ground and cooperation that they developed with their traditional enemies, the next chapter will analyse the UVF and RHC's papers, statements, articles in *Combat*, *Loyalist News*, and the creation and failure of the VPP. This is necessary to understand how these men, who were pariahs in their own communities, 'deluded Irishmen' to the PIRA, and a nuisance to the British government, attempted to create the foundations for a 'new' Northern Ireland that included all the people, including the working class of both traditions.

Finally, beyond illustrating the evolution of certain elements of the RHC and the UVF's politics, what this chapter clearly shows is that the stereotype of the 'knuckle dragging' Loyalist without a political thought in his head does not hold when examining this period of the conflict. The evidence on the role of education in the UVF and the RHC compounds refutes the throwaway line that Loyalists came out of prison only with muscles. The following chapters will put that myth to rest.

# 4
# The Emerging Light: Political Loyalism, 1973–75

The POLITICAL prisoners and the paramilitaries cannot be made the scapegoats for our society's ills because ours was a sick society long before the fighting men came on the scene.

Gusty Spence[1]

We didn't go to bed one night as ordinary family men and wake up the next morning as killers. Conditions were created in the country whereby people did things they shouldn't have done.

Billy Mitchell[2]

Did stinking polluted politics come before paramilitarism? I think the answer to that is "Yes."

David Ervine[3]

## INTRODUCTION

While some would argue that Spence, Mitchell and Ervine's quotes are nothing more than rationalisations or a way of avoiding responsibility for their actions, the work in this and the following chapters will clearly demonstrate that these insights were part of a larger rethinking and analysis of how Northern Ireland descended into violence in 1969. This study argues that these three quotes were not rationalisations, but rather encapsulate how these UVF political leaders accepted Spence's analysis of Unionist rule as '50 years of misrule', and came to understand how this 'misrule' led to the violence of the 'Troubles'. Subsequent analysis led these men to question the entire political structure of Northern Ireland prior to 1969. In doing so, they came to realise that the violence had not happened in a vacuum; ordinary people, who never committed a crime in their lives, did not suddenly go mad in 1969 and become murderers. Something happened that had led to the violence and the decision of many young men to kill during the conflict. As a result, this political cadre of Loyalist thinkers concluded that the violence in Northern Ireland was the symptom of a 'sick society' and this sick society bred the 'men of violence'.

In his study of mass violence in the twentieth century Volker Berghahn asks, 'How was it possible that the men of violence were capable of the atrocities they committed?' He also asks, 'Are we all capable of such behavior?'[4] Citing the two great wars of the twentieth century and the accompanying mass slaughters as evidence of humanity's ability to descend into barbarism as well as the many studies of mass violence and the 'human soul' that claim that all people are capable of violence, Berghahn concludes that, 'if this is correct, the social milieu and the ideological and legal context become all the more important.'[5]

Although the thinkers in the UVF and RHC did not have the benefit of Berghahn's work or the studies he cites, their own insights led them to the same conclusion. The people of Northern Ireland did not suddenly go mad; the ideological and legal context of Northern Ireland led to the violence. Once they came to this conclusion, they then began to engage 'in a debate which raised fundamental issues on all aspects of their identity and on the nature of society.'[6] From this debate and exploration, they concluded that Northern Ireland was an 'abnormal state', and that abnormal state had created the conditions that led to the violence of the Troubles.[7] Therefore, to eliminate the causes of violence, they had to change the social, political, and legal context within Northern Ireland. They had to create the conditions where the 'men of violence' could no longer lure young men and women 'with the promise of radical change and permanent salvation.'[8] To accomplish this they had to embark on the journey in search of a new way forward, one that would include everyone in Northern Ireland in the creation of a new and just society. However, before they could move on to reshaping Northern Ireland they first had to find a way to end the conflict.

In 1974, Billy Mitchell argued for reaching out to the Republican and nationalist population to find a peaceful resolution to the conflict.[9] In both 1975 and 1977, Gusty Spence called on the paramilitaries of all sides to sit down and end the conflict. In fact, Spence argued in 1975 that a united Ireland was unobtainable, and that the Loyalist paramilitaries had to find a way out of the conflict that was not simply a return to the past of political serfdom that the Loyalist working class had endured.[10]

Throughout the 1970s, the UVF issued challenges to the PIRA to put down their guns and come to the negotiating table. In 1979, it called on the Provisionals to end their armed campaign and work towards a new devolved government. The UVF believed that the IRA had to understand that they could not win militarily, and that the 'Provisionals are not naïve enough to realise the futility of their aims.'[11]

Another important part of this process was the UVF's and the RHC's leap into politics. They embarked on a concerted effort towards a political settlement between 1973 and 1975, publishing conciliatory statements, calling for a ceasefire in 1973 to facilitate talks as well as meeting secretly with both the OIRA and the PIRA. To get its political message out to the public, the UVF created the Volunteer Political Party (VPP) in 1974. For its part, the RHC published an important document in the autumn of 1974 entitled, *Within the Context of Northern Ireland*, which put forward proposals that would eventually find their way into the GFA. In other words, the UVF and the RHC in particular sought to create an environment that would end the violence and ensure that Northern Ireland would never again experience the violence of the Troubles.

To understand how they did this and what they proposed, this chapter examines the development of the political thinking of the RHC and the UVF in this period, their foray into politics, and a brief analysis of why their work failed to create a political solution. What this work will make clear is that it was the UVF and the RHC who actually developed the idea of a compromise peace that involved a voluntary power-sharing government in Northern Ireland that also included the warring factions. They did this long before Sinn Féin and the Democratic Unionist Party went into government on 8 May 2007. In fact, in the early 1970s the UVF and RHC in Long Kesh, along with their allies on the outside, began work on a document that eventually became *Sharing Responsibility*,[12] a document which envisioned working together with the nationalist/republican community to make Northern Ireland a peaceful and prosperous society.

## THE RISE OF POLITICS

Even though they put a great deal of effort into their political analysis and solutions these men faced many difficulties in securing support for their initiatives. On the streets, the conflict continued apace: nearly 500 people died in 1972 alone. Over the next four years, the number of deaths averaged 285 a year before dropping dramatically in 1977 under the impact of criminalisation.[13]

While the prisoners, prior to criminalisation, had the space and the time to reflect, think and analyse, for those outside the prisons the world was very different. The UVF/RHC on the outside did not have the time, inclination or wherewithal to consider what Spence was saying and what was coming out of the prisons. In particular, the Brigade Staff of the UVF dismissed some of Spence's writings as not fitting the situation in which they found themselves.[14] Plum Smith explained what happened for those on the outside:

> You can't talk about jobs and things when someone's getting ... killed, and neighbours getting killed. I mean, in the intensity of war it's very hard to talk rationally to people who are totally submerged in their grief.[15]

David Ervine agreed with Smith's assessment: 'Against a backdrop of violence and fear and siege, our politics would not be heard.'[16] Billy Mitchell spoke of how those on the outside thought that prison had softened Spence. Sometimes this led them to tear up his writings.[17] At one point, the UVF leadership sent back a position paper with the words 'Fuck Off' on it.[18] Hutchinson argues that the brigade staff on the outside 'couldn't be bothered with our political debates'. The UVF brigade staff essentially told those inside, 'Don't talk to me about politics. Give me a gun.'[19] As one long-time observer of the conflict put it, 'I guess that a lot of positive words were lost on those who lost themselves in the fog of war.'[20]

Although the political thinkers/activists faced these problems, they did have allies on the outside who worked with them to help develop political programmes and give them political advice and support. These were David Overend, Hugh Smyth and Jim McDonald. They did not belong to the UVF, but they did represent the interests of working class Loyalism. They worked with the UVF/RHC both inside and outside the prisons on the development of a political programme. Hugh Smyth explained how these men began to work together:

> Jim and I had been friends for many, many years from school days and we were both always socially minded. David Overend was a member of the Labour Party [NILP]. I was then a Councillor, and one of the reasons we actually got together in those early days was, again, we felt the Unionist leaders was not doing enough for working class areas. So, David with his labour roots, Jim McDonald with his labour roots and also because of the political

situation, at that time the Troubles were starting. Neither of us wanted to go down the path of violence. So, we all three of us wanted to remain on a path that would take us on a political direction because we knew even then that, at the end of the day, there was going to be no military solution, there had to be a political solution. So, we came together for that reason.[21]

Another man who was significant for Loyalism and Loyalist thinking outside the prisons was the Rev. John Stewart, a member of the NILP, the minister at the Woodvale Church on the Shankill and a former shipyard worker. Jim McDonald remembered Stewart as someone who played a significant role in the development of his political thinking and someone who was an enormous asset to the loyalist community and the working class.[22]

In *Principles of Loyalism: An Internal Discussion Paper,* Billy Mitchell writes that in,

> late 1972 a number of key figures within the UVF began to engage in dialogue with members of the Northern Ireland Labour Party. One of the NILP members was the late Rev. John Stewart, then Minister of Woodvale Methodist Church in the Greater Shankill area. Rev. Stewart met regularly with senior members of the UVF during the next few years and encouraged them to think in terms of "bread and butter" politics as well as the constitutional issue. He also encouraged them to respond to republicanism through non-violence and dialogue.[23]

However, Stewart died in 1977 and his death was a terrible loss not just for Loyalism, but also for Northern Ireland.

Though they did not belong to the UVF, Mitchell argues that both Stewart and Smyth had 'an impact on the leadership of the UVF', and their influence was crucial in this period.[24] Their influence and support helped people like Billy Mitchell and others in the UVF and RHC who,

> thought there was a genuine need for a political voice because we thought Craig and Paisley didn't represent us. ... so we felt we needed a political voice ... There was genuine thinking within elements of the UVF that there had to be a political voice.[25]

The NILP did have its influence on the UVF and the RHC and could have been that voice, but with the onset of the conflict, the

NILP began to disintegrate and left a political vacuum for both the Catholic and Protestant working class.[26] That left those who wanted to find a way to end the war and to build class based politics searching for a new way forward. This led these Loyalist thinkers to look for a new way to represent working class Loyalism and end the conflict.

## 'ENLIGHTENED ULSTERMEN'

Unionists are always able to say "no" ... and effectively block political institutions they don't like, but they're not very imaginative in coming up with pragmatic solutions to the political problems.

Tom Roberts[27]

1972–75 was the worst period in the history of the Northern Ireland conflict. 1,680 people lost their lives in the violence and many more suffered terrible injuries and trauma.[28] Bombings and shootings occurred daily and the situation in Northern Ireland looked set to descend into a cycle of even more horrible sectarian violence. However, in this darkness, and against all expectations given the stereotype of Loyalism, the UVF and the RHC attempted to move beyond the politics of 'no' and began to think in terms of compromise, power sharing, or in their terminology 'sharing responsibility', and reaching out to their traditional enemies.

In the previous chapter, we learned that Spence and the UVF/RHC inside Long Kesh had begun to rethink the armed struggle, focusing on politics as the only solution to the violence in Northern Ireland. At the same time, Nelson argues that outside Long Kesh,

Informed sources suggest that, at this time, a number of more senior UVF men (at least in Belfast) were moving more firmly to the view that sectarian warfare was undesirable, that both "extremes" might be involved in some political settlement and share certain social aims.[29]

Evidence for Nelson's claim came in 1974 as the UVF began to publish conciliatory statements in the *Sunday News* and articles condemning sectarianism in its journal *Combat*. The UVF also called a ceasefire in 1973 to facilitate a political solution and then in 1974, it created the Volunteer Political Party.

In the same period, the RHC began to develop its own political thinking, publishing proposals in 1973 and 1974. Then in 1975, it published a ten-point plan for peace, along with proposals for a new assembly in Northern Ireland. The RHC, like the UVF, did this against the backdrop of the bullets and the bombs, and the opposition of the mainstream Unionist politicians and other forces in society. In particular, the DUP maintained its intransigent position of 'We don't want Catholics in government' and as Hugh Smyth put it, 'in their ignorance thought, that they could go back to a situation where we were going to get Stormont back, with the one-party rule.'[30]

Although the UVF published conciliatory statements in the *Sunday News* as early as 1973, this new thinking really went public in a press conference in 1974. At this press conference, Billy Mitchell outlined how the UVF's thinking had evolved in this period. He said,

> We want to see peace but we want peace that will satisfy both the Ulster Protestants and the Irish nationalists. Some solution will have to be worked out between what the media call "the men of violence". The politicians can never give us peace. The men who pull the triggers are the only ones who can take their fingers off the triggers. The Provisionals will have to accept the fact that the Protestant people of Northern Ireland will not give up their Protestant liberties. Our objection is to the Provisional IRA and their supporters who are trying to take away our liberties and our traditional way of life at the point of a gun.[31]

Statements such as these conveyed to the public the thinking that the UVF/RHC and their allies had begun to develop. It was neither a complete political programme nor a fully developed ideology, but it did lay out what they believed was necessary before the violence could stop. What they realised, even in the early 1970s, was that there had to be a compromise with the nationalist/republican population and that peace was not possible without involving the 'men of violence'. The collapse of the first attempt at power sharing with the Sunningdale Agreement proved this. Mitchell's comments, as did many of the other statements analysed below, also recognised that the PIRA could never attain its aims, another assertion eventually proved correct. Although it was not explicit in this statement, as we will see below, political Loyalism recognised Irish nationalism/republicanism as a legitimate aspiration.

In looking back at this period, Mitchell stated in 1997 that, 'they [UVF] had the "feeling" that there had to be some sort of resolution ... there had to be a different way.'[32] Consequently, 'they [UVF] made the decision to meet with the Provos and Official IRA in exploratory talks that came to naught, but did show how far the UVF was prepared to go in this period.'[33] An example of how far the UVF was prepared to go is evident from its own notes from the secret talks it held with the PIRA in 1974. The UVF delegation stated that,

> No solution to the Ulster problem would be acceptable unless it –
> a) guarantees the Protestant people their distinctive liberties and way of life will be maintained for all time.
> b) satisfies the nationalistic aspirations of the Irish people.
> c) rejects forever, government by the landed Gentry.[34]

As noted earlier, for political reasons, the UVF would later deny these talks ever took place. However, as Mitchell pointed out, 'We didn't have a strategy and we didn't have a political philosophy. We had a gut feeling the politicians weren't going to resolve it.'[35] This was evident in a 1974 article in *Loyalist News* entitled 'Pure Frustration'. Obviously written by the UVF, it stated:

> The militant organisations could produce the answer... What is needed and what is asked for ... is to make the necessary arrangement to bring together without fear of arrest, to a conference table those who can bring about peace ... . There can be no peace unless the Ulster Volunteer Force is also present.[36]

As for strategy and philosophy, that would come later in the documents that began to emanate from the RHC in 1973, the conciliatory statements coming from the UVF in 1973 and 1974, and the documents they would eventually publish through the PUP from 1977 onwards. Interestingly enough, as we will see, the three points made in the secret meetings with the PIRA would eventually underpin the UVF's and the RHC's political statements and policy documents.

Even before the UVF statement read by Billy Mitchell in 1974, Nelson claims that political movement was afoot, and that the UVF and RHC had begun to develop their political thinking. Evidence for this exists as early as 1972. In December 1972, *Orange Cross* published an interview with 'Captain William Johnston', the name that all UVF leaders use when sending out communiqués. While claiming that the UVF had never committed sectarian assassinations, a fact not supported by UVF actions in 1971 and 1972, 'Johnston's' words did provide a glimmer of hope for the future and an indication of the thinking that was taking place in the UVF and RHC. He supported freedom of religion, while calling on Catholics to 'disown the IRA terrorists'. Once Catholics did that, he promised that Loyalists would accept Catholics as 'fully and comprehensively as British people'. Then, both sides could work to secure a 'great future for us all – irrespective of religion'.[37]

Another indication that something was happening within Loyalism is evident in the work of Aaron Edwards. In his research, he came across a May 1972 document that showed that the NILP acted as a go-between for prisoners in Crumlin Road and the British government. The document that came out of these meetings put forward the following proposals:

- To urge a 3 months' truce – to commence at the earliest possible date and thus secure a hasty end to violence.
- During the Truce – an urgent review of Internment, and, if possible, the release of all detainees who are NOT being charged with offences against the State.
- Release of Detainees and Internees.
- Amnesty for Political Prisoners – to include all sides, and to embrace [the] entire United Kingdom, The Republic of Ireland, and Northern Ireland.[38]

This document suggested a way forward, at least in terms of creating a breathing space to allow the politicians to get around the table and hammer out some sort of agreement. The next year the RHC would put forward policies that built on these proposals. That this set of proposals came out of the discussions in Crumlin Road Gaol, especially in 1972, may confound some because of the stereotype of Loyalist paramilitaries. However, no one should be surprised. As the last chapter illustrated, a great deal had already taken place within the UVF, the RHC and Crumlin Road Gaol that led to this type of thinking.

These 1972 talks and proposals did not arise in a vacuum; but rather unfolded against the backdrop of the agitation and cooperation that involved all the paramilitaries. We know that a certain level of cooperation had already taken place in Crumlin Road, as P. J. Monaghan (OIRA), Spence (UVF) and Billy McKee

(PIRA) worked together on issues common to all prisoners. Spence took the lead as they developed the 'no-conflict' policy and began to consult each other about such issues as political status, with all factions eventually agreeing that they should fight for political status together.

However, the PIRA leadership outside the prisons would not allow the PIRA prisoners to fight for political status.[39] Eventually, the PIRA prisoners launched their own campaign for political status when McKee went on hunger strike. The OIRA then took action and the UVF joined in the prison strike, which eventually ended when the British government granted special category status to the prisoners, acknowledging them as politically motivated prisoners rather than common criminals.[40]

Aaron Edwards argues, 'Throughout the conflict the UVF ... frequently chose to seize the initiative rather than to lose ground to its republican opponents', and did this 'with support from the NILP'.[41] That the NILP had significant input in these discussions became clear in July of 1973 when the RHC published its 'Proposals for the Assembly' on the front page of *Loyalist News*.[42] These new proposals have an obvious link with the 1972 proposals brought out of Crumlin Road by the NILP. It is worth noting that these proposals stood out from much of the writing in *Loyalist News* at the time. Articles in the paper could run the gamut, although anti-Catholic, anti-Communist, pro-National Front ones tended to comprise the majority of the articles. The 'Proposals for the Assembly' were decidedly different. That these proposals appeared on the front page illustrates their political importance and conveys the journey on which some elements of Loyalism had embarked.

The 'Proposals for the Assembly' were an obvious attempt to influence the new Northern Ireland Assembly, an assembly based on the British White Paper 'Northern Ireland Constitutional Proposals.'[43] The RHC's proposals attempted to provide guidance on how the Assembly could work to end the conflict. In its first four points, addressed to the members of the assembly, the Proposal called for a return to democratic government, preventing Westminster from forcing through any legislation against the will of the majority in the Assembly, working for the welfare of all sections of Northern Ireland, and acting together to bring about a cessation of terrorist acts. It also recognised that 'peace cannot be restored unless all interested parties and factions take part in talks to end the sectarian conflict'.[44]

Under the first proposal, it is not clear what they meant by return to democratic government. One might assume they meant 'majority rule' again, but Proposals 3, 4 and 5 do not support that analysis. Proposal 2 does contain a warning to the British government about imposing a solution over the heads of the majority in Northern Ireland. In light of what happened during the Ulster Worker's Council Strike, when the Protestant working class aided by the paramilitaries rose en masse to bring down Sunningdale, this was a very prescient warning and made it clear that the Loyalist working class and/or their representatives in the UVF/RHC and UDA would have to be part of any solution.

What is interesting about Proposals 3 and 4 is that they called on the Assembly to act on behalf of the entire nation and how the new Assembly might end the sectarian conflict. These points directed the Assembly to act not just in the interests of one section of the population, but to act 'for the welfare of all sections of Northern Ireland.'[45] Furthermore, Proposal 4 acknowledged, even before Billy Mitchell said it in 1974, 'that peace cannot be restored unless all interested parties and factions take part in talks to the sectarian conflict.'[46] In other words, the authors acknowledged that whatever form the new government took, it had to represent all sections of the country, not just Protestants or the Unionist establishment. Although the RHC does not state that explicitly here, later documents make it clear, that is what it was thinking.

The RHC also acknowledged the reality that no peace process could work unless those doing the fighting were at the peace talks, an assertion that appears again in the 1970s in various documents and speeches. Except for the brief experiment in legalising the UVF and Sinn Féin in 1974, which was too little too late, government initiatives, instead of bringing the paramilitaries into the political process, generally tried to marginalise them and deal with the so-called moderate politicians and 'constitutional' parties.

The fifth point in the proposal echoed an idea that came out of the Crumlin Road talks and expanded on that thinking. Following up on Proposal 4, the authors proposed a series of confidence building measures to develop the trust in the word of both the paramilitaries and politicians. Like the Crumlin Road document, the RHC proposals called for:

a) A ceasefire of all parties for a period of time – six months.
b) In the event of such a ceasefire being honoured, the immediate release of all internees.

c) To be followed in three months with a political amnesty.
d) On the announcement of a political amnesty, all explosives and firearms to be handed over to the RUC, without fear of arrest or charges made.[47]

Furthermore, the proposals called for the army and the RUC to cease operations against any of the paramilitary organisations involved in the conflict.

Why did the RHC think they could make these proposals at this time? There were several reasons. It recognised that the Republic of Ireland's attitude had changed and that the Republic of Ireland had realised that no one could force Loyalists into a united Ireland. Loyalists also believed that the Republic was now actively pursuing and prosecuting the IRA. The RHC also perceived a shift in the SDLP, the main nationalist party in Northern Ireland, which they now viewed as willing to work for the good of all sections of society in Northern Ireland. Finally, the authors asserted that the 'Loyalist Coalition members of the assembly are no longer of the "old school boy type", it is possible for the will of the people to hold sway.'[48] In other words, these new politicians were in a better position to represent the interests of the working class.

In the same period, the UVF created a leaflet that it distributed on the day of the 1973 Assembly elections. Entitled 'THE MYTH EXPLODED: THE TRUTH ABOUT THE U.V.F. (The Organisation with a Social Conscience)' (emphasis in original), it laid out seven reasons to 'BACK UVF', that dealt with many social issues and illustrates its emerging ideas on social justice. While the leaflet discussed defeating the IRA it also pointed out what the UVF did to help old age pensioners, those who could not afford burials, policing (which meant paramilitary justice) and the Black Taxi service.[49]

More RHC proposals appeared in 1973. In August, an article in *Loyalist News*, called for a parliamentary act to create integrated schools:

The World, let alone Ulster, is too small a place for a religious divide. God does not want it, neither does the majority of this country. If the new Parliament would take the courage and pass such an act, in years to come, it would be remembered as the greatest public act since the abolition of Slavery.[50]

In the next edition of *Loyalist News*, the RHC argued that, 'The working class men and women of this country have rights, the right to work and live in peace and hast what the majority want'. This document also called for laws that would 'bring the full wealth of these six counties ... for the benefit of the people.'[51] Interestingly it made no distinction between Catholics and Protestants.

Clearly, those who wrote these documents had travelled very far from the traditional ways of thought within Unionism. While they had not thoroughly thought out their politics, nor had they developed an ideology or a political programme, they had become politically aware enough to analyse for themselves what was happening politically and to make it clear that there would be no going back to the '50 years of Unionist misrule'. Obviously, they did not just wake up and think the Republic and the SDLP had changed. They had studied, analysed and recognised there was a substantial political shift in both the Republic and the SDLP, and decided that this had created space for them to find a way to end the conflict.

They returned once again to the fact that the 'Big House' no longer totally dominated politics and that the new Assembly more closely represented the ordinary people. While the Ulster Unionists still dominated with 31 seats, the VUP had gained seven, the DUP eight and the West Belfast Loyalist Coalition had three, along with one independent Unionist, which gave them 19 members, as well as some politicians such as Harry West in the UUP who represented the thinking of many within the Protestant working class. Recognition of this shift also allowed them to contemplate entering the political arena and no longer bowing to their supposed betters.

Nevertheless, the authors believed that Northern Ireland needed proposals like this because,

> this terrorist war could go on indefinitely, one force that will [not] dictate the terms, for a cease fire, nor the politician alone, it must be done with the cooperation of all concerned in this struggle, for the survival of Ulster.[52]

They also admitted, 'The proposals we have suggested are radical to the extreme', and then asked 'but are they?'[53] When examined in the context of 1973, when the sectarian war began to accelerate and some traditional Unionist politicians continued to demand a return to majority rule and the crushing of all 'terrorism', these ideas in the 'Proposals' were very radical indeed, and they also show a great deal of reflection, change and foresight. In the end, they asked 'CAN SUCH AN OPPORTUNITY BE MISSED?' and they replied 'THE ANSWER IS – NO'.[54] Unfortunately, this proved to be another of those lost opportunities to which no one listened, assuming that anyone even knew that these proposals existed.

### 1973–74: The First Steps

On 14 October 1973, a communiqué appeared in *The Sunday News* announcing the formation of the Ulster Loyalist Front (ULF). This new Front was to serve as the political voice of the UVF, which was still an illegal organisation. In its statement, the ULF claimed to 'express the views and opinions of grass-roots Loyalists' and put forward proposals that would benefit the poor and the working class, such as better housing, the restructuring of education amongst other proposals.'[55] It also stated that 'it will uphold the right of "genuine Ulster Loyalists" to hold and bear weapons of self-defence', More importantly, 'its declared aims are to act as a ginger-group, and to express the views and opinions of grass-roots Loyalists'. The ULF also pointed out that it placed a 'priority on the defeat of both wings of the IRA – together with their front organisations – and calls for the introduction of tougher penalties for violent crimes'.[56] It also laid out its thinking on devolved government, a call for devolved majority rule, the return of jury trials, and the release of 'all Loyalist "prisoners of war" who have been detained or imprisoned because of 'anti-terrorist offences'.[57]

Hugh Smyth who participated in the ULF, claims that the ULF existed,

> to ensure naturally that Northern Ireland remained part of the United Kingdom ... But it was also to ensure that the interest of the working class people, come what may, whatever settlement there was going to be, that their working class voice was going to be heard. And so, that was a vehicle in which that voice could be heard, that we went around expressing what we expected from future political leaders or from a political settlement.[58]

Other researchers agree with this and point out that this short-lived Front, although still promoting the primacy of the constitutional issue, focused on social issues, jobs and the welfare of the working class.[59] This is clear in the announcement where it also focused on 'better services for the old, the very young, the sick, and disabled,' called for changes in the housing allocation and educational structures, and it pressed 'for the introduction of workers' partnership schemes as an incentive in factories,' favoured 'private enterprise', but wanted to curb 'international monopoly capitalism.'[60] The ULF also provided the foundation for the UVF ceasefire of 1973, which Cusack and McDonald argue would provide a breathing spell for the ULF and other Unionist parties to work towards a political solution, while the security forces dealt with the IRA.[61]

What was happening in this short-lived enterprise, which was in no way conciliatory and in some ways even very reactionary, was that the UVF and those associated with it had begun to try to find their own way in politics and move into the space opened up by the collapse of Stormont and the 'Big House'. The ULF thought that this was necessary because it believed 'that the Unionists, the VUP [Vanguard Unionist Party] and the DUP have failed their supporters and it will be affiliated to none of them.'[62] Consequently, Loyalists on the ground had to start finding their own way, and as retrograde as some of the ULF's proposals were, this was at least a start to the development of real working class politics within Loyalism.

With the development of this political voice, the UVF then declared a ceasefire on 17 November 1973 to facilitate talks towards a political settlement of the conflict. The UVF also wanted to make clear that the Unionist politicians no longer controlled the UVF:

This will also point out to the politicians who advocate the use of force that they do not control the Ulster Volunteer Force and that we will not be used by them in order to achieve by militant means, that which they have failed to do by democratic and political means.[63]

The UVF was serious about the ceasefire and about what it hoped to accomplish and prove. The ceasefire also marked a public break with the Unionist politicians, whom it believed had used and disappointed them. The UVF did not intend to let Unionism use it anymore. While still not ready to put forward its own agenda, the UVF now knew and said what it would not do.

Sarah Nelson agrees that this ceasefire was not a cynical exercise to get the UVF's men released from prison, or to reorganise the UVF for a new offensive. She argues it 'reflected the influence of the "doves" at "brigade staff" and "officer" level'.[64] Nelson believes that the UVF was genuinely interested in ending the conflict and was even willing to countenance some form of power-sharing. Even before the ceasefire, the UVF released statements to the press focusing on conciliation and peace. However, the UVF was also clear that it was prepared to go back to war if it believed the Assembly and/or the British government was prepared to force them into a united Ireland.

A major problem confronting the UVF in getting its message out was the reticence and/or resistance of the media to publishing its statements. According to Nelson, 'the media, apart from the *Sunday News*, declined to publicise them'.[65] This would seriously hinder the UVF from getting its message heard and would help to keep it marginalised.

Another factor that undercut the UVF's political message and its proposed ceasefire was the continuation of the PIRA bombing campaign aimed largely at England. In fact, Bruce argues that the IRA violence undermined greater political involvement by the UVF in this period.[66] At the same time, according to Cusack and McDonald, the UDA in January 1974 launched sectarian attacks, aimed at undermining the UVF ceasefire. They quote a UVF statement, the day after the UDA murdered two innocent Catholics, in which the UVF called on the UDA to 'desist from their present murder campaign' and work to 'bring about peace and prosperity to our beloved Province.'[67]

The initial communiqué announcing the power-sharing Sunningdale agreement, which contained the 'Council of Ireland', a proposal giving the Republic of Ireland a political role in Northern Ireland and that all Loyalists opposed, also put a strain on the UVF, particularly between those who argued for political involvement and those who counselled simply defeating the 'enemy'. Eventually the UVF, while still nominally adhering to the ceasefire, drifted back to killing. Between 10 January 1974 and the 2 May 1974, the UVF killed at least 22 people. The worst was yet to come on 17 May 1974 with the Dublin-Monaghan bombings when the UVF killed 33 innocent people in a 'return of the serve'.[68] Many of these killings took place after the British government had legalised the UVF. Confusingly for many, the UVF continued to issue a number of conciliatory statements aimed at reaching out to its traditional enemies while it continued to kill in 1974.

One might ask, why the confused and contradictory nature of UVF actions and politics in this period? This study will deal in depth with this question later in this study. For now, a few comments will suffice to address this seeming contradiction. On the simplest level, especially in this period, one can argue that the UVF adhered to its emerging politics while continuing to conduct the 'war', perhaps a precursor to the PIRA's 'Armalite and Ballot box' policy. It is also possible that this simply reflected the tension inside the UVF between those who wanted to move towards politics and those who believed their primary purpose was to defend the Union. The provocations it faced from the IRA while on ceasefire would have exacerbated these tensions. However, a more sinister explanation has recently surfaced that claims that MI5 was involved in sectarian assassinations in 1974 and these 'were designed to destroy [then Northern Secretary Merlyn] Rees's attempts to negotiate a ceasefire, and the targets were identified for both sides.'[69]

Even in the face of these obstacles, the UVF undoubtedly continued to evolve politically and eventually began to seek a political accommodation with its enemies and to develop its own political solution to the conflict in Northern Ireland. The UVF communiqué sent to the *Sunday News* for publication in February 1974 provides strong evidence for this claim.

On 3 February 1974, the *Sunday News* published a set of reflections prepared by the UVF Brigade Headquarter Staff based on work by various members of the UVF. This communiqué made clear that, even with the violence of the UVF and its RHC allies, a real change in the political thinking had taken place within the UVF. One of the most telling sections stated that,

> The Ulster Volunteer Force leadership has a new outlook on life. They see Ulster, not simply through the eyes of sectarian bigots and gunmen, but through the eyes of enlightened Ulstermen. Ulstermen who now see that life in Ulster can only be enjoyed to the full by the creation of a new society based upon, the Unity and sovereignty of the ordinary rank and file Ulster people – Protestant and Roman Catholic alike.[70]

The UVF's statement argued that the conflict forced the Protestant working class to re-evaluate its deference to Unionist power and the failure of those politicians to take effective action to end the conflict. In fact, the UVF's disillusionment is clear from its questions: 'What the hell are we fighting for? What is the sense of bombing the IRA when our political leaders are incapable of working out a political solution?'[71] The UVF also complained that the political leaders with whom they met did not have 'any sound constructive policy to put forward'.[72] In frustration, it complained that, 'No one gave a damn' and no one acknowledged the UVF ceasefire. Having called the ceasefire to create the breathing space to find a political solution, the UVF found, as it would throughout its political journey, that

Unionist leaders preferred to, at best, marginalise Loyalists and at worst attack them.

Although the UVF fiercely opposed Sunningdale, in its 3 February 1974 statement, it exhibited the first insight into the political ideas that would later manifest itself as *Sharing Responsibility*. Under the heading, 'All must consent', they posited, 'the people of Ulster must realise that sooner or later they are going to have to live together. They must sink their differences and decide upon a common policy for peace and good government.'[73] The UVF also argued, 'It is utterly impossible for any one section of the community to produce an alternative that would be acceptable right across the board.' Furthermore, the UVF stated, 'If we are to have a real and lasting peace in Ulster then no alternative will be acceptable unless it has the consent of the vast majority of the ordinary rank and file people.'[74] Therefore, the UVF called for a Council of Ulster that would 'give organisations and parties an opportunity to meet their political and military opponents and learn of each other's fears and opinions.'[75] The UVF ended this communiqué by stating that,

> The Ulster Volunteer Force appeals to all Ulstermen, to pause, to stretch out the hand of forbearance and conciliation, to forgive and forget, and to join in making for the Province which they love, a new era of peace, contentment and goodwill.[76]

These statements, like the RHC documents examined earlier, convey clearly that within the UVF, elements of that group who had gone through a political reassessment and arrived at a very different understanding of what caused the conflict and how the conflict might end. In essence, for the UVF and its allies the scales had fallen from their eyes. What is notable is that the paramilitaries would not go back to their past blind support for the Unionist state. They now knew that all the people in Northern Ireland must have rights and enjoy life to its fullest in order to live without violence. Consequently, the UVF called for reaching out to its traditional enemies to create a society that all could enjoy.

Aaron Edwards' argument that the UVF frequently 'led' in politics in this period was on display in *Loyalist News* a week later. A front-page article in *Loyalist News* on 9 February 1974, entitled 'U.V.F. TAKES THE LEAD' reiterated the UVF's hope that its traditional foes would take the hand of reconciliation they offered. Furthermore, it stated that, 'it would not be the politician who would bring peace to Ulster. Peace can only come through the agreement of all those who have taken part in the war.'[77] While still arguing, at this point for majority rule, the UVF also called for full employment, good housing, and freedom of religion and of one's political views.[78] This statement sparked some interest from both the PIRA and OIRA and led to talks among the various organisations. However, these talks went nowhere in large measure because the UDA launched new attacks and portrayed itself as the defender of the Protestant faith and Ulster, the 'super-Prods' within and without the UVF undercut the talks, while the Provisionals clung to their demand for a 32-county united Ireland. Republican violence also increased during the year.[79]

At the same time, instead of acceptance from its own community, the UVF found itself under attack almost immediately after its February communiqué. Patrick Riddell, a *Sunday News* columnist, in a column that appeared on the 10 February in the *Sunday News*, blasted the UVF's 3 February article and criticised it for its 'muddle-minded nonsense', focusing mainly on the UVF violence and calling for the UVF to use the assembly that they already had.[80] Besides attacking the UVF for its violence, he also attacked it for its 'Woolly Socialist phraseology' which he argued 'is evidence of woolly thinking.'[81] Other reactions were no better. In its 17 February 1974 edition, The *Sunday News* published comments from various political leaders. These were generally negative. Tara, a radical, fundamentalist Protestant organisation, in particular unleashed a vicious attack on the UVF, which we will examine in depth in the next chapter.

The education minister and 'Unionist member for South Belfast, Mr Basil McIvor said he was not in the least impressed by what the UVF had to say', while 'SDLP leader Gerry Fitt said that the UVF suggestion that there should be a Council of Ulster at which militants from both sides should talk could not be taken seriously.' The VUP, at the time the most extreme of the Unionist parties, would not comment on a statement from a proscribed organisation and the DUP refused to support the UVF's Council of Ulster idea.

To appreciate the real political shift that began in this period, one need only look at the UVF journal *Combat*. In April 1974, while the UVF was ostensibly holding to its ceasefire, a front-page editorial appeared entitled 'Sectarianism: Who Stands to Gain?' The editorial attacked the middle class 'Unionist fur coat brigade' and 'Unionist misrule'. It also argued that recent sectarian attacks 'all point to the involvement of "hired mercenaries" working under the direction of the faceless degenerates who urgently require a renewed spate of sectarian violence.'[82] While demonstrating the UVF's emerging political awareness, the article also supported Spence's analysis on the founding of the UVF and the conspiracy within Unionism to foment a sectarian war. The argument that someone or some organisation stoked sectarian war by carrying out random sectarian killings will also play a prominent role later in this study as it helps to explain why the Loyalist political thinking and initiatives failed.

Another example of the UVF's emerging political sensibilities came in the same issue of *Combat*. The East Antrim Volunteers and East Antrim Workers Council inserted a sidebar, probably written by Billy Mitchell, entitled 'Combat Violence' which is worth quoting in full:

COMBAT The violence of the Provisional IRA; the senseless bombings, murders and mutilations.

COMBAT The violence of the Security Forces; the dawn swoops, the wrecked home, the Kitsonian torture, the distraught wives and heartbroken mothers.

COMBAT The violence of repression and injustice; the crime of Long Kesh, the taking away of a man's liberty without trial, the no-jury trials, the politically motivated sentences and the use of criminals as paid 'touts'.

COMBAT The violence of unemployment; the degradation of the dole queue, the meanness of handouts and the 'charity' of the state.

COMBAT The violence of bad housing and no housing; the overcrowding of home, the high rise flats, the damp walls, the high rents and the rapacious landlords.

COMBAT The violence of sectarianism; the division of a community for political gain, the murder of citizens on account of their religion, and the paid sectarian mercenaries of the upper-middle class tories [sic].[83]

It was such statements and the ceasefire that encouraged the British government to legalise the UVF on 14 May 1974. The government also legalised the PIRA and Sinn Féin in the hope that by bringing the paramilitaries together politically, it could get them to abandon the armed struggle.[84]

In conjunction with the legalisation of the UVF, the Ulster Workers' Council (UWC) Strike broke out. This strike initially appeared to stymie British plans. The Loyalist working class rose en masse, supported by the Unionist middle class and Unionist politicians in the form of the United Ulster Unionist Coalition, and brought down the hated, by Loyalists, Sunningdale agreement.[85] One might have expected that this strike and its aftermath would have ended the experiment to engage armed Loyalism and Republicanism in politics. However, just the opposite happened, at least in regards to Loyalism. The collapse of Sunningdale, like the fall of Stormont, opened the door to alternative visions of restructuring Northern Ireland and in a sense freed the paramilitaries to explore alternative structures for bringing the two warring communities together.

For people like Hugh Smyth one lesson of this strike was that they could have really made progress, but for the terrible mistake Loyalism made after the strike:

> We gained a victory through the workers strike and assembly, but immediately after having got the victory, we handed it back to the same politicians who had been doing nothing for us for years. I believe that at that stage if we had formed a workers' party out of that workers strike that I believe would still be in power today.[86]

Gusty Spence also noted of one of the more interesting lessons that Loyalism learned from this episode. He argues that,

> If the Ulster Workers' Council had said "we want the dissolution of the Council of Ireland, we want to co-operate with the power-sharing executive ... We want to be consulted." Then there is no doubt in my mind that the power-sharing executive would have co-operated with them ... Now that would have been a good thing for society because I couldn't have seen the executive forming a liaison group with working-class unionism without forming one with working class nationalism.[87]

Whether either Spence or Smyth is correct here in their analysis, the lessons that came out of this strike for the Loyalist paramilitaries was that they had to develop their own power-sharing plan, to create the space to implement it, and to move all armed groups towards politics. After the UWC Strike, the break that had begun during 1969–72, was in many ways now complete for the UVF and RHC.

### The Birth of the VPP

Bruce argues that the success of the strike encouraged the UVF leaders to move into political action, a decision that dovetailed with British policy at that time,[88] and coincided with the Northern Ireland

Office White Paper entitled *The Northern Ireland Constitution,* which the government published on 4 July 1974. The White Paper's goal was to find 'what provision for the government in Northern Ireland is likely to command the most widespread acceptance.'[89] At the same time, Stanley Orme, the Northern Ireland Office Minister, was also engaged in discussions with Loyalists and Republicans in Long Kesh.[90] Based on its analysis of the paramilitaries, the British government believed that the opportunity for détente now existed between the paramilitaries and that evidence existed of an emerging working class consciousness that the government could use to move the paramilitaries towards ceasefires. The government also believed that Loyalism was moving towards a form of 'Ulster nationalism'.[91]

While the government launched its initiative to create a devolved administration in Northern Ireland and to bring the paramilitaries into the political process, we now know that the Wilson government also flirted with the 'Doomsday Scenario' in which Britain would 'cut all constitutional ties with Northern Ireland and turn it into an independent dominion territory'.[92] Put simply, the government hoped for the best but prepared for the worst.

The UVF responded to these developments, its legalisation, and its perceived new power after the UWC strike, engagement by the British government, and the call for a new Constitutional Convention by launching the Volunteer Political Party on 22 June 1974. In a statement on the front page of *Combat*, signed by Billy Davison and Ken Gibson, the UVF announced the launch of the Volunteer Political Party with the following words:

> This week the Ulster Volunteer Force has taken another positive step forward by forming our own **Volunteer Political Party** (**V.P.P.**). This step was taken with a two-fold aim in view, firstly to encourage all Volunteers to think both objectively and politically, as to the type of Ulster they want and secondly, to ensure that the general public will easily identify that the voice of the **Volunteer Political Party** is also the voice of the **Ulster Volunteer Force**.[93] [Emphasis in original]

The statement asserted that the UVF had emerged 'from the shadows into the bright sunlight'[94] to fight those who had attacked and attempted to marginalise the UVF and its political evolution. Furthermore, the UVF 'required all Volunteers to join this Wing', telling them, 'It is not enough to know that you can fight physically without knowing as to why you are fighting.'[95] It also called on all within the Party to help formulate a policy document.

Beyond the many other problems that the VPP encountered through October 1974, the lack of a political programme that the party could rally around caused serious problems when things went badly for the Party, especially as the 'UVF was a broad political church. There was [sic] all sorts of ... political viewpoints in it and none.'[96] Without a party programme, the political leadership had a very hard time, as it would even if it had a political programme, in getting members to support it.

Nevertheless, the VPP eventually published its *Manifesto of the Volunteer Political Party* before the October election and called a ceasefire for the 12 August 1974, stating,

> This decision comes in accordance with UVF Policy and in direct response to the progress presently being made by the Volunteer Political Party in their sincere efforts to replace the war being waged in Ulster with lasting peace with justice for all people.[97]

Despite the pluralistic nature of the organisation, this document reflected a shift to the left economically and socially, and represented a move towards social democracy. In the section 'Ulster at Westminster', the VPP recognised that the days of shouting 'No surrender!' and ignoring the economic health of Northern Ireland 'are now over.' They argued that it was 'necessary to send to Westminster representatives who will make common cause with other MPs from other out-lying regions to defend economic interests common to all of them.'[98] The manifesto also called for securing the link with Britain by becoming an equal member within Great Britain and on parity with Scotland and Wales.

What is also interesting in the manifesto is that the VPP rejected the 'fur coat brigade' of the old Stormont government as well as any attempt to force Northern Ireland into a united Ireland, or contemplate a unilateral declaration of independence (UDI). The VPP stated its goal explicitly, 'we will support any evolution that will work for the good of all the people of Ulster.'[99]

Under '*Internment and Security*', the VPP called for the immediate release of all internees whose organisations were on ceasefire. It opposed the Diplock Courts and called for 'an expanded Ulster Defence Regiment and the return of the RUC to strictly policing activities.'[100]

In looking to the future, while preferring devolved government, the manifesto made clear that it could accept complete integration into the United Kingdom. However, it rejected unification with the Republic fearing that the Catholic Church would exercise its power over the Protestant people in religious, social, and educational policies and that economic policies would be those of an agrarian nation at the expense of an industrialised Ulster.

While rejecting a united Ireland, the manifesto also rejected a unilateral declaration of independence as injurious to the working class, in particular, saying that only the 'fur coat brigade' (the middle and upper classes) would benefit from such a declaration.[101] The manifesto recognised that breaking the economic link with Britain would only exacerbate the sectarian violence in Northern Ireland and would cause more suffering as the demand for limited jobs would increase if Northern Ireland went it alone. Therefore, in order to prevent even more sectarian violence and a descent into total anarchy, the VPP believed that Northern Ireland had to maintain the link with Britain.

Moreover, the manifesto and VPP's analysis anticipated Ron Weiner's landmark work *The Rape and Plunder of the Shankill – Community Action the Belfast Experience*,[102] in that it recognised that the interests of the 'fur coat brigade', would override the interests of the working class if Great Britain cut Northern Ireland loose. The VPP needed only look at the behaviour of the Unionist state over the period of 'fifty years of Unionist misrule' to understand this.[103]

The section dealing with UDI exhibits a great deal of political insight on the part of the VPP. Weiner's work pointed out that the Unionist state could only survive in isolation, without ties to international capitalism and only if Westminster left Northern Ireland alone. The thinkers behind the manifesto of the VPP recognised this also and knew that if Northern Ireland returned to the isolation of the past 50 years, the Protestant working class and the working class as a whole would suffer even worse deprivation and violence. Not surprisingly then, this document reflects the evolving political thinking of the UVF and its allies. Armed with their understanding of the past and the ramifications of the different 'unacceptable' alternatives, it went beyond the immediate constitutional issue and instead looked to the future of Northern Ireland, concentrating on the economic and political policies that affected the working class of both communities.

Interestingly enough, a week before the VPP published its manifesto; the *Loyalist News* published an interview with an anonymous RHC prisoner in Long Kesh. In the interview, he laid out his personal views on the various aspects of the conflict, including his views on religious freedom and power sharing. In regards to religious freedom, he argued that, 'it is only wrong when a person's beliefs impinge upon the rights of others.' When asked about power sharing with the SDLP, he replied,

> I believe that someday the Loyalist representatives, be they politicians or the various representatives of the Para-Military organisations, will sit down, face to face with other representatives of varying opinion to formulate whatever agreement there exists in order to set Ulster on the road to peace with justice, freedom, and comparative contentment for all people. In these circumstances, I would not disagree with the possibility of power sharing. If the SDLP are truly representative of the RC [Roman Catholic] population, then they must be given the responsibility to fully represent their voters.[104]

While none of these individuals and documents put forward any concrete proposals for the future in the manifesto, it is clear that there was a progressive political movement within both the RHC and the UVF. The UVF/RHC, or at least their leading elements, had moved towards not just ending the conflict and securing the border, but making sure that Northern Ireland did not return to violence or give political power back to those they believed benefitted from the '50 years of misrule'.

However, as we will see at the end of this chapter and in the next chapter, the VPP and its leading thinkers often went too far for the majority of UVF and RHC volunteers. Many volunteers were simply not ready for this type of thinking. At the same time, many outside the UVF, including those in Loyalist communities, did not believe gunmen could become politicians. More importantly, the Loyalist political analysis and solutions posed a threat to the forces that had a stake in keeping the working classes apart, the Protestant working class in its place, and the sectarian war alive. These forces would attack them not only for the threat they posed to their personal interests, but also for having the impertinence to step beyond their expected role in the Northern Ireland conflict. Consequently, as the politics of the paramilitaries threatened the control of the Unionist establishment over the Protestant working class, this establishment would attack the progressive thinking and thinkers in the UVF, RHC and VPP, undercutting, some would argue destroying, Loyalism's move towards politics, thus prolonging the conflict.

### Within the Context of Northern Ireland

Continuing to analyse and look for a political solution to the conflict, the RHC launched a document entitled *Within the Context of Northern Ireland*, which set out what the RHC believed should be the 'aims and beliefs of political representatives who would stand in the 1975 Northern Ireland Convention Elections.'[105]

*Within the Context of Northern Ireland* built on the thinking of the UVF and RHC, which had published a series of articles in *Loyalist News* under the title 'Proposals for the Assembly' in August 1973. In these documents, the early outlines of *Within the Context of Northern Ireland* and *Sharing Responsibility* appeared. In its proposal for the government, the authors argue that they wanted power sharing that was not mandatory. The proposal called for a government that would include all and would create 'a Parliament without "Border" or "Religious" issues'. The document also called for a reformed police force acknowledging that policing 'had been one of rancour ... for fifty years for the minority.' It also dealt with the issue of employment speculating that Northern Ireland could realise 'full employment' for all. In perhaps the most important section, the proposals argued that integrated education 'is one of the keys to the future'.[106] These ideas eventually found their way into *Within the Context of Northern Ireland* and *Sharing Responsibility* and illustrate once more the progressive nature of UVF and RHC in this period.

A member of the RHC, who requested to remain anonymous for this study,[107] with input from other RHC thinkers and reportedly with contributions from the UVF, wrote *Within the Context of Northern Ireland* before the October 1974 elections; *The Sunday News* announced it on 3 November 1974.[108] This document built on and fleshed out the concepts from the 'Proposals for the Assembly' and the VPP manifesto. In contrast to the manifesto of the VPP, which laid out general principles for a 'Progressive and Forward Thinking Unionist Party',[109] it laid out concrete proposals for the maintenance of the Union and proposed the 'radical changes' necessary to allow Northern Ireland 'to survive the next fifty years'.[110]

On the front cover of the document, the authors laid out how radical this would be arguing, 'Religion and politics are the two major factors in the lives of the people of this country. We must try and separate them. Past history has proved they cannot mix.'[111] In

Northern Ireland in 1974, nothing could have been more radical than to call for a secular society, as secularism would have attacked both the ethos of Catholic Nationalism and that of the conservative Protestant state.

The RHC addressed the prospective members of the Convention and appealed to them 'to make decisions that fulfil the political and religious aspirations of the *whole* [my emphasis] of the population of Northern Ireland.'[112] This represented a clear break from those who wanted a return to the majority rule of the old Stormont and was a warning that there would be no going back to the past. The rest of its programme made it clear that these thinkers had broken not just with the past, but also with the Unionist establishment. In the most important sections dealing with the Constitution, the link among Northern Ireland, Ireland and the UK, as well as security and the role of religion in Northern Ireland, the RHC had indeed embarked on some radical, innovative thinking.

Acknowledging that Northern Ireland 'had a long history of violence and political intrigue',[113] *Within the Context of Northern Ireland* called for a new Constitution that would embrace all citizens and work for the benefit of everyone. This new Constitution had to be,

> fully conscious of the principle of 'peace at home' with a view to founding a political and democratic state with judicial and ... with social reforms, to restore and guarantee human rights, social justice, serenity and well being for the individual and collectively.[114]

Regarding the link between Northern Ireland and the UK, the document laid out clearly that Northern Ireland's place was in the UK and that a 'sovereign Ulster must be the deciding factor in the link.'[115] However, it also called for a link with Dublin 'on a basis of friendship', which would eventually overcome the years of mistrust and build a relationship based on equals and common economic interests.[116] Anticipating that a more federal system within the British Isles would exist in the near future, it stated that the interests of England, Ireland, Northern Ireland, and Scotland dictated that they be on friendly terms.

Two other points deserve mention. The RHC argued that in this new federal system, 'It would be the aim of residents of Northern Ireland to woo the Southern residents within the bounds of an all-Ireland within a federal system in the British Isles.'[117]

Interestingly, this is a reversal of the Sinn Féin policy of using the British government as a 'persuader' to get Loyalists to enter a united Ireland.

The second point was the call for people in Northern Ireland to rid themselves of the 'inferiority complex and let the nations of the world know that the word "British" does not mean Englishmen ... alone.'[118] This is an acknowledgement that many in Northern Ireland still felt inferior in relation to not only Britain but in dealings with the Republic and the rest of the world. Yet, it also indicates that Loyalists were now determining their own identity and embarking on their own political journey. The self-confident cadre that had begun to develop inside and outside Long Kesh had now moved into the political arena, ready to engage as equals with their neighbours to the South and East as well as their fellow citizens in Northern Ireland. Still, it would take more than overcoming the divisions that existed and the problems facing both parts of Ireland. They stated that, 'Only time and tolerant understanding is the answer to our problems North and South of the Border.'[119]

As its cover page made clear, the RHC took a very strong stand on the negative impact of the intersection of religion and politics. This document also attacked all those who roused the working classes of both sides to fight and then stood above the fray to maintain their political and social position. The RHC, or at least elements of it, were now 'enlightened Ulstermen' prepared to reach out to their opponents and no longer prepared to follow those traditional leaders who had led them to the top of the hill and then left them there.[120]

By calling for separation of religion and politics, the RHC offered a vision of a new Northern Ireland that was secular and run in the interests of all the people, not one religion or the other. While accepting the right of any individual to worship however he or she wants, it refused to go further because to do so would, 'give credibility to the clerics who in past history have claimed more deaths and destruction to further their particular sectarian aims.'[121] The RHC concluded that, 'Religion and Politics must be parted forever.'[122]

*Within the Context of Northern Ireland* also dealt with a wide array of social and economic issues – housing, issues of nationalised industries versus the private sector, employment, taxes, tourism, farming, child welfare, pensioners, prison reform, radio and television, and judicial reform. These proposals indicate that the men who had written this document had adopted a programme very similar to mainstream European Social Democracy. More importantly, this document, and other proposals to come, reflects the fact these thinkers had totally broken with the past and traditional Unionism.

As stated above, the entire proposal reflected the thinking that Northern Ireland would not go back to the past. For instance when dealing with housing, the RHC, contrary to the policy of the old Unionist state, claimed that 'It is every man's right to have a house, either to rent or own.'[123] After the disastrous experience of urban renewal that involved building concrete high-rise flats such as Unity Flats, Divis Flats, and the Shankill Flats, they argued against making this mistake again. If anything like these had to be built again, the planners would set a limit of three storeys. The proposal also called for overcoming the housing shortage, while at the same time making sure the houses were inhabitable and stayed within the budget of the people who lived in them.

Integrated education was another area in which the RHC had moved beyond most people in Northern Ireland in 1974 and even 38 years later. Recent statistics bear this out. In a study done in 2006, only 5 per cent of the population attended an integrated school.[124] The RHC recognised the destructive nature of the segregated school system and, in fact, believed that the educational system was the root cause of sectarianism in Northern Ireland.[125] The goal of this part of the proposal was to make sure that children would grow up together rather than living their whole lives with no contact with someone from the other community. They also sought to end the tradition that where one went to school played a role in getting a job or any type of position.[126]

The RHC proposed that funding for education be radically changed so that only integrated state schools would receive state money and both public (private, in the British usage) and religiously-based schools would have to finance themselves with no state aid. Finally, within the new integrated state schools the proposal said that, 'Religious education should be taken out of the school syllabus.'[127] The far-reaching and extremely progressive ideas presented here also make it plain why it has been so difficult, even today, to reform the educational system. The proposals that the RHC put forward here would, as did much of Loyalist thinking, come up against too many entrenched interests.

As for the RHC's other proposals in this document, they all meant to help the economy, the worker, the families, the farmers, the pensioners; in short, to benefit the ordinary and working class people. The proposal called for making sure that old age pensioners could live out their lives in comfort, that families with children would get financial support, that farming practices would undergo a review to see how to make farming more efficient, and the state would reform the tax rates to help the working class and businesses. In essence, this document proposed a total restructuring of the social and economic base of the country.

The RHC also believed that the judiciary was in need of substantial reform. Again, having studied the history of Northern Ireland, in particular the 1969–74 period, the RHC concluded that politically motivated men had used the court system for their own ends and to protect their own interests. As a result, the RHC demanded that law and politics be divorced, and that all sitting judges immediately resign their seats. While not clear on how to reform the judiciary, the authors did recognise that those in power had used the legal system for their own ends.

Henry Patterson found evidence of this corruption and abuse of political power in research for his book on the Orange Order and the Unionist Party. He cites the case where, at a UUP Executive committee meeting in 1958, Brian Faulkner explained why universal suffrage could not come to Northern Ireland. Faulkner justified the exclusion of thousands of working class Protestants from the voting rolls as necessary to maintain control of areas in which Catholics made up the majority of the electorate. He boldly laid out the Unionist Party's thinking when he said,

> We cannot publicise our views on this matter ... The socialists can go out on the highways and by-ways and air their views but if we were to allow universal suffrage . . .... we may lose Derry City and ... lose Fermanagh ... . The trouble in telling people that they ought not to have the vote – it was important that it should be impressed upon them that the real reason behind it is Derry, Tyrone and Fermanagh.[128]

The laws clearly gave those who had money or property the vote while disenfranchising not only Catholics, but also the Protestant working class who did not own a home or paid enough in taxes to have the right to vote in local elections.

What we can then discern from this document is that those on the ground involved in the violent aspects of the conflict, those 'knuckle-dragging Neanderthals', had evolved towards a social democratic worldview; and moved light years ahead of Unionism and the IRA in this period. Tragically, for their political experiment, they had moved much too far and much too fast for their own constituency. They paid the price in October 1974.

## THE DEMISE OF THE VPP

In the October 1974 elections, Ken Gibson, representing the VPP, stood against two others: Johnny McQuade, a former UUP member who had defected to the Democratic Unionist Party (DUP), and Gerry Fitt, SDLP for the Westminster seat. The result was disastrous for the VPP. Gibson not only failed to win the seat, but he received only 2,690 votes in his own constituency and lost his deposit.[129] McQuade received 16,265 and Fitt won with 21,821 votes.[130] The VPP had put itself out there and had suffered a massive and humiliating political defeat. This defeat marked the end of the political experiment of the UVF and the RHC in this period.

In the wake of this defeat, the UVF withdrew from politics and issued a statement on 1 November 1974 that appeared on the front page of *Combat*:

Following consultations between Brigade Staff and the Chairman of the Volunteer Party, it has been agreed that the Ulster Volunteer force shall cease its involvement in party politics and shall not, therefore, be contesting the proposed Convention Elections.[131]

The statement continued, 'the low poll for the Volunteer Political Party candidate ... indicates that the general public does not support the political involvement of the Ulster Volunteer Force.' It then went on to say that the VPP would pledge 'full support to the established pro-Unionist parties' as long as they met certain requirements.[132] Those requirements represented a massive pullback from its previous positions.

The focus now shifted back to security of the Union, and the right to bear arms in defence of the Union against Republicanism and communism. The UVF also changed its position regarding prisoners. Where in their earlier statements, it took into account all prisoners, now the UVF declared that the state should only free those prisoners who had engaged in anti-Republican activities.[133] The new policy kept the argument for a return to democracy and devolved government, but the statement differed from earlier ones. It referred to any new political actions as good for the Province rather than the good of 'all' in the province. It did retain the call for civil and religious liberty for all, but that was about all that was left from the progressive thinking that appeared in June and over the previous year.

In a later edition of *Combat*, responding to queries from the many people who wanted to know the UVF's stand on politics and political action, Billy Mitchell wrote, 'The UVF is first and foremost a military organisation with politics taking a secondary role.'[134] After the elections, it left the politics to the mainstream politicians. Although this was clearly a setback for those who sought to create a political voice for Loyalism and in an effort to get its place at the negotiating table as an equal, Mitchell attempted to portray this as a move for the better. He wrote,

> Those who feel that the UVF has betrayed its supporters by scrapping its political wing should look again at the situation. Under the present system the force gives more freedom and scope to those of its members who feel politically inclined while, at the same time, it gives the same freedom for others to opt out of political action.[135]

This is consistent with the UVF's earlier statement in which it allowed its members to join any party they wanted and/or stand for election. However, what this meant was that the UVF had relinquished power once more to the very politicians who many in the UVF and RHC believed had created the situation in Northern Ireland in the first place.

This was not the only ramification of the VPP's electoral defeat. Not long afterwards, the UVF, although still nominally on ceasefire, raised the level of its violence and, as time went on, embarked on a vicious sectarian campaign in 1975. One of the reasons that the UVF returned to violence was in response to new Republican violence. The PIRA had unleashed a new bombing campaign in the autumn of 1974, blasting pubs in Woolwich, Guildford and Birmingham, killing at least 26 people and injuring many more.[136] With the UVF's stated aim of acting as a military force to fight Republicanism and communism, its return to violence to counter Republican violence fits its stated mission in this period. However, other factors also led it away from politics and back to a 'military solution'.

There was never strong support in the UVF for the political path that its leaders, including Spence, had tried to take. This was evident in the reaction of the Belfast Company and Platoon Commanders when news of the secret talks the Brigade staff held with the PIRA leaked out. At a meeting in the Liverpool Club in Belfast, these leaders rejected any agreements made by the Brigade Staff and blamed Billy Mitchell and Jim Hanna for these talks.[137] This fact reinforces Sarah Nelson's argument that the chief problem 'was that the radicals were trying to impose a top down policy – not responding to a wave of grassroots feeling.'[138] Consequently, with the defeat of the VPP at the polls, the dissatisfaction with the 'politicals' manifested itself in a coup that took place in the UVF. This is a murky episode, about which no one has really spoken.[139]

According to an anonymous source in Cusack and McDonald, Gibson wanted to put the UVF under the control of the VPP, himself and his lieutenants, thus putting decisions on military operations in the hands of the political, not military leadership.[140] Looking back on this period Hutchinson says, 'It was my particular argument at that time that we needed to remain in control of the politics, I'd no problem with people trying to influence what was going on but not to be in control of it.'[141]

As part of this conflict over control within the UVF, elements of the UVF killed Jim Hanna, one of its own members, on 1 April 1974 for reasons that are still not clear. Some speculate it was because he was a British agent, others speculate that it was because he took part in talks with both the PIRA and OIRA,[142] still others believe he fell victim to an internal rival in the UVF.[143] One UVF volunteer believes that Gibson ordered Hanna's killing to establish political control over the UVF.[144]

No matter the reason behind Hanna's killing, it was not until the defeat in the elections that the tension boiled over and enabled those opposed to the political movement in the UVF and/or the attempt by Gibson to establish political control of the UVF, to launch a coup and replace the Brigade staff. This coup, Hutchinson acknowledges, clearly represented a rightward lurch by the UVF.[145] Furthermore, Cusack and McDonald argue that after the coup the UVF plumbed new depths of violence.[146] The UVF's return to violence and the extreme sectarian nature of that violence left the UVF, by the end of 1975, in disarray and disrepute even among its own supporters, and sent those hoping for a political solution into despair.[147]

Sarah Nelson, who had access to the UVF and VPP leadership in this period, writes that the 'pink' (socialist or communist) elements moved out of the movement, or found themselves marginalised within the organisation.[148] She cites the UVF's return to the offensive against communism and its flirtation with the National Front as evidence of the backward step the UVF had taken.[149]

To see how far rightward and backward it had moved, one need only examine the 'UVF Military Policy' published in November of 1974. There is nothing in this document that would lead anyone to think that the UVF had ever flirted with politics and a compromise solution. It reiterates the statements made in the 1 November 1974 UVF communiqué in *Combat*, stating that the UVF would seek out and destroy the enemy, and aid the forces of the state. Furthermore, when the forces of the state were too weak to deal with the enemy, the UVF reserved the right to take matters into its own hands.[150] Much of the rest of this policy document concerned itself with the conduct of the UVF and when the UVF could legitimately use force against the state, against subversion and against its own members. In anticipation of the IRA's eventual policy of defining legitimate targets, Article 16, of the 'UVF Military Policy', declared, 'that all individuals, associations and business concerns which support the enemy are legitimate targets for procurement operations.'[151]

Articles 10 and 11 also illustrated the UVF's rightward shift. Article 10 declared that Provisional Sinn Féin and the PIRA were the chief short-term enemy and that the 'Provisionals could only be defeated by military means and any form of détente is out of the question.'[152] Article 11 is worth quoting in full:

> The most dangerous and deadly enemy in the long term will prove to be the Official IRA and its Marxist-Leninist associates. In the struggle against these Republican socialists the ULSTER VOLUNTEER FORCE [emphasis in original] recognises the need for both political and military action. To the end the UVF shall seek to expose the errors of doctrinaire socialism and to expose the myth of the supposed class struggle. At the same time the UVF shall gear itself to resist the upsurge in violent revolutionary socialism which will be unleashed throughout Great Britain and Ireland in the near future.[153]

Gone was the cooperation with the Officials and recognition of their common grievances with the 'fur coat brigade'.

This was such a turnaround that even the OIRA commented on it in its journal, *United Irishmen*. The OIRA recognised that the 'heady days of UVF aspirations for workers who supported them' were over and that 'bread and butter has been replaced ... with Faith and Heritage.'[154] In October 1975, the journal *Fortnight* commented on the shift that had brought 'harder men: more brawn than brain, "apolitical" rather than "right wing" ... their qualifications had more to do with prison ... . records ... than with intellectual abilities.'[155]

Simply put, the coup and the rightward shift left the UVF in disarray. Without a doubt, it led to the horrible year of 1975 during which the UVF embarked on a sectarian murder campaign. Hutchinson himself accepts that, 'Whenever they [brigade staff] were "right-of-centre", the strategy was "to kill Catholics".'[156] The year 1975 validates Hutchinson's argument. The UVF and RHC combined killed over 100 people, mostly innocent Catholics.[157] The UVF carried out the Miami Showband massacre, an act that revolted its own community. This massacre, along with many other actions eventually led to the proscription again of the UVF in October 1975. Even worse, according to the Dillon, this coup and the reaction against the political path also led directly to the formation of the Shankill Butchers, who took the violence to new and horrific levels.[158]

In response to the UVF actions, Merlyn Rees, the Northern Ireland secretary, proscribed the UVF on 4 October 1975; the next day the security forces rounded up dozens of UVF volunteers.[159] At the same time, the disgust within the UVF at the 'new direction' began to become public. Writing the week after Rees once again proscribed the UVF, one UVF volunteer from East Belfast published an article 'Ashamed of the UVF' in the *Sunday News* on 12 October 1975. *Loyalist News* republished this piece on 18 October 1975. He criticised the 'present Brigade [staff]' for 'debasing the name of the UVF' and 'misusing funds.' This volunteer wrote that he 'felt deeply ashamed' for the 'atrocities carried out against innocent men and women, Protestants and Catholics', and felt guilty for doing nothing to 'help the men on the Shankill who were trying to stop it.' He went on to call these men 'gangsters', who wrecked the UVF. He called for an 'honest and able man as brigadier' who 'will be given a chance to work for Ulster.'[160] He would not have long to wait as a counter-coup took place within the UVF at the end of October 1975, a coup that removed the more right-wing and militant leadership.

The militant and reactionary leadership had done much damage to the UVF that would take a long time to repair. For instance, Spence said that this was the period that 'I began distancing myself from the brigade staff and they from me',[161] eventually leading to his resignation from the UVF in 1978. Communities such as the Shankill turned against the UVF in horror at its actions. Nelson points out that prisoner aid groups, such as Orange Cross, found it very difficult to raise funds to help prisoners' families, sell prisoner handicrafts, or even continue to publish their paper.[162] The new leadership did reduce sectarian killings and for the UVF and Loyalism, it was an improvement. However, the new leadership did not involve itself in politics in the same manner as it had in 1973-74. Nelson claims that the new leadership behaved cautiously and kept relatively silent about politics, although it engaged with Loyalist political thinkers.[163] Billy Hutchinson supports Nelson's claim, stating that,

> they [UVF leadership] began to think about the future and how they'd move forward and they began to allow people like Hugh Smyth and Jim McDonald to go away and debate things politically and bring papers forward politically. They'd have been very supportive of their meetings and the outcomes of their meetings and would've used Hugh Smyth and Jim McDonald to negotiate with the NIO around a number of things. There was a very different attitude but at the same time they continued their military campaign but had more of a focus.[164]

## CONCLUSION

One could write more about the damage done to the UVF, the RHC and the people of Northern Ireland because of the electoral defeat, the coup and the rightward lurch. The terrible killings that took place, and the dangerous political drift of the UVF when the pure militarists took control of it, vividly demonstrates what happens when politics fail, especially within the context of Northern Ireland of the mid-1970s. Aaron Edwards' argument is on the mark:

> In this sense "war" for these volunteers became divorced from political life: "when this occurs in our thinking about war", wrote Clausewitz, "the many links that connect the two elements are destroyed and we are left with something pointless and devoid of sense."[165]

This is exactly what happened after the collapse of the political experiment of 1973-74. Politics would return later, in a very different form, but would take much longer to have any impact on ending the conflict.

# 5
# Darkness at the End of the Tunnel: The Failure of Politics

The previous chapter analysed the UVF's and the RHC's new thinking and how they tried to enact their ideas. That chapter showed clearly that the traditional narrative of all Loyalists as 'backwoodsmen' and/or 'Neanderthals' does not hold, and that by putting forward very progressive and inclusive political proposals some elements of Loyalism stepped beyond what everyone expected of them. Furthermore, the last chapter demonstrated that, contrary to the accepted wisdom, Loyalism was not simply reactive. In this period, progressive Loyalist political thinkers led the way in terms of politics and sought a way to end the conflict in a compromise peace in Northern Ireland. Unfortunately, for Northern Ireland, they failed in this enterprise.

Although the last chapter dealt briefly with why it failed, in particular the VPP's electoral disaster of 1974, an initiative that Hugh Smyth points out was a terrific idea, but whose 'timing was horrible',[1] to date a detailed analysis of why the political Loyalism emanating from some quarters of the UVF, the VPP and RHC failed does not exist. This chapter seeks to fill this gap in historical knowledge by examining the many factors, forces, and actors that aligned against the Loyalist political experiment and actively or passively helped to cripple or destroy the progressive politics emanating from the UVF and the RHC.

To accomplish this task, this chapter will examine and explain why the Provisional IRA could not constructively engage with political Loyalism in this period. It also asks and addresses the following questions: Why were political Loyalism and its representatives unable to get the votes or support from the communities that they claimed to defend and represent? Why did the UVF/RHC and the VPP encounter resistance from mainstream Unionist parties when they put forward ideas to end the conflict and what was the nature of this resistance? What role, if any, did some elements of British intelligence play in undercutting the movement towards compromise and cooperation? If sections of British intelligence did undercut the development of Loyalist thinkers, then how did they do so and why?

Answering these questions, in particular the alleged role and actions of certain sections of British intelligence, goes a long way to explaining why the Loyalist political experiment failed, why this conflict lasted so long and why it was so difficult to end. Doing so provides a very different view of the nature of this conflict.

## PROVISIONAL REPUBLICANISM

The easiest question to answer is why the PIRA could not engage constructively with political Loyalism in this period. The simplest explanation is that, after 50 years of living in what they viewed as a failed sectarian state, what sense did it make for Republicans to accept a new partitionist assembly or anything that would maintain Unionism and the link with Britain, regardless of how inclusive and just this new assembly would be? At the same time, believing itself to be the legitimate government of Ireland and the generation that would finally realise the Republic, there was no reason for the PIRA to compromise with its enemies. Consequently, PIRA did not see the need to develop a plan for a compromise peace because it believed it would throw the British out of Northern Ireland at the point of a gun.

Bowyer Bell and Cusack and McDonald point out that the PIRA did engage in secret talks with the UVF in 1974 to find some form of common ground, and recent evidence shows the PIRA was willing on some levels to talk with and compromise with the UVF.[2] However, those talks went nowhere.[3] One reason for this failure, among many others, was the fallout from the PIRA's continued violence and 1974 bombing campaign. As we will see, these actions only strengthened the hand of the hardliners within the UVF who opposed talking to Republicans and helped undercut any possibility of compromise with Loyalism.[4]

Echoing Clausewitz's warning, the OIRA pointed out that 'a terror campaign ... without a political corollary was a mindless and deadly exercise.'[5] Liam McMillen of the OIRA pointed this out at the annual Bordentown speech commemorating Wolfe Tone, the father of modern Irish Republicanism, in June 1973. In response to the Provisionals continued reliance on exclusively militarist tactics, McMillen, restated, 'We stand not on the brink of victory but on the brink of sectarian disaster.'[6] Tomás MacGiolla had already used this term in a speech given in July 1972 called 'Where We

Stand: The Republican Position.' MacGiolla also responded to the PIRA's declaration of 1972 as the 'Year of Victory' by clearly stating, 'We are not on the brink of victory, but on the brink of sectarian disaster and sell-out.'[7] Ignoring these warnings, the PIRA continued its armed campaign, which weakened the position of the UVF delegates to the secret talks and led to a violent backlash from Loyalist paramilitaries who embarked on their own campaign of 'counter-terrorism' and of 'terrorising the terrorists.'[8]

Another important factor that stymied political accommodation with Loyalism was that the Provisionals had little in the way of political thinking in this period. The Provisionals really did not begin to develop this until 1977, at the earliest,[9] and it took the PIRA until 1992 to publicly countenance a compromise peace. Even with the political development within the PIRA, most PIRA volunteers like many Loyalist volunteers, had a very low level of political sophistication and this included the early PIRA leadership.[10] This created a situation, in which no matter what Loyalists might do to seek accommodation within the context of Northern Ireland, in this period and in the future, the PIRA, because it was still 'committed to a United Ireland', could not really contemplate a compromise solution. As Smyth put it, 'You can't extend the hand of friendship, if somebody's not prepared to accept it.'[11]

The works of Bowyer Bell, a leading authority on the Provisional IRA, supports Smyth's argument. He claims that the 'The IRA leadership was ... narrow, parochial, committed to the simple dream [of a united Ireland].'[12] The recent work, *Abandoning Historical Conflict?*, supports Bowyer Bell's contention. In a series of interviews with ex-Republican and Loyalist volunteers, the authors claim, 'their [PIRA volunteers] initial motivation "wasn't anything to do with politics, really."'[13] This is also reflected in the more common attitude of one PIRA volunteer who said, 'I hadn't a political thought in my head ... other than it was to get the "Brits" out of Ireland.' He added, 'We just want to shoot.'[14] Another IRA volunteer, Gerard Hodgkins joined for the same reason. He told Alonso that his, 'motivation was that I was young ... there is an excitement to it ... "fuck, somebody give me a gun, this is great."'[15]

The stories of Anthony McIntyre (see Introduction) and Gerard Hodgkins may stand out, but they are not unusual. Alonso cited many other examples of this attitude and the lack of political awareness among the IRA volunteers. His work revealed that the motivation for most of them did not come from well thought out Republican ideals: like McIntyre, many volunteers were very 'pro-Republican without knowing what Republicanism actually was.'[16] Instead, according to Alonso, family histories, Republican mythologies, and indoctrination played the major role in the decision to join the IRA.[17] Like the Loyalist paramilitaries, it was not until prison that most of these volunteers began to study history and politics and began to understand the conflict and what it would take to end it.[18]

Tommy McKearney, a former IRA prisoner and socialist thinker within the IRA, argues,

> What was missing ... was a coherent analysis and what it meant to be a socialist or how it might be implemented, apart from a broad and sometimes uncertain view that the details could be worked out in the aftermath of an IRA victory.[19]

He continues claiming that, 'The Provisional IRA was composed largely of young men and women in a hurry, who were focused on prosecuting the insurrection and often viewed political education as an optional extra.'[20]

What political thinking that did exist among the Provisionals came from the 1971 *Éire Nua* document, which the Provisional IRA scrapped after the 1981 Hunger Strikes. *Éire Nua*'s fundamental proposals called for 'a federation of the four historic provinces of Ireland, Ulster, Leinster, Munster, and Connacht, with each having its own provincial parliament under the coordination of a national government.'[21] It also called for 'devolved powers through provincial parliaments to local councils', as well as a 'citizen participation in their own governance at all levels of government.'[22] To appeal to the Unionist/Loyalist population in the North, the authors of *Éire Nua* called for an 'all-Ireland constitution incorporating: A Bill of Rights, Separation of Church and State, and An Independent Judiciary.'[23] Coincidentally, Desmond Boal, a lawyer and co-founder, along with Ian Paisley of the Democratic Unionist Party, came out in favour of a two-state federal Ireland, which would consist of one 26-county and one six-county state.

*Éire Nua* did appear to represent a genuine effort to end the conflict and it did gather some interest, in part, because it attempted to address the concerns of the unionist population by protecting their rights within a Federal Ireland. However, many factors worked against it as a practical way of ending the conflict.

Hugh Smyth contends the 'the Loyalists said ... "look, we don't want that. We're not taking that."'[24] Recent revelations support

Smyth's argument. This new information points out that progress did take place around *Éire Nua* and other issues in the secret meetings between the IRA and the UVF in 1974, including the possibility of a permanent ceasefire, but the 'super-Prods' within the UVF and many groups outside of it opposed and prevented any compromise.[25]

Although these talks were productive, it is questionable how far they would have gone even if the 'super-Prods' had not intervened. For one, while the PIRA welcomed and considered some accommodation with Boal's federal plan, the reality was that it did not envisage a compromise peace with Loyalism within a Northern Ireland state.[26] At the same time the PIRA, as mentioned earlier, 'simply kept up the pressure of their campaign.'[27]

McKearney also claims that this initiative went nowhere for a number of other reasons, not the least of which was the fact that when the UVF and PIRA met to discuss this 'a Provisional IRA negotiator behaved aggressively and undiplomatically.'[28] Furthermore, even though the Dublin based IRA representatives put forward *Éire Nua* as a possible basis for a settlement,[29] Bowyer Bell argues that Northern Republicans would have little use for *Éire Nua*, claiming that in the midst of armed conflict, 'militant Northerners ... saw it as an unnecessary concession to intransigent unionist opinion.'[30] This fact is important, as the 'militant Northerners' did not believe in 'federalism' or a compromise peace with Loyalism.[31]

Bowyer Bell also contends that *Éire Nua* represented an older generation of Republicans, mainly the Dublin based leadership, who saw it as the way forward, while Northern Republicans only viewed it as an expedient that by 1981 had served the PIRA's purpose.[32] Ed Moloney agrees with Bowyer Bell and claims that that *Éire Nua* was not a policy statement that the left-wing or urban elements of Republicanism could or would accept and that this document appealed mainly to the Catholic and conservative elements of Southern Republicanism.[33] Henry Patterson is harsher in his analysis; he views *Éire Nua* as a cynical ploy by the Republican movement to prove they 'were not just reactionary militarists.'[34] According to Patterson, the only reason the PIRA accepted *Éire Nua* was to provide 'constitutional froth' that could deflect the critics who claimed that the PIRA had no real politics.[35]

Although a UVF document from 1977 points out that the PIRA claimed to oppose clericalism and stated 'that under the Eire *Nua* religious intolerance and clericalism would be non-existent',[36] Richard Davis argues that *Éire Nua* was based on 'Irish and

Christian values' and 'fell within Catholic guidelines' when dealing with social and political issues.'[37] If Davis and Maloney are correct, then *Éire Nua* would have had little attraction for most unionists. At the same time, *Éire Nua's* concessions to unionism and its inability to establish a 32 county Irish Republic increased 'northern [Republican] disquiet with central aspects of *Éire Nua*.'[38] Beyond these many problems, the Republic of Ireland's government would have had little stomach for it, as *Éire Nua* would have meant the end of the Republic of Ireland in its present form.[39]

As the PIRA in the North gradually distanced itself from *Éire Nua*, a strategic reappraisal came about and new politics did begin to develop around Gerry Adams, Martin McGuinness, and Danny Morrison in the late 1970s, after the UVF and RHC had already pulled back from active involvement in politics. Jimmy Drumm signalled this shift in the 1977 Bodenstown speech. In words similar to that of the IRA before the 1969 split and the thinking of the OIRA after the split,[40] Drumm said,

> The forging of strong links between the Republican movement and the workers of Ireland and radical trade unionists will create an irrepressible mass movement and will ensure mass support for the continuing armed struggle in the North.[41]

The difference between this speech and the OIRA was that the PIRA left out any reference or consideration of the Protestant people or the Protestant working class.

In 1977, this thinking also found its way into the IRA's *Green Book* (the IRA manual), which was more reminiscent of IRA thinking before the 1969 split, again except for excluding the Protestant working class, than PIRA thinking after the split. This document stated,

> Sinn Féin should employ full time organisers ... Sinn Féin should be radicalised (under Army direction) and should agitate around social and economic issues which attack the welfare of the people.[42]

It would take the PIRA until 1982 to develop a new, political ideology known as the 'Armalite and the Ballot Box',[43] which combined military and political action to achieve a united Ireland. When it did make this shift towards politics, Gerry Adams 'drew on the past to point the way forward.'[44] For the Adams leadership, the goal was still the Irish Republic proclaimed in 1916. Only now, the IRA would achieve the Republic in a very different way than it had intended in 1970, albeit one that still focused on victory and did not involve compromising with or even talking to Loyalism. This would also eventually lead to a shift in the movement from the armed struggle towards a political settlement and would cause the IRA trouble with its own volunteers. One set of commentators argues that,

> the leftist posturing of the late 1970s and early 1980s was eventually displaced by a Sinn Féin political programme which, whilst left of centre, is bereft of revolutionary pretensions, ditched amid the prospect of entrance into government during the 1990s.[45]

Like the UVF and the RHC, when they embarked on a political path, ordinary IRA volunteers did not universally support the political thinking and evolution of the IRA leadership. In fact, it took a great deal of cajoling and manipulation for the IRA leadership to get the organisation to agree on a ceasefire in 1994 and again in 1997.[46] As a result, even when the leadership realised that the conflict had to end in a compromise peace, according to Ed Moloney, they had to manipulate ordinary volunteers to achieve their ends. As a result, they lost many members who disagreed with their political direction.[47]

Another significant factor militating against compromise with Loyalism was the Provisionals' view of Protestants as 'deluded Irishmen'. As noted briefly in the 'Introduction', the IRA viewed Protestants in Northern Ireland as Irish men and women who had not realised their 'true' Irish nature. They believed and, as recent work indicates, continue to believe, that once the British pulled out of Northern Ireland and unification took place, the scales would fall from the eyes of Protestants.[48] Once that happened, Protestants would realise they were truly Irish and belonged to the Irish nation. Bowyer Bell illustrates this point when he argues that Republicans believed that they possessed the truth and that the only reason that Protestants did not understand they were Irish was the fact that British propaganda had blinded them.[49] Therefore, according to this narrative,

> a united Ireland would convince the unionists that they were Irish and the Loyalists that sectarian murders was futile. A united Ireland would, somehow, be united not by the conversion of the

Protestant workers to class interests ... but by the power of the old dream.[50]

This conviction, if for no other reason, led the IRA to believe that it did not need to participate in an internal compromise settlement with Loyalism.

Even though the IRA leadership met with the UVF in 1974, the IRA really could not engage with the Loyalist thinkers as equals or partners as this went against its narrative that this was a struggle for national liberation, a war of the Irish nation against British imperialism, and the IRA was the legitimate government in Ireland. David Ervine accurately portrayed IRA thinking when he said,

> They [the IRA] were formulating a policy that effectively was typified by the suggestion that they weren't fighting us. They had an illusion of themselves as the legitimate government of the island of Ireland, *à la* the 1918 vote ... So, they saw themselves as the legitimate government of Ireland. Of course, if you are the legitimate government of Ireland, your enemy is not the people on the island of Ireland; your enemy is the British Government.[51]

A 1974 PIRA document reinforces this view. In it, the author justifies the use of violence stating that, 'the primary objective of the IRA is to achieve freedom and unity of Ireland by forcing a British withdrawal.'[52] It argues against compromising with the 'other quarter' of the population in order to fulfil the wishes of the other three-quarters.'[53] Armed with this narrative, the IRA, although it did engage at various times with Loyalists, did not have to negotiate with and compromise politically with Loyalists or the Protestant population as the war was not against them, but against the British government.

This narrative also posited that Loyalism and Loyalists, if not deluded Irishmen/women, were nothing more than agents of the British state fighting to maintain British colonial rule. For Republicans this meant that Loyalists were not independent actors. Instead, the IRA characterised them as 'Loyalist death squads', 'unionist death squads', 'pawns' or simply agents of the British state.[54] In essence, the IRA believed or utilised the narrative that Loyalism could not have done anything on its own and that the British used them to do their dirty work, a practice known as 'collusion.'[55]

There is no doubt that collusion did exist on various levels. The Pat Finucane murder, the lawyer killed by the UDA for defending

IRA suspects, and also the murder of Laughlin Maginn, an innocent Catholic also killed by the UDA on leaked security information, both in 1989 are evidence of this.[56] Furthermore, the Steven's Inquiry, the panel set up to investigate collusion, found 'that Security force collusion with Loyalist paramilitary killers led to a number of murders in Northern Ireland.'[57]

However, Loyalists have a different take on collusion. One narrative that this author has heard in numerous conversations is that it was not really collusion in all cases. Their argument was that they had deliberately put men in the UDR to 'obtain weapons, training and access to files on the nationalist community and IRA.'[58] While many are sceptical of this narrative, recent revelations in the Belfast Telegraph have given traction to this argument. According to Liam Clarke,

> Martin McGartland, a former RUC Special Branch agent within the IRA, has confirmed claims that the Provisionals got co-operation from people working for the RUC. It is claimed a honey trap involving one of the Provos' very own Mata Hari was used to seriously compromise police security.[59]

Tom Roberts says he has 'great difficulty with the word collusion because our experiences of the security forces was more like collision. You know, as in any conflict the security forces will infiltrate and manipulate insurgent groups.'[60] In a private conversation, another former member of the UVF said, and this is paraphrasing, 'It didn't look like collusion when they knocked down my door to arrest me.'[61]

They also view the accusation of collusion directed against Loyalists as hypocritical and that Republicans 'overplay this [collusion].'[62] Roberts cites the 'Stakeknife' case as a glaring example of Republican collusion. In this case, the head of the IRA's Internal Security squad was responsible for up to 40 killings while in the employ of the British state. He argues that,

> if the Provos were willing to admit it, they were pretty well infiltrated themselves. And they don't refer to that as collusion. I think the example of Freddie Scappaticci sitting at the top of the internal security squad in the IRA, in the pay of the British. How much higher can you get?[63]

Hugh Jordan's work supports this claim. He cites one particular case of collusion involving the IRA, where an IRA operative called

Maurice Gilvarry was 'turned' by the RUC. While in the employ of the RUC, Gilvarry participated in the double murder of a retired prison officer and his wife and then turned in his accomplices.[64]

The Smithwick Tribunal, which is investigating possible collusion between the IRA and the Gardaí in the fatal shootings of RUC Chief Superintendent Harry Breen and RUC Superintendent Robert Buchanan in 1989, recently received a 'dossier of evidence from Ian Hurst, a former member of British military intelligence.' In this dossier, he claims that, 'half of all senior IRA members were working for various intelligence services.'[65]

Clearly, the RUC and the British forces 'ran' and/or colluded with the paramilitaries on both sides. However, the existence and the extent of 'collusion' on the Loyalist side has allowed the IRA to frame the conflict in terms of a war against British presence in Ireland. In this narrative then, it is not a battle between those who want a united Ireland and those who want the union with Britain; it is an anti-imperialist struggle, with Loyalists as part of the imperialist state apparatus. Dawn Purvis recognises this, as do most, if not all, political thinkers within Loyalism:

> Republicanism was quite happy to join this peace train and that it would be they and the British government because that suits their ideology. To have the other warring faction in there didn't suit because it fed into this notion of two warring tribes and left the government out of it.[66]

In an interview with Alonso, a former Republican validates Purvis' argument and admits now that this was a simplistic view that led to many mistakes by the Republican movement:

> The big issue that is never discussed in the Republican movement in my view is the sectarian nature of the conflict ... although in the minds of the sort of purist Republicans it was a conflict between the Republican movement and the British, and the British army.[67]

This analysis of Provisional Republicanism does not seek to minimise or downplay what the Provisional movement eventually did to end the conflict and move Northern Ireland into the present era of relative peace. However, what this study of Provisional IRA attitudes and political thinking from this period illustrates is how the PIRA, even though it met with the UVF in 1974, was not ready to engage with the political thinking coming out of Loyalism in the 1970s.

This period also provides us with one of those 'grand ironies' of history. While the leadership of Loyalism developed political programmes for power sharing within the context of Northern Ireland, reached out to their traditional enemies and recognised that all warring parties had to sit at the negotiating table in the 1970s, it took the IRA many more years to realise that the politics of compromise, not military might, would end the conflict. Only in 1992 did the IRA, or at least the leadership of the IRA, accept the need for compromise in a political settlement that would not result in immediate unification. By then, the UVF and RHC, while still engaged politically with the PUP, had retreated to their traditional role of defending the community and leaving the politicians to find a solution to the conflict.

Nevertheless, one can argue that even if the PIRA was not so politically naive and if it had responded to the UVF and RHC political initiatives, Loyalist politics would still have failed. Examining all the forces and obstacles aligned against political Loyalism and its political ideals, its success, or even its ability to have an impact on the politics of Northern Ireland would have been nothing short of miraculous. That miracle did not occur.

## PROTESTANT ATTITUDES AND THE PROTESTANT WORKING CLASS

The above analysis clearly illustrates why, even beyond Republican ideology, Republicans were not ready to compromise with Loyalism in this period to achieve a political settlement in Northern Ireland. However, another problem confronted those who wanted to create progressive politics within Loyalism. They encountered resistance and active opposition to their ideas within their own organisations and their own community. This did as much, if not more damage to the Loyalist political experiment than the attitudes and actions of the Republican movement.

The previous chapter's examination of the failure of the VPP and the coup that took place within the UVF in 1974, illustrated how little support there was within and without the UVF for it becoming and acting as a political movement. In the form of the VPP, The UVF had, in Hugh Smyth's words 'went too soon … . We weren't prepared and we got a bloody nose out of it.'[68] After this failure, the UVF lurched rightward and went back to its professed role of defending Northern Ireland's constitutional position and killing its enemies to preserve that position. From that point onwards, the UVF's political policy was to engage with politicians on its own terms and eventually liaise with the Loyalist politicians, accepting advice and analysis, but no longer actively engaging in politics.

Gusty Spence had met this same resistance to his political thinking. Many of the volunteers did not understand his politics and viewed their own role as that of 'defenders' and 'soldiers' not as politicians and thinkers. The violent and sectarian nature of the conflict outside the prisons helped reinforce those attitudes and undercut support for any political thinking.

The attitudes within the paramilitary organisations are not surprising when examined within the context of the community from which they originated. The 'politicals' for want of a better term, within these organisations had stepped beyond the expectations and the accepted role of those from the working class Loyalist community.[69] Therefore, while they might put forward grand ideas about compromise, progressive politics, and thinking as 'enlightened Ulsterman', their own community had not travelled down that road with them.

The documents and interviews referenced so far in this study indicate that there was a very high level of analytical thinking taking place among a small cadre of the RHC and UVF, mostly those in Long Kesh, who had the time to step back and deliberate on the conflict.[70] Their work was significant and could have made a difference in another context, but their programmes and ideas clearly did not represent the majority within their organisations and their communities.

As Steve Bruce points out, using just these documents and arguing that they represent the thinking of everyone in the UVF and RHC, can present a somewhat skewed vision of how deep the political thinking penetrated the RHC and UVF.[71] Here Bruce is somewhat accurate. Even Billy Mitchell thought the Loyalist thinkers were not representative of the Loyalist community as a whole.[72] While this is essentially correct, it does not take away from the work done by these men to develop new ways of thinking to end the conflict. However, the fact remains – the lack of popular support was a crucial reason that these men failed in their attempt to bring peace to Northern Ireland.

One example of how far the leadership was ahead of its membership and its community and how little support it received appears in a nine-page document that Boston College recently purchased from the Gusty Spence archival collection. This document records that

in the secret talks that took place between the UVF and the PIRA
in 1974, as noted above, the leadership of both organisations made
significant progress, which eventually led the UVF to write, 'The
agreements between the two organisations could have led to a better
understanding and to a permanent ceasefire.'[73] However, it is not
clear from the notes of this meeting whether this meant a ceasefire
between the PIRA and the UVF or a general ceasefire as there was
no mention of a general ceasefire or the ending of the PIRA's armed
struggle. Instead, what came out was the UVF's insistence that if
the IRA's war was against the British then the IRA should restrict
'their military campaign to that end.'[74] Regardless, nothing came
of this initiative for the reasons outlined in the previous section
and, as stated earlier, because 'the super-Prods would not wear it.'[75]

There are many other examples from *Orange Cross*, *Loyalist
News* and *Combat* of the retrograde thinking within the UVF
and the RHC, and the kind of resistance and problems that those
who tried to move their own organisations into the politics of
compromise faced. Reading these journals confronts the reader
with a dizzying array of opinions, from the far right to the far
left. Articles appeared supporting the right-wing National Front;
at various times, some articles would attack socialism, while others
would seem to support socialist ideas. At the same time, the majority
of these articles exhibited very little sophistication and depth of
thought and some argue that these articles were more representative
of the thinking of the ordinary volunteer. For purposes of this study,
it will serve to mention just a few here.

In the May 1971 edition of *Loyalist News*, the front-page lead
article demanded the return of the B-Specials, claiming that they
needed to 'ANSWER WITH THE ONLY SOLUTION ... THE
GUN'[76] (emphasis in original). The August 1973 edition of *Loyalist
News* also published a favourable story about the far-right National
Front. At the same time as the UVF condemned sectarianism, a
full-page article also appeared in *Combat* praising the National
Front as 'a party of British Nationalism', while wishing them 'every
success in Northern Ireland.'[77]

Just a month earlier, *Orange Cross*, published a story called 'just
"ned" a true story'. This article told the story of a hard working
Protestant who fought in World War I, came back to poverty,
re-joined the army to survive, served in Sierra Leone and then
came back to fight the IRA in 1922. The point of the article was
to attack Bernadette Devlin and John Hume for benefitting from
the welfare state and then attacking the 'Protestant ascendancy',

while Ned scraped by in two-room house off the Shankill Road.[78] This is an example of the thinking that fuelled the populist rage against Catholics.

Throughout 1975, various articles in *Loyalist News* denoted a threat from the non-white world to Western Civilisation while at the same time referring to a theft at a Chinese Restaurant as a 'Chinky Restaurant Theft'.[79] It ran a long series of articles attacking the Catholic Church and communism, and ran another article supporting the National Front. It also continually warned of the 'Red Menace'.[80] When talking about the various and contradictory articles in *Combat*, Hugh Smyth said,

> You know you would have had the 'No surrender!' 'Not an inch!' But, at the same time another article saying 'Look, we're no better off than the people on the Falls Road. We have bad housing. The Catholics have bad housing. We have unemployment. The Catholics have unemployment. Our health problems are bad.[81]

Although these are just a small sample of the retrograde thinking within the UVF and the RHC, these examples clearly illustrate that the mass of these organisations had not moved as far as the thinkers in Long Kesh who were writing manifestos and proposals at a sophisticated level. This meant that the ordinary volunteers did not always understand or support their own leaders and in the case of the VPP did not even vote for it.

When asked why many in the UVF would have voted for the DUP instead of the VPP, Hugh Smyth replied, 'The UVF's a big, big organisation. It's a big church. I daresay that you've people in it who agreed with what Paisley was saying "Not a Taig [Catholic] about the place."'[82] One senior UVF official agreed with Smyth's analysis, arguing that the VPP 'was a coalition of sorts – fascists, socialists, liberals etc., all under one umbrella.'[83] Regarding the problem of leading the UVF to progressive politics, Billy Mitchell noted that,

> in many ways we were too far ahead of our time. The volunteers just wouldn't have been ready for it. The problem was if you try to lead too far from the front the people are that far behind you that you are not really leading at all, you're out on your own.[84]

Sarah Nelson's work here is invaluable. She had first-hand experience with the Shankill constituency and an understanding of why the VPP and progressive politics neither penetrated the Protestant working class nor connected with those outside the Loyalist community.

Nelson points out that on a structural level there were many forces aligned against the VPP and that they spanned the political spectrum. Focusing on factors that lay outside the Protestant community, Nelson cites one member of the OIRA who was not certain about the socialist bona fides of the VPP and argues that the SDLP, whose policy was to exclude the gunmen from politics, opposed the VPP. Although some members of the NILP worked with the VPP, it generally opposed the VPP, not wanting gunmen in politics. Moderate Unionists feared and opposed the VPP because it might be socialist or, as Nelson puts it 'because of social snobbery and class hostility.'[85] To illustrate her point Nelson cites an article that had appeared in *Fortnight*, which questioned 'the intellectual and moral capacity' of the VPP to take part in politics.[86] Interestingly, *Fortnight* published this article within a week of the UVF's conciliatory statement in the *Sunday News* of 3 February 1974. Finally the VPP candidate Ken Gibson, a member of the UVF and former prisoner, stood against, John McQuade of the Ulster Unionist Coalition, who was working class himself and very popular on the Shankill. Even without all these problems, the VPP would have had a difficult time winning an election and taking root in its own community.

The VPP confused the very people that it wanted to reach by departing from the traditional line of Unionism and focusing on more than just the border. Nelson claims that many people on the Shankill commented that the articles in *Combat* and the VPP manifesto were too hard to understand. The articles about Irish history and economics had a red tinge to them that 'looked suspiciously ... Republican minded.'[87] According to Nelson, the traditional Unionist parties had the voters' ears, as they always had, and the VPP could not break this hold and get people to see what they saw, that the traditional Unionist politicians did not care about or have the best interests of the working class in mind. Nelson recounts one episode where Ken Gibson pounded a table in frustration because he could not get the Protestant working class to see its own self-interest. Reportedly, he said, 'Scum, rats [i.e. the politicians and Orangemen] I've told the people out there, but they're afraid. I've told them, you can run this country, you can have anything you want.'[88]

Another important factor that brought down the VPP,

> was the reaction of the influential Loyalists in Belfast, UUUC [United Ulster Unionist Coalition] politicians, Orangemen and religious fundamentalists [who] far from ignoring the VPP, like the media, gave it attention out of all proportion to its size or strength.[89]

These were the 'super-Prods' 'who went into hysterics fearing communist subversion'[90] with any move towards politics from within Loyalism. This led to a vicious disinformation campaign against the VPP, in which these 'super-Prods' attacked the VPP for communism, republicanism, and all sorts of 'vices.'

At the same time, a rural-urban split existed within Unionism. When talking about the left-wing politics that Spence and others developed in the 1970s, Roberts notes that the type of politics coming out of the VPP in the 1970s and then later the PUP never 'made any inroads outside of Belfast in terms of electoral support.'[91] He argues,

> it really didn't take root in rural areas ... . it is much like any, sort of other society. Socialist type politics normally take root in the major centres of population where there is more deprivation.[92]

A study done by T. K. Daniel supports Roberts' claim. In a 1976 article called 'Myths and militants',[93] he argues that a split within unionism took place between rural and urban Protestants. He also claims that evidence exists to prove the unionist middle class held more extreme views than the Protestant working class. Daniel claims that 'the extent of working class "moderation" can be demonstrated' by studying voting patterns, in particular, the June 1973 Assembly elections.[94]

Daniel shows clearly that the Protestant working class tended to vote for more moderate candidates; candidates who were prepared to negotiate solutions rather than be intransigent. Their rural and sometimes even middle-class counterparts tended to vote for a much harder line.[95] In particular, he cites the result in South Belfast, where a VUP candidate, at the time the most extreme Unionist party, won a middle class area as an example of middle class extremism. His explanation for this is reminiscent of the *Manifesto of the Volunteer Political Party* and the RHC document, *Within the Context of Northern Ireland*. He writes,

It seems likely that the benefits of the Welfare State, which it is feared may be lost if Loyalist militance leads to a break with Westminster, weigh more heavily with the Belfast working class than with their fellows in the country districts. ... Agricultural subsidies ... do not seem to exert the same influence on the politics of the farmer, whose wholehearted support, despite the fact that he, of all members of the community had the most to lose, was such a prominent feature of the Ulster Workers' Council strike. It may well be that the urban worker feels that, should the province be absorbed into a United Ireland, he could leave for Britain, taking his skills with him. The farmer, owning his land, has no alternative. He must stand and fight.[96]

Another factor that prevented any move towards progressive politics was the nature of the Protestant working class itself in its attitudes towards its social betters. The deferential nature of the working class in its relationship to mainstream Unionism, that is those who were 'born to rule' because they had the money or the education, held the Protestant working class back from politics. These same attitudes played a role in undercutting the Loyalist political enterprise as many working class Protestants, even if they were more moderate than their middle class and rural counterparts, often voted for the traditional parties, their 'betters' when they went to the voting booth. Finally, progressive Loyalist politics failed because of the Protestant attitude to law and order, and the inability of most Protestants to accept paramilitaries becoming politicians. Nelson points out that 'most people remain unhappy about their soldiers becoming politicians.'[97]

Beyond the problems that the VPP and progressive thinkers faced within their own community and the inability of the Provisional movement to constructively engage with political Loyalism, other factors, some of them sinister, played a major role in destroying the VPP and its allies, and in crippling the evolution of Loyalist political thinking. Furthermore, this alliance of forces, and what they did to undercut the political thinking within Loyalism in this period, prolonged the conflict by 20 years, and made it all that more difficult to finally make peace in Northern Ireland.

## BRITISH POLICIES: CRIMINALISATION, ULSTERISATION, MARGINALISATION

Another factor in the failure of Loyalist politics stemmed from British government policies that served to undercut the cooperation and understanding that the UVF and RHC had begun to develop with the OIRA and to a certain extent with the PIRA. The most significant, was criminalisation. True, with Roy Mason, the new Northern Ireland Secretary, in charge, the Labour government from 1976 to 1979 lowered the violence dramatically and increased the prison population. However, as David Ervine pointed out, 'It set the peace process back 20 years.'[98] Criminalisation broke down already fragile relationships among the groups in Long Kesh as the focus now went from cooperation to survival and fighting for political status. It also broke down the system that had aided in the development of a new and politically sophisticated cadre of Loyalist prisoners and eventual politicians. Without new prisoners going into the compounds of Long Kesh, the process of the long-term prisoners mentoring the younger ones ended. The positive experience that Hutchinson, Ervine, and many others had under the Spence regime in Long Kesh gave way to a battle for survival in the H-Blocks.

Examining the membership and ethos of Loyalist organisations such as the PUP, EPIC, and Alternatives, the UVF initiated Restorative Justice Programme today; one can clearly see the impact that the political and social education in Long Kesh had on members of the RHC and the UVF, especially those in Compound 21 under Spence.[99] Former prisoners, who were in Long Kesh during the Spence era, now staff these organisations and work tirelessly to transform the conflict and to ensure that the conditions that led them into Long Kesh would never return. Therefore, it is not hard to speculate on how this conflict may have ended without criminalisation.

These policies also shifted the focus of the military and political conflict that was taking place in the streets to the prisons.[100] Tom Roberts points out that the British government mishandled the battle over political status and 'prolonged the conflict in terms of the hunger strike ... I believe it gave the IRA a whole new impetus for possibly another thirteen, fourteen years. It was my view that the IRA conflict was waning towards 1980, say 1981.'[101] Richard O'Rawe makes the same point:

Adams, if not [Ivor] Bell, was pragmatic enough to realise the limitations of the armed struggle approach; hence the "long war" strategy. But, while Adams recognised that the war could not be won militarily, he also saw that simply to call it off would have made the Republican movement directionless and politically irrelevant ... . It would have been another "glorious defeat" for Republicans to sing about as we faded into obscurity.[102]

O'Rawe also claims that, in this period, Adams was hoping for some 'unforeseen event' that would 'transform the fortunes of the Republican movement.' That came, as Roberts argues, in the 1981 Hunger Strikes and the rise of Sinn Féin and Republican electoral politics.[103]

At the same time, the British establishment really did not know what to do with political Loyalism in this period. This confusion manifested itself in the wild shifts in policy in the 1970s. Rees' policies of first legalising the paramilitaries to bring them into the political process, then proscribing them again is one aspect of this. The granting of political status in 1972 and then eliminating that in 1976 is another. Putting forward proposals for power sharing while at the same time toying with jettisoning Northern Ireland from the United Kingdom also reflects this confusion or exasperation. More importantly, for this study, the contradiction of talking to the IRA while ignoring Loyalism and its representatives in this period also reflects the government's inability to come to grips with the situation and Loyalism. Billy Hutchinson believes that,

> the British government thought Loyalism was a thorn in its side and would not play a role in resolving the problems. Quite frankly, I think the British didn't know where Loyalists fitted in all of this and I think they hoped they'd waken up some morning and they'd all be gone.[104]

Beyond the British government's shifting and contradictory policies, one can discern either an inability to agree on a solution or bureaucratic infighting in the government. Examining this period, Catney does not believe that, 'the British government, operated with joined-up thinking.'[105] He believes that there was no obvious linear connection from one policy to the next and that many of their initiatives were a result of particular circumstances rather than a well thought out plan to end the conflict. Catney contends, 'that the initiative of criminalisation, normalisation, and "Ulsterisation" had a lot to do with the impact that the [IRA] execution of Airey Neave, [Margaret Thatcher's close friend and advisor, in March 1979] had on the British.'[106] Billy Hutchinson agrees with this analysis. He argues that after attempting to work towards a political solution the British wanted 'the Ulsterisation policy in the prisons and they wanted no nonsense, no talks, no negotiations, no nothing. Just crush them.'[107]

When examining this period, 1972 to 1975, Catney's and Hutchinson's arguments explain a great deal. Clearly, the British went from engaging the paramilitaries, granting 'Special Category Status', attempting to bring them into politics, and facilitating paramilitary cooperation. Just as clearly, the British government ended political status, disengaged with the paramilitaries and embarked on a security solution over a political solution. These shifts, especially the shift to a security solution, seriously undercut the development of a politically aware and confident cadre of Loyalist thinkers prepared to engage politically with any and every actor involved in the Northern Ireland conflict.

Dorril and Ramsay in their work *Smear!: Wilson and the Secret State*,[108] which focused on the anti-communist political campaign to oust Harold Wilson, agree. They also see many factors preventing the British government from acting with one voice or a coherent strategy. Examining the Wilson government when it came face to face with the situation in Northern Ireland they argue that,

> Wilson and Rees inherited not an agreed bi-partisan policy on Northern Ireland with a united state apparatus, but a state machine wracked not only with normal bureaucratic 'turf' wars, but split along ideological lines: wet/dry, hard/soft, destroy/negotiate.[109]

The British government's lurching from one policy to another, was not the only force and factor that drove British policy. Evidence suggests that certain British policy makers and the policies that they developed aimed to make sure that no real political thinking and political activism emerged out of Loyalism, and that any cooperation that developed among the paramilitaries would never find expression in an organised, armed and politically aware working class movement.

Before moving onto an analysis of this facet of British policy making, this study must briefly examine the Unionist attitudes towards the development of political awareness among working class Protestants and the emergence of political thinking within the paramilitaries. This interlude is necessary because Unionist attitudes and its treatment of working class Loyalism will dovetail with those within the British establishment who actively worked to destroy any political development within the UVF, RHC and working class Loyalism.

## UNIONISM AND LOYALISM

> Unionism saw political Loyalism as a threat ... not, political Republicanism but political Loyalism. To have an articulate voice representing the working class. . . was not what Unionist political elites wanted.
>
> Dawn Purvis[110]

There is no doubt that Unionism feared a challenge to its position. After 50 years of total domination over the Catholic population and near total control over the Protestant working class, mainstream Unionism, after 1972, found itself faced with an intolerable situation, facing not just a threat from Republicans, but facing a political challenge from its own people. Spence, in particular, argues that Unionism feared the UVF not only because it had guns, but more importantly, 'because the U.V.F. were thinking outside the ideological railway lines of traditional unionism' and this posed a threat to the established order.[111]

Throughout the history of Northern Ireland, Unionism did not tolerate any challenge to its supremacy and rule. When faced with a threat to its position, it played the 'sectarian card' and rolled out the threat of an IRA invasion or the subversion of the Northern Ireland state. Then Unionism attacked its critics and crushed the emerging thinking; any move towards political progress or compromise 'would be scuppered.'[112] This was necessary for Unionism. The paramilitaries had their place, as 'bully boys', but not in the field of politics. As David Ervine once put it, Unionism wanted a 'Smart shop assistant ... But, not too smart.'[113]

As noted in Chapter 2, this is not a recent phenomenon. The violence of the 1919–22 period, the changes in the voting laws, the Outdoor Relief Riots in 1932, the sectarian riots of 1935, and the destruction of the first PUP in 1938 indicated to what lengths Unionism would go to maintain control over its own working class. The next section of this chapter analyses the lengths that the Unionist establishment and others went to undercut and destroy political Loyalism in the 1970s.

## THE 'RED SCARE'

Resistance to the politics of the UVF and RHC did not come simply from within their own groups and their communities, nor simply from within Unionism. Based on the evidence from studies about this period, it is clear that a vicious disinformation campaign and possible deliberate sectarian violence took place. The express purpose was to destroy the emerging working class politics of the UVF and the RHC. This section therefore addresses two important questions, 'Who attempted to destroy the Loyalist political initiative?' and 'Why did they do this?' Answering these two questions leads us into the very dark shadows of this conflict. What we can speculate on and surmise is that forces within Unionism and within the British intelligence community, mainly MI5, worked to enact their own agendas and actively pursued policies that made sure that Loyalist working class politics would not survive and that the sectarian violence would continue. Having said that, the reality is that it will take many more years and a great deal of archival research to get at the truth of the campaigns waged against the UVF/RHC and the VPP when they attempted to act politically.

When discussing what happened to those Loyalists who stepped outside the 'the ideological railway lines of traditional unionism',[114] Sarah Nelson concludes that Loyalists 'found they had walked into a fire.'[115] This fire started even before the RHC and the UVF went public with their political analysis and continued for two more years, crippling the political initiative of Loyalism.

When political Loyalism raised its head above the parapets, vested interests within Unionism and elements of British intelligence launched an all-out attack against the UVF and its allies. No one, including Spence, escaped this attack. As we will see in this section, articles and letters appeared in *Combat*, *Loyalist News*, the *Sunday News* and the *Belfast Newsletter* attacking the UVF for either becoming a communist organisation or having communists infiltrate it.

One anonymous online commentator believes that an alliance developed within Unionism to destroy any moves towards political independence of the Loyalist working class:

In response to the tentative emergence of Loyalist working class identity, and potential cross-sectarian alliances, the DUP and Vanguard [VUP] alike worked to maintain sectarian divisions and to crush any signs of "communism" or left-wing activism, because in order to maintain their favoured position in society unionists could not afford for Protestants to see Catholics in a sympathetic light.[116]

Nelson concurs and points out that once this alliance of entrenched Unionist interests realised the threat coming from below,

> A virulent anti-VPP campaign was waged in the press via anonymous letters, which newspapers seemed only too eager to print. Traditional organisations were used to spread the word.[117]

Recognising that with the fracturing of unionism, independent thinking could develop within the working class, these powerful groups and individuals whose interest were served by the status quo did not wait until this new political thinking went public. Even before the UVF published its new analysis in February 1974, *The Sunday News* reported in September 1973 that, 'Loyalist organisations had already started a "witch hunt" for "communists" who have infiltrated their ranks.'[118] The 'red scare' within Unionism had reared its ugly head again. However, the statement went further and laid down the markers of how far Loyalism could move politically without facing attacks:

> The United Ulster Unionist Council (U.U.U.C.) composed of the Democratic Unionist Party, Vanguard [VUP], a section of the Unionist Party and Orange delegates, were being asked by North and West Belfast delegates to adopt a motion. This stated that there could not be an honourable settlement with the leaders of the Roman Catholic community.[119]

Essentially, the mainstream Unionist parties propagated the 'red-scare' campaign to maintain their traditional role as leaders of the Protestant working class and to pre-empt any discussion of a compromise peace. Nelson believes that part of this campaign resulted from class hostility, fear of a paramilitary takeover and fears of a communist revolution.[120]

There is also evidence of a coordinated campaign beginning in July 1974 'to scare the population off new leaders.'[121] According to Purvis,

> Paisley started to plant the notion of communism within political Loyalism ... Trying to force political Loyalism out of the tribe. In other words "You're not the same because if you were the same as us you wouldn't be talking about communism. It's only them awful people over there [Republicans] that talk about communism."[122]

This equation of communism with political thinking within Loyalism was devastating, because within the unionist community,

> communism was equated with Republicanism ... in other words anti-state and subversive. So, when you had political Loyalism talking about the social issues, talking about the state of working class people, Paisley started to plant the notion of communism within political Loyalism.[123]

This is not to say, that some Unionist leaders may not have really feared a communist revolution. What is evident is that whenever a challenge to Unionist power emerged, as it did in 1919, 1932–35 and 1938, Unionism played the 'sectarian' or 'red' card and sometimes both. As Hugh Smyth has pointed out, this happened to the original PUP in 1938: 'What happened to those boys was that they were branded "communists" and "socialists".'[124] As we have seen, it happened to the VPP in 1974 and it has happened again to the modern PUP.

A letter that appeared in the *Belfast News Letter* on 27 August 1974 illustrated how this campaign worked. The anonymous letter writer claimed that the Protestant people needed to know that the UVF and sections of the UDA were now under communist influence and that the UVF leadership had been brainwashed 'into Marxist thinking'.[125] This letter was not unusual in this period. A series of letters appeared in various papers attacking the UVF, the RHC, and the VPP for going 'Red'. One particular letter appeared in *Loyalist News* from a woman who claimed her husband had become a communist after joining the UVF.[126] Even before the emergence of political Loyalism in 1973 and 1974, articles appeared attacking individuals as communists. For instance, in *Loyalist News* Paisley attacked John McKeague as a 'communist'.[127] Bill Craig, along with Paisley and the main Unionist parties, claimed that communist workers dominated the Ulster Workers' Council and Craig made speeches in 1974 that warned of communism as a great threat to Ulster.[128]

After the coup in the UVF, *Loyalist News* published a series of articles in 1975 on the communist threat, while, at the same time, publishing a positive article on the National Front.[129] *Loyalist News* even published a front-page article in 1975 entitled 'RED GREEN OR ORANGE', warning that, 'The Red Peril is amongst us.'[130] However, even these articles did not spare the organisations from the anti-communist attacks. Even after the coup in 1974 and the shift to a more militant and right wing position the attacks continued. As Garland argues,

> The U.V.F. "retreat" [coup] did not absolve it from continued attack. Jim Kilfedder M.P. was reported as saying, "It is well known that paramilitary groups on both sides of the divide are infiltrated by communists" and that "power hungry" men controlled Loyalist paramilitary organisations ... . They hinted that "some U.V.F. members were considering a temporary break with the Shankill until the Marxist leadership was removed." They went on to say that "The article in the Sunday News ... by the U.V.F. last year clearly indicated that their political thinking was identical to that of both the provisional and Official I.R.A."[131]

Faced with such concerted and possibly coordinated attacks, Loyalists attempted to protect themselves by explaining their positions, and stating clearly what they wanted for all the people of Northern Ireland. At other times, according to Billy Mitchell, they actually had to attack those with whom they had a working relationship, in order to cover their flanks. In discussing their relationship with the OIRA, he said,

> Even though we had a working relationship with the Stickies [OIRA], many times we came out and said they posed a greater threat than the Provos. All to offload the idea that we were Communists – the accusation was hurting us in our own communities.[132]

This put the UVF in a difficult position. As Mitchell pointed out, they had to deny any contact with Republicans otherwise Unionist leaders would use those contacts to prove that the UVF and the RHC were not true Loyalists.

The RHC and the UVF tried other ways to deal with these accusations. In an article in *Combat* in 1974, entitled 'time to end the nonsense', the writer fought back by accusing those smearing political Loyalism of using a well-worn strategy to maintain their position:

> Basically, Communism might be called a 'scapegoat word' used to smear people ... For 50 years and more our politicians sat pretty, secure in the knowledge that Loyalist people would vote for a goat decked in a Union Jack. Suddenly, they were faced

with people fed up with this, who demanded: proper protection against bomber ... better representation, better houses (or just hot water). Horrors! What could they do to defend themselves? Answer – call those upstarts "Communists".[133]

Ken Gibson attempted to turn the accusation of 'communist' to his advantage by arguing that this slur was a tool for bosses. He argued, 'The communist slur is one that shall return to those who invented it. Who is not a communist, who does not believe what "Boss Cat" instructs?'[134] In a 1973 article 'Reds Under the bed', *Loyalist News* reacted the same way in responding to the United Ulster Unionist Coalition's, the anti-Sunningdale coalition of Unionist parties, anti-communist attacks on the UVF. Like Gibson, it took the offensive and directly addressed the 'diabolical rumour to the effect that Loyalist organisations have been infiltrated by REDS or communists.'[135] The authors then wrote that it was 'the duty of all Loyalists to ensure that everyone incorporated in the Ulster Society has a job and a house and a reasonable level of existence and we dare anyone to argue against this ideology.'[136] Such challenges implicitly attacked those who had 'misruled' Ulster for 50 years and created the terrible conditions that the working class of both communities suffered. Finally, Loyalist leaders wanted to know why such attacks took place against the UVF. They rhetorically asked,

> Is it because the Loyalist Para-military organisations have become so powerful as to pose a threat to the power driven aspirations of the accusers. For too long have the accusers' wielded absolute sway with the Loyalist people.[137]

At other times, they took a strongly anti-communist position while defending their economic and political policies.[138] They published articles defending their bona fides as Loyalists, distancing themselves from the ideologies that they found themselves accused of holding, while at the same time attempting to get their readers to think for themselves. An example of this appeared in a front-page article in *Combat* entitled 'Smear Allegations Answered!' as a response to an anonymous letter writer, who had accused a *Combat* writer of being a communist.[139] In an undated article, the 2nd Battalion of the UVF devoted an entire page to explaining the dangers of communism and the duty to 'expose the dangers of left-wing politics in Ulster'.[140] *Combat* also published articles calling for more attention to social issues, while at the same time publishing articles such as 'Communism – The Enemy of the Working Class',[141] and 'Working Class Politics Not Communism'.[142]

No matter how hard they tried to defend themselves, or to frame the narrative, they could not overcome this disinformation campaign. Nelson points out how this effectively crippled the VPP campaign in 1974:

> Weary VPP canvassers would return to base and tell of their doorstep experiences: "Time and again the same thing: 'Are you communists? My husband's lodge was warned last night' or, 'Have you had talks with the IRA?' and we'd be saying patiently 'no, love', and seeing they didn't quite believe us."[143]

As we know, the results at the poll devastated the VPP and the 'politicals' in the UVF, leading to the coup in 1974.

In essence, the anti-communist campaign had done its job. According to Garland,

> The right-wing scare-mongering had been effective. Even the U.D.A., which had been involved in a vicious feud with the U.V.F. issued a call to the Shankill U.V.F. to "Stop Marxist rot." They suggested to the Volunteers that they should, "rid themselves of the Marxist thinkers in their ranks."[144]

Garland also points out that this campaign did not end there. Citing an article in the *Sunday News* from 3 June 1975 in which the UVF suffered more anti-communist attacks, he tells of how their 'weekly collections fell by over £1000 the week immediately following ... that article.'[145]

Thus, when looking back at this period, it is clear that the anti-communist disinformation campaign was effective and played no small part in destroying the political initiative of the UVF, the RHC and the VPP in their attempts to bridge the sectarian divide and negotiate a compromise peace with nationalists and Republicans.

## TARA AND MI5

The above section examined the attacks and the nature of the attacks directed against the political thinkers in the UVF, and how and why Unionism used these attacks to maintain its position and control over the Protestant working class. While it is clear why Unionism would use these attacks, it is not clear if they were acting on their own, or whether they were part of a concerted attack on political Loyalism. The evidence discussed below suggests that these attacks were not just part of Unionism's inherent conservatism, nor fear for its position, or of communism. Although all played an important role here, it is possible that they were also part of a much larger campaign waged by elements of the British Security forces against the emergence of Loyalist working class politics.

Most of the discussion about collusion, dirty tricks, extra-judicial killings has tended to focus on what the British and RUC security forces did to the Republican movement and how it used Loyalism to do its dirty work. However, this is not the whole story. Elements of MI5 and MI6 may have run operations, such as the anti-communism campaign, that effectively crippled the politics coming out of Loyalism. Therefore, the attacks on the UVF and progressive Loyalism will only make complete sense when one takes into consideration the possible role of the security forces.

In trying to make sense of the attacks that the UVF/RHC and VPP faced, Billy Mitchell argued that a great deal of the attacks 'came from Tara',[146] 'a strange body'[147] created by William McGrath, a shadowy figure with suspected links to MI5 and/or MI6.[148] Citing Moloney and Pollak's work *Paisley*,[149] Garland claims that McGrath 'was said to have "worked for MI6 in the 1950s when associated with an evangelical group which smuggled Bibles across the Iron Curtain."'[150] Other researchers have linked McGrath to MI5 and/or Army Intelligence in Lisburn.[151] What we know for sure is that McGrath created Tara in 1966, which represented an extreme form of evangelical fundamentalism that viewed the conflict in Northern Ireland as one 'between fundamental Protestantism and Romanism for the soul of Ireland.'[152] Believing that this conflict would culminate in an apocalyptic struggle, McGrath envisioned Tara as the organisation that would arm and prepare Protestants for the coming final struggle with Catholicism, liberalism, Republicanism, communism, and ecumenism so that 'Ireland might be saved and that Britain be reborn.'[153]

Initially, McGrath created links with the UVF in the early 1970s when PIRA launched its offensive. For its part, the UVF entered Tara primarily to see what weapons it could get. However, the UVF did not stay in Tara for long. McGrath's homosexuality, and about which the UVF already knew, his paedophilia, which later came out in the 'Kincora Scandal',[154] the bizarre nature of Tara's ideology, its militarily inaction in the conflict, suspicion that McGrath was a British Agent, and a lack of guns led the UVF to leave Tara en masse in the summer of 1971.[155] After the UVF left Tara, Tara continued to adhere to its fundamentalist and apocalyptic vision of the 'final battle', while the UVF went its own way and continued to develop very different and radical political ideas.

In 1973, following its religious fundamentalist and right wing political vision, Tara issued its 'Proclamation', according to which, Tara existed to prepare all Protestants for the final battle, the 'doomsday situation' against all those that Tara believed represented the 'international conspiracy ... to undermine the union with Britain and force "Rome Rule" on the Protestants of Ulster.'[156] Tara believed that this conspiracy involved 'Communism, the IRA, the Vatican, the ecumenical movement, the British and Irish governments, most mainstream Protestant churches and liberal elements of the Unionist Party.'[157] This Proclamation also illustrated the extreme and illiberal nature of Tara. In it, Tara claimed,

> It is our task to educate the Forces as to the nature of the conflict and the rightness of our cause, so that in the final battle the Army and Police will be fighting side by side with us against a common foe, namely Romanism and Communism.[158]

Tara also called for proscription of the Catholic Church and demanded that, 'All Roman Catholic centres of education must be closed.' Once the state made the Catholic Church illegal, then the state should institute integrated education, on the condition that 'religious education must be provided only by Evangelical Protestants.'[159] Finally, the Proclamation stated clearly that compromise was not possible. Under Article 10 Tara claimed that,

> Conflict is inevitable. We would not choose this path but the forces of Romanism and Communism will. It is imperative therefore that every Protestant should be prepared to bear arms so that all our resources may be in a state of readiness to be placed under the command of the proper Authorities in the hour of need.[160]

In 1974, Tara stated, 'There is not the basis for peaceful co-existence'[161] with the Catholic population. Therefore, Tara branded those who counselled compromise, 'traitors', meaning those in the UVF, VPP and RHC.

Tara responded to the publication of the UVF's conciliatory statement of February 1974 in the *Sunday News*, with a strongly worded statement attacking the UVF. According to Tara, the UVF had carried out 'an act of treachery' by claiming that unionism had committed 'fifty years of sectarian indoctrination'. Tara also attacked the UVF for adopting a non-sectarian stance in 1972, and blasted Spence for dropping the sectarian labels of Protestant and Catholic and instead using the terms Loyalist and Republican. Furthermore, Tara condemned Spence for his conciliatory and heartfelt letter to Joe McCann's widow as evidence of the UVF's shift towards Republicanism.[162]

Tara went further and pulled out the 'red card', claiming that communists had infiltrated the UVF. As illustrated above, within the conservative Protestant working class and among Protestants as a whole in Northern Ireland, no other accusation could do more damage to the UVF or call its legitimacy into question. However, this was not all the UVF faced from Tara and others early in its political evolution.

Beyond the differences between the secular UVF and the religious fundamentalist Tara, when we consider McGrath's connections to MI5, then the nature of Tara's attacks on the UVF's political thinking become more sinister. Paul Foot's study of Colin Wallace, a controversial MI5 agent in Northern Ireland through 1974, suggests that MI5 had a great deal of use for McGrath and Tara and that the attacks on the UVF in this period were part of that relationship.[163] Tim Pat Coogan agrees and argues that,

> stratagems such as falsifying "IRA records" to show misappropriation of funds, involvement with communism and other pieces of information... designed to show a pro-communist slant ... . The Orange paramilitaries were subject to the same treatment. For example, the Tara organisation was used to fabricate links between the UVF and communism.[164]

In the same edition of the *Sunday News* that Tara used to attack the UVF, the UVF claims that unnamed agents attempted to destroy the UVF by forming 'a militant breakaway "Provisional" UVF', and claimed that these agents offered bribes to get members to defect, with the goal of breaking the UVF Ceasefire. Furthermore, the UVF believed that the elements that tried to create this breakaway group 'require UVF violence so that they can justify their existence.'[165] While the article speculated that self-serving elements within the UVF attempted to do this, there is a clear hint that it viewed this as an attempt to drag the UVF into a sectarian war.[166] The UVF made this clear in a March 1974 article in *Combat*, which claimed, 'that certain elements in the Loyalist camp were working for an end to the ceasefire.'[167]

The UVF, who had contact with the OIRA at this point, knew of what happened to the IRA in 1969 and 1970 when elements of the Dublin government allegedly played a role in splitting the IRA and setting up and arming of the Provisional IRA. Even without contact with the OIRA, information on this had already appeared in the *Sunday Times* and the *Orange Cross*.[168] It was easy for the leadership of the UVF to believe that certain forces beyond Unionism feared the emergence of a 'political' paramilitary movement it could not control. These same forces would have no problem collaborating with or controlling a purely military organisation, because that organisation would not question its place in the conflict: it would simply follow orders, and as will become evident below, possibly serve the agenda of others.

Another significant factor exists that ties together the anti-communist attacks on the UVF and the RHC, and the increase in sectarian killings in this period – domestic British politics. A number of works (*Spycatcher*,[169] *Who Framed Colin Wallace*,[170] *War Without Honour*,[171] *Smear!*,[172] *The Dirty War* and *The Troubles*) claim that an anti-communist plot originated from within MI5 and elements in the army to undermine the Wilson government and even help to install a more right-wing leadership in the Conservative Party.[173] *The Daily Mirror* addressed this in 2006, writing that, 'In the view of hard-right MI5 mavericks like "Spycatcher" Peter Wright, who later confessed his role in the plot, Socialists were the same as Communists – intent on delivering the UK to the Kremlin.'[174] Setting a context for this, journalist Barrie Penrose argues that we,

> need to bear in mind the backdrop to the alleged plots ... Our establishment, from the intelligence services down to parts of Fleet Street, were paranoid about the threat of communism. So paranoid it seems, they were prepared to believe a prime minister of Britain was an active Soviet spy.[175]

Given the context of the Cold War and post-war Britain, Wilson and Labour were 'very vulnerable to the allegation of Communist or Left-wing infiltration.'[176] Therefore, according to this narrative, the security services had to stop Wilson and Labour by whatever means necessary, otherwise they would sell Britain out to the Soviet Union.

Recent work by Christopher Andrews rejects this claim. In his work *Defend the Realm*, Andrews argues that the plot never existed.

He claims that the man who did the most to publicise this plot and keep the notion of it alive, Peter Wright, a former MI5 agent and author of *Spycatcher* eventually undercut his own argument when he admitted there was no grand plot in MI5, and that there was only one other agent who would join him to remove Wilson.[177] To further support his claims that the plot against Wilson did not exist, he cites a 'stringent internal inquiry' ordered by the Director General Sir Anthony Duff that found that no plot against Wilson existed, nor was there a dirty tricks campaign aimed at him or any involvement in the UWC strike.[178]

Whether an actual plot against Wilson, known as 'Clockwork Orange', really existed or not, would take us far afield and so this study will leave the topic of a plot against Wilson for other researchers. However, taking into account Andrews' own work, one cannot help but see that extent of paranoid fear within the security establishment of subversion and of a communist plot that existed long before the conflict in Northern Ireland broke out and which became a major factor in MI5's activities in Northern Ireland.[179]

From the evidence presented in the various sources, MI5 and others involved in Northern Ireland may not have been involved in a plot to overthrow Wilson and Labour, but the evidence does suggest that that they were involved in undercutting Wilsons' and Rees' initiatives in Northern Ireland and undermining any political initiatives by the paramilitaries.[180]

Some evidence also suggests that MI5 may have actively involved itself in the UWC strike,[181] as well as worked to undercut Merlyn Rees' policy on internees and his attempts to bring the paramilitaries into the political arena.[182] When the threat of the strike loomed, Wallace claims that his superiors instructed him to make sure that the strike failed. Wallace claims that, for whatever reason, 'London had a change of mind and that they wanted the Ulster Workers' Council Strike to succeed.' He then argues,

> I later discovered that this new strategy was part of the overall policy to discredit Harold Wilson ... . It also became clear that during the strike false intelligence assessments were being given to the government so that incorrect decisions were made.[183]

Dorril and Ramsay also believe that,

> the Army and MI5 were happy to allow the Ulster Worker's Council strike to succeed, there were lessons to be learned from the dispute ... and the next time the strike might be from the left.[184]

While Andrews dismisses these claims, Martin Dillon believes that Wallace's allegations 'provide a compelling argument to explain the reasons why the strike was allowed to proceed.'[185] Claiming that the fear of a two-front war with both Republicanism and Loyalism if the army intervened as less than compelling evidence for not stopping the strike, he claims that 'there may well have been a hidden agenda of which the Wilson government was unaware.'[186]

Such activities or 'dirty tricks' by the security forces also aimed to keep the conflict going until the security forces defeated the IRA and all terrorists. According to this narrative, MI5, like Paisley and his hardline allies, would not accept a compromise solution such as Sunningdale.[187] Again, Colin Wallace states that,

> the sectarian assassinations [in 1974] were designed to destroy [then Northern Secretary Merlyn] Rees's attempts to negotiate a ceasefire, and the targets were identified for both sides by Int/SB [Intelligence services and the RUC Special Branch]. They also believe some very senior RUC officers were involved with this group. In short, it would appear that Loyalist paramilitaries and Int/SB members have formed some sort of pseudo gangs in an attempt to fight a war of attrition by getting paramilitaries on both sides to kill each other and, at the same time prevent any future political initiative such as Sunningdale.[188]

Fred Holroyd supports this analysis. He accuses MI5 and MI6, and the R.U.C. of 'dirty tricks' in 1974 and 1975, claiming that these 'were carried out on both sides of the border and ranged from the professionally disreputable to murder.'[189] Holroyd's work lays out in detail the actions taken by the security services that led to many deaths.[190]

These are interesting accusations and ones that have particular resonance for this section. The UVF itself recognised something sinister happening in this period and believed someone or some group had targeted it with the goal of increasing the violence and destroying its movement towards politics.

Not long after the *Sunday News* article detailing the attempt to set up a 'Provisional UVF', the 18 March 1974 edition of *Combat* carried an article condemning sectarian killings. This article stated unequivocally, 'We cannot justify the murder of any man simply because his concept of true religion is different from ours.'[191] The April 1974 edition of *Combat* carried a front-page article entitled 'Sectarianism: Who Stands to Gain?'[192] that highlighted some recent, inexplicable and clearly sectarian attacks that took place in both communities.

The UVF believed that the express purpose of these attacks was to stir up a sectarian war because those behind the attacks realised that there was a 'growing movement amongst the paramilitary organisations towards seeking a political solution.'[193] The editorial pointed out that the attacks had the hallmarks 'of "hired mercenaries" working under the direction of the faceless degenerates who urgently require a renewed spate of sectarian violence.'[194] Even the police may have been confused about the murders taking place in this era. A *Sunday News* article claimed that, 'Police are known to be more puzzled about the most recent series of murders' because they believed that in a number of the murders 'the killers could not have known the religion of the victim.'[195]

Given their own knowledge of the paramilitary world, the UVF realised that something very sinister was at work in these attacks. The UVF speculated that these attacks were the work of elements of the security forces and political actors who opposed any compromise solution, especially coming from the paramilitaries. Another likely explanation is that a rogue element within Loyalism carried out these attacks. In either case, the UVF believed that the goal of the killings was to create a sectarian war in order to prevent a political solution emerging from the paramilitaries themselves.

Further evidence of these dirty tricks and the desire to foment a sectarian war appears in a letter by Colin Wallace dated 30 September 1975. This letter demonstrates that the UVF was right to be concerned about the setting up of a 'Provisional' UVF in March that would shift the UVF back towards militarism. When referring to the UVF, Wallace wrote that MI5,

> wanted the more politically minded ones ousted. I believe much of the violence generated during the latter part of last year was caused by some of the new Int [intelligence] people deliberately stirring up the conflict.[196]

Although MI5 may have fuelled the violence, Garland argues that it is not clear that MI5 had anything to do with the 1974 coup within the UVF and that 'Volunteers now say there was no political motivation but a hard line element had taken over.'[197] At the same time Garland points out that, a Ministry of Defence document showed "clearly that the army regards its operations in Ireland as counter-revolutionary aimed at rooting out the Communist menace." This lends support to the views of Colin Wallace (Foot 1990) Holroyd (1989) and others, that elements in the security forces were fighting their own war and fighting it within the same ideological framework as Tara. The U.V.F. had been one of its victims.[198]

This evidence supports the UVF's analysis of the sectarian killings in March and April 1974 and, along with Wallace's admission, clearly points to a campaign to undercut the emerging working class politics of the UVF and the RHC. Their movement to the left, in the context of their war with the IRA alarmed elements within the security apparatus enough to undercut this political development and to make sure that politics did not emerge from the paramilitary organisations. Based on paranoid fears of some within the security forces, achieving total victory over the paramilitaries was more important than finding a compromise solution to the conflict.

## CONCLUSION

This chapter opened with the challenge of answering the following questions.

1. Why the Provisional movement could not engage with the political Loyalism?
2. Why could political Loyalism, unlike Sinn Féin, not get votes or make an impact in the communities from which they came?
3. Why did the political thinkers in the UVF and RHC encounter resistance from mainstream unionist parties?
4. What role did elements within British intelligence play in undercutting the movement towards compromise and cooperation?
5. If sections of British intelligence did undercut the Loyalist thinkers, then how did they do that and why?
6. In whose interest was it for Loyalist politics to fail and why did those actors actively work to make sure working class Loyalist politics never succeeded?

The answers to questions one and two were relatively straight-forward. As this chapter has pointed out, even with the secret talks and areas of agreement between the PIRA and the UVF, there were numerous reasons that the Loyalist vision of a compromise peace within the context of Northern Ireland failed to reach the PIRA. For one, the PIRA still viewed Loyalists as agents of the British state, members of death squads or deluded Irishmen who once they went into a United Ireland would realise that they were Irish. It also believed, at least for a brief time, that the British were going to leave Northern Ireland and so there was no need to engage with Loyalism. Furthermore, negotiating with and compromising with Loyalism would have undercut the PIRA narrative of the war as one of national liberation against the British.

This study believes these are all good explanatory points, but believes that something no less important was at play here, something most analysts of the conflict either ignore or downplay. The PIRA had its ideology and its view of unionists as 'deluded Irishmen', which kept the Provisional leadership from making a realistic assessment of the conflict and how it would end that resulted from its own low level of political development. Consequently, in this period, the leading elements of Loyalism found themselves too far ahead of the PIRA in understanding how the conflict would have to end in a compromise peace within the state of Northern Ireland.

Loyalist political thinkers of this period also found themselves too far ahead of their own membership and their own working class community. These political thinkers within Loyalism had stepped out of their traditional roles, the 'scales had fallen from their eyes', and they had become 'Enlightened Ulstermen'. However, they had gone too far, too fast. The majority of volunteers and the majority of the Loyalist population did not really understand the political thinking emerging from the leading elements of Loyalism. Consequently, in this period of conflict, they could not and did not support those who came from their own communities to represent them. The VPP electoral disaster was proof of this.

Many other factors came together in this period to sabotage Loyalism's political experiment, some of them cynical, such as the Unionist and security forces actions, and some of them simply bad policies that had dramatic and terrible consequences. One policy that did the most damage to budding working class cooperation and moves towards peace was 'criminalisation.' Although, it lowered the scale of violence, criminalisation ensured that the conflict lasted into the 1990s as this policy inadvertently shifted the battleground from the streets to the prisons, thereby changing the face of the conflict and prolonging it.

British attitudes and actions also played a large role in undercutting Loyalism. We now know that one of the reasons that Rees' and British shifts in policy appeared schizophrenic in this period is because they were. The British never really knew how to engage with Loyalism or paramilitaries as a whole, and shifted policies from engagement to disengagement, from criminalisation to legalisation back to criminalisation. In particular, the one shift that really damaged Loyalist politics was the shift from a political to a security solution that took working class and paramilitary politics out of the equation.

Unionist attitudes are not surprising, given the history of Northern Ireland. Simply put, from the earliest days of the Northern Ireland state, Unionism never tolerated any challenge to its authority. Catholics knew this from the founding of the state and learned this lesson again in 1968 and 1969. However, it took the collapse of Stormont and the Unionist State for working class Protestants to find out to what lengths Unionism would go to maintain its power. Unionism would only tolerate Loyalism as the 'bullyboy' who would do its bidding. Once working class Loyalists began to think and act for themselves, and in the interest of the working class of both communities, they found themselves under attack politically in the papers, in speeches and letters to the editor.

Finally, if these factors were not enough to undercut the political development of Loyalism, political Loyalism faced a coordinated campaign equating any political thinking inside the working class with communism. This attack came from all sides, the Unionist establishment, Tara, the British security establishment and their own organisations. This campaign seems to have had its origins in MI5, which developed it for its own agenda and deep-seated fear of communism. Unionism also used this tactic to keep working class Loyalism in its place and to save its version of Ulster. Ultimately, these were all successful in preventing the development of Loyalist working class politics.

Evidence presented here also suggests that elements within MI5 wanted Rees and Wilson to fail in Northern Ireland, and at the same time worked against any solution that smacked of compromise. Viewing the world through their paranoid, anti-communist lenses, they could not tolerate compromise of any sort. They could only accept victory over perceived communists and terrorists.

The UVF also faced a threat from forces intent on undercutting it that went beyond simple political attacks on it. These forces, if we accept this argument, came from elements of MI5 and the security forces, who attempted to split the UVF and undercut its political activists. If the UVF was correct these forces attempted to cripple the UVF by creating a non-political, military movement they could control. While, much more work needs to be done on this, the evidence presented in this chapter suggests that rogue elements within MI5 attempted to do this by stoking the sectarian killings of 1974 and 1975. If true, the goals of these actions were to ensure that any cooperation or understanding among the paramilitaries would end, and that the conflict would only result in a military victory over both the Republican and Loyalist paramilitaries.

After examining all the forces and factors aligned against political Loyalism in this era, it is no surprise that their political experiment failed. What is surprising is that it survived long enough to put out all the forward thinking documents and offers of conciliation and compromise. Even more surprising is that even though the forces of reaction defeated political Loyalism in this period, those who survived the political attacks attempted to keep the dream alive. They worked hard and tirelessly to find a way to end the conflict, to create a just and lasting peace, and thereby to create a Northern Ireland where everyone would 'share responsibility' for the running of the country. The next chapter examines how they kept those dreams alive, and how they eventually created a very progressive proposal for a compromise peace in Northern Ireland.

# 6
# The Light in the Darkness: Political Loyalism, 1975–77

Throughout the last thirty years a curious contradiction has run through Loyalism. On the one hand these paramilitary groups have been responsible for some of the most blatant sectarian carnage. On the other, their political representatives have articulated policies that seemed more imaginative than anything coming from the Ulster Unionist Party or the DUP. That is, the UVF and UDA were prepared to support such policies which were anathema to many unionist politicians who simply wanted the old Stormont regime to return.[1]

With the defeat of progressive Loyalist politics in 1974–75, some elements in the UVF, the RHC and those outside those organisations, continued to work on ideas and documents to end the conflict and speak out against the continuing horrible, sectarian and mindless violence. After the failure of Loyalist politics and the PIRA ceasefire, violence raged throughout 1975 and into 1977 with the UVF and RHC as well as the UDA continuing to kill at a terrible rate, and in fact outkilling the PIRA in 1975.[2] In the 'curious contradiction' mentioned above, while the UVF and RHC continued to carry out this brutal sectarian campaign, political elements within the UVF and RHC engaged with trusted Loyalist politicians, people like Hugh Smyth, who worked with them to develop policies that could end the conflict. Spence claimed that,

> Whilst the V.P.P. went to the wall, there were those of us who were absolutely determined that the start that was made would never be allowed to wane entirely and that once we could, we would do something about it.[3]

After the political disaster of 1974, the prisoners in Long Kesh, away from the bullets and the bombs continued to dream of 'progressive ... moral organisation which could show working class Protestants the way forward' and 'work out a settlement with their Republican opposite numbers.'[4] With this determination, and with their counterparts outside the prisons even in this violent period, they continued to work on a far-reaching proposal for a new assembly that they eventually published in 1977 under the title 'Devolution: The Plan for Ulster'.[5]

Before 'Devolution: The Plan for Ulster' saw the light of day, a number of thinkers within UVF and RHC showed that not all was lost in terms of political development. A month after the coup in 1975 and a month after proscription, an unsigned article appeared in *Combat* entitled the 'The Futility of Violence'. Even though this study discussed this article earlier, it is worth revisiting. The author argues that in using violent means, 'we have been defeating ourselves' and that 'political and sectarian violence is wholly inconsistent with the goals of freedom in society, the value of human life and the dignity of the individual.' The author even referenced Albert Einstein's quote that violence 'attracts moral inferiors', and finishes by calling on 'all patriots to make a declaration of intent to forsake the gun (at least for a spell) in favour of dialogue.'[6]

In discussing the work of the new Constitutional Convention that sought to create a new and workable devolved government, Billy Mitchell wrote in July 1975, 'The building of a new Ulster will unite all the people in support of the Union.' He cites an NILP policy document and argues 'the Union RESTS NEITHER ON "NATIONALIST" NOR "SECTARIAN" CONSIDERATIONS' (emphasis in the original). He concludes by saying,

> If we are to see a new era of peace, prosperity and contentment in Ulster we must strive to break down the traditional political and religious differences which divide the two communities in Northern Ireland.[7]

In his traditional 12 July speech in 1975 inside Long Kesh, Spence applauded the 1975 PIRA ceasefire as a welcome respite provided the politicians did not compromise any principles. At the same time, he acknowledged that the PIRA could never achieve a United Ireland. He pinned his hopes, as Billy Mitchell and many others had, that 'a political solution will be found ... wherein all men of whatever calling can live in peace and justice with equal opportunity.'[8]

Although no formal political party existed to represent political Loyalism during this period of terrible sectarian killing, against all odds these men continued to think, write, speak, and work on a viable political solution, holding out the hope that somehow they could end the conflict.

## POLITICS OF COMPROMISE

One of the most interesting and forward thinking documents to come out of Loyalism in this period appeared in *Loyalist News* on the 18 January 1975. Written by two members of the RHC in Long Kesh, it carried the title of 'A TEN POINT PLAN FOR PEACE WITH HONOUR AND JUSTICE'.[9] They wrote this document while waiting to hear if the PIRA would extend its ceasefire and prolong the period of relative peace in anticipation of the upcoming Constitutional Convention. While some Unionists and Unionist parties still sought total defeat of the PIRA, these thinkers understood that to end the conflict the PIRA needed to leave the battlefield with 'a certain amount of returns.' Since no other group was giving a lead on this, they developed this ten-point plan in the hopes of creating a situation where Northern Ireland could realise a lasting peace.[10]

Arguing that, 'it is foolish to demand that which is impossible, i.e. total victories and total defeats', they criticised those on the 'Loyalist side ... who talk of betrayals and of utterly defeating the IRA' while they stood on the sidelines. They laid out a proposal that they believed was 'practical, realistic and necessary' and that would possibly satisfy all sides in leading to a lasting peace.

Because of the nature of these proposals and their prescience, it is worth laying them out in full:

1. In the situation that exists at present the British Army must maintain a low level profile so as not to endanger a permanent peace, both Nationalist and Loyalist areas to be included in the low-profile plan. There must not be any specific raids for arms, ammunition or 'wanted men' in any areas and general security duties, including routine patrols etc., to be continued with utmost care to ensure that precipitive [sic] action is not used.
2. In view of the low profile attitude in response to the situation, all warring factions continue to pursue a non-violent policy aimed at peace. The temporary ceasefire of the Provos to be continued "indefinitely" as a gesture of their sincerity to the people of Ulster and the British Government.
3. Within a short time the British Government to respond to the "new situation" as promised. We suggest the phasing out of all Detainees, Loyalist and Republican, in small numbers, at first but in a steady stream until there are no detainees left in Long Kesh or Armagh Jail.

4. If the peace continues to hold the British Government to reduce the numbers of troops on the ground, as was again the intention of Rees once the situation no longer needed such large numbers. To ensure the people of Ulster that security will not be endangered the role of the Northern Ireland security force, the UDR be increased but stay at a low level.

5. Within a short time the British Government should implement the two-thirds remission of sentences for all prisoners in N.I. thus bringing the prison laws into line with those already pertaining to the rest of the U.K., therefore this move cannot be construed as a compromise but as a step towards equal treatment for all U.K. citizens. The two-thirds remission must be operated right across the board, with all prisoners being released immediately after having completed one-third of their effective sentence. This move will remove the sting from the political situation and also ease the vast over-crowding and abnormal administration problems of the N.I. Office. When considering this plan it must be remembered that all prisoners will eventually walk into freedom, and they may as well walk out without embitterment. Regardless of their political persuasions each believe they fought for what they genuinely believe in. Also, there can never be any peace in Ulster while there are men in prison camps who believe they were right in the action they took.

6. A statement of intent to be issued by the Government to the effect that: After a period of, say, one year, without violence the British Government to introduce a process whereby "politically motivated Special Category" prisoners be released. This process to be taken in stages releasing first those men with the longest amount of time already served, followed by men whose sentences are of medium term, followed by the long term and indefinite period Prisoners, i.e. men serving life sentences. Finally, an amnesty to be introduced that will clear the books of all men who engaged in political action.

7. Political action as opposed to military action to be greatly encouraged by the British Government. The proscription orders of the presently illegal groupings to be lifted thus allowing for these groups to partake in political discussion.

8. At the forthcoming Convention elections, all political parties and groups to be given the opportunity to stand for seats. The number of seats to be increased from 78 to 100 to facilitate the rise of further political groups.

9. The Convention is to be held along democratic and constitutional lines to be designed so as to include the views and opinions of the various political parties and groups, including all warring factions.
10. If progress is made through the Convention and peace still prevails then the implementation of the Government's intentions to further reduce the numbers and commitment of British Forces in N.I. until the level of armed forces is along the lines that were in operation prior to the troubles.[11]

Most of this proposal built on or reiterated ideas that the RHC and UVF had put forward earlier. As before, they wanted these proposals applied equally to all sides. They also accepted that the paramilitaries of both sides had acted for political reasons and that acknowledgement of this fact was necessary in creating the breathing space needed for future negotiations and for their involvement in those talks.

Proposal 8 recognised that the Convention had to be larger in order to bring in the 'warring factions' to the table. They recognised that a reduced Convention froze out the smaller parties as well as those who were involved in the armed struggle. What these writers did was to recognise that no solution was possible without all parts of society represented and more importantly, without the men with the guns at the table. It would take nearly 20 years before this would happen.

To understand how prescient and forward thinking this document was, two anecdotes are worth repeating here. In 2009, a few days before meeting with one of the authors of this document, I had a meeting with someone from Sinn Féin, who shall remain anonymous. This person asked me to explain what type of research I was doing. I explained the present work and my analysis of political Loyalism. This person did not accept what I was saying and wanted proof of my arguments. I pulled out this document and let him/her read it. After this person read it, he/she put it down and then said, with a look of incredulity on his/her face, 'This is the foundation of the Good Friday Agreement'.[12] A few days later, I met with one of the authors of this document, Plum Smith. When he read it, after all these years, he said, 'If you look at this, you'll find the Good Friday Agreement in this.' Smith went on, 'When you look at that ... that's very radical. This is more radical than what Republicans were doing ... at the time.'[13] Regarding the IRA, he was correct. It still clung to its hopes that the British planned to disengage from Northern

Ireland and did not entertain any political thinking that involved a settlement with Loyalism and Unionism within the context of Northern Ireland.

Smith then explained what underpinned their thinking when writing this document. 'We knew all along that what people wanted was fairness, what people wanted was acknowledgment of each other.'[14] Then, expanding on what they hoped to gain by these proposals, Smith made it clear that it was about creating a breathing space so that politics could then work. He argues, 'Your first thing was your ceasefires, then your talks, and then your agreement.'[15] Creating this breathing space would then allow the politicians to find a way to meet the desires of all the differing allegiances in Northern Ireland. Their hope, similar to what happened after the ceasefires in 1994, was that once this breathing space allowed politics to take over, all parties to the conflict could then work out an agreement among their competing political visions. Clearly this thinking on the Ten Points was 20 years ahead of its time, yet Loyalism never received any credit for putting these ideas forward. Even today, observers, and analysts either continue to ignore their contribution or do not know about it.

As Smith notes, the RHC thinkers here were far ahead of the IRA in terms of an inclusive political settlement. The IRA's agreed 'twelve points' in 1975 with the British government ignored Loyalists and Loyalism, and concentrated only on IRA and British relations. Where the Loyalists called for amnesty for all and pulling back the army and police from all areas and that all factions had to sit at the negotiating table, the IRA, consistent with their belief that Loyalists were 'deluded Irishmen' and/or agents of the British state, only concerned itself with dealing with the British. For instance, Article 12 called for 'Further talks to take place between IRA leaders and senior British representatives.'[16]

Despite how progressive these ideas were, the reality is that, even if the British had paid attention and the IRA had had a more realistic analysis of Loyalism, the outcome would probably have been the same. In the context of this period, the increase in UVF and RHC violence, the ending of the PIRA ceasefire, the new more militaristic leadership of the UVF along with the coming security crackdown by the British government all weighed against any form of compromise peace in this period. Furthermore, as is clear from above, there was little stomach for political thinking among the paramilitaries outside the prisons after the failure of 1974. Those doing the political thinking at this time were in prison when they wrote their pieces and found themselves isolated from the reality outside. Nelson quotes one of the disillusioned 'politicals' on the outside, saying that 'Gusty, X and Y [UVF prisoners near release] would be better staying where they are, writing their pamphlets and dreaming their dreams.'[17]

In 1975, many issues obstructed those in the UVF and the RHC trying to move politics forward and end the sectarian violence. One problem was getting anyone to listen to any constructive proposals. For instance, The Ulster Citizens Civil Liberties Centre, a UDA sponsored group, published its version of a bill of rights in 1975. This group worked with a member of the California State Bar and Mr David Lowry, a Lecturer in the faculty of Law at Queen's University. Like all other paramilitary proposals, it went nowhere and the national press ignored it and its proposals.

Even though this initiative came from the UDA, *Loyalist News* published the proposals as some of these proposals mirrored much of the UVF and the RHC thinking in this period. The bill of rights would protect human, social, political, and economic rights, as well as guaranteeing the right of assembly, conscience, expression, assembly, privacy, liberty, life, and security. *Loyalist News* published it because it believed that, 'if it was introduced in Northern Ireland', the document 'would bring radical change.'[18] However, that did not happen.

Garland chronicles many other problems, ranging from the 1974–75 coup through the reorganisation of the UVF after the 1975 counter-coup as reasons why the UVF and the RHC could not move forward.[19] Billy Hutchinson agrees and believes the internal problems in the UVF eventually led Spence to resign from it as he and the outside leadership remained at odds over the future direction of the movement.[20]

Before Spence resigned from the UVF though, he attempted to break through the political stasis of this period, both inside the UVF and outside of it. Like the authors of the RHC document, Spence attempted to provide leadership and ideas in a period where none existed. One significant initiative took place when Spence, along with Republicans in Long Kesh and with the support of Merlyn Rees, organised and then participated in an 'Anti-Sectarian Assassination Conference' in February 1976 inside Long Kesh.[21] This conference aimed to reign in the sectarian killing. Although it did not put an end to them, there was a reduction of killings by the UVF. This, along with the Brigade change in 1975 and the Mason crackdown, as reflected in the criminalisation and Ulsterisation policies, significantly reduced UVF killings from 100 in 1975, to 71 in 1976 and then down to 14 by 1977.[22] However, the Shankill Butchers had begun their vicious campaign in 1975, and IRA killings actually increased in this period.[23]

A year after this conference Spence made two calculated and very important speeches in his continuing attempts to move the political situation forward. The first took place on the 12 July 1977, when Spence, as the UVF OC, gave his traditional speech. The other came in his Remembrance Day Speech on 11 November of that same year. The tone of these speeches was very radical, confrontational and visionary all at the same time, and marked a clear break for Spence with those on the outside and inside who did not want to move politically, and in particular with traditional Unionism. At the same time, he laid down a challenge to the PIRA to engage politically with Loyalism to end the conflict.

## THE SPENCE ORATION 12 JULY 1977

These [unionist politicians and clerics] are the men who cunningly and purposely fused religion with politics and fostered fear amongst the Loyalist community for their own design and to maintain power. No fascist or bigot can expect sympathy or understanding in the UVF.

Gusty Spence[24]

12 July is the sacred day in the Loyalist calendar, the day when King William of Orange famously defeated the Catholic King James at the Battle of the Boyne in 1690. For Unionists and Loyalists celebrating that day serves as a reminder of, 'when William of Orange achieved for us ... Civil and Religious freedoms.'[25] Therefore, it is significant that Spence chose this day to denounce the Unionists that he believes created the 'sick society', the 'conditions' and the 'stinking, polluted politics' that led to his and his men's incarceration in Long Kesh. This speech was also significant in that not only did he attack 'official Unionism, but he also attacked what he considered the retrograde elements within the Loyalist movement, those who, according to Bruce, Spence considered 'dwarfs'.[26]

Spence attacked Unionism not only in his speeches, but also by his actions inside Long Kesh. Harry Donaghy, a former OIRA prisoner tells of an incident that he claims to have witnessed from his adjacent compound that involved Spence and Paisley:

I think it was 1977, the same year that Gusty made the famous speech in July ... we were in compound 20 ... [A] sympathetic prison officer had tipped the UVF off that Paisley was coming to the prison for a pastoral visit. We saw a lot of activity in the UVF compound. Again, at that particular time ... when you came into that particular part of the camp ... you had to enter one way and then leave another way. Well, apparently the good doctor [Paisley] had appeared with one or two of his helpers ... And they were walking up ... a roadway ... By that time the UVF were on parade in compound 21 ... . [I]f memory serves me right, they [UVF] were all lined up. He [Spence] says "I've asked everyone of you why you were here when you entered the UVF compound." He [Spence] says "Here's one of the reasons why you're here, we're all here." Gusty had nailed him.[27]

Although Spence 'had nailed him' [Paisley] in Long Kesh, it was in his 12 July speech, that he really nailed him and all the retrograde elements in both Unionism and Loyalism.

Addressing the causes of the conflict and the role of the paramilitaries in the conflict, Spence argued that the paramilitaries did not start the conflict; rather they were the symptom of the sick society from which they sprang. He argued that when the civil rights movement tested Northern Ireland in the crucible of the 1960s, 'the scaberous [sic] cracks began to show through.' Spence attacked those who brought on the violence by the creation of that 'sick society' and created the climate of fear among all sections of the population. He argued that 'it is fear which makes one people oppress another' and that the people of Northern Ireland had to 'abolish fear' to create a normal society.[28] He rejected the narrative of traditional Unionism, which blamed the Troubles on a Republican plot. He understood and stated clearly that it was the '50 years of misrule' and the fear and hatred created by that misrule that had led to the present conflict.

Spence then attacked those who he believed had created the conditions that led to the violence, and those who, believing that they could achieve a military victory over the IRA, only prolonged the conflict. He challenged them in the following words:

Victory over whom – the IRA? Or do they mean victory over the Roman Catholic community? Over whom do they really want victory? The fears of Roman Catholics will not go away because a bunch of bigoted Unionist politicians say so ... we could never agree with those fascists who hold the reign of power. Do they not realise that the I.R.A. was a natural manifestation of Catholic fears just as the U.V.F. and U.D.A. were born from Loyalist fears?

In no uncertain terms, he condemned the tactics that enabled Unionist politicians to maintain their control over the Loyalist working class:

> We, in Northern Ireland are plagued with super-Loyalists who are not content to be ordinary. These people are the witch-hunters – the Ulster Senator McCarthys – who enter debate and newspaper columns armed with the tar brush, the innuendo, and the lie … if one does not agree with their bigoted and fascist views then one is a "taig lover" at best, or a "communist" at worst.[29]

Such tactics had marginalised those in the paramilitaries who wanted to move forward and only led to more deaths.

Spence's attacks did not stop with Unionist politicians. He openly criticised elements of the UVF and those within Loyalism who he saw as no better than those bigots and fascists within Unionism. Spence stated that 'we have too many of these people in our own ranks' and went on to stress that 'No fascist or bigot can expect sympathy or understanding in the U.V.F. compounds of Long Kesh.'

In this speech, he not only rejected the accepted Unionist narrative of the conflict, he attacked the methods of Unionism to maintain power. He also clearly stated that the UVF prisoners could no longer hold the narrow, xenophobic, and insular thinking that Spence believed had led to the conflict. Furthermore, rejecting both the retrograde thinking and the Unionist narrative, Spence told the UVF and its allies that they would have to 'fend for ourselves politically and to commence articulation in that direction.' Just what that direction would be, Spence made very plain in the rest of his speech.

Echoing the 1974 article 'Pure Frustration', Spence argued that, 'the politicians, seemingly cannot or will not give us the peace we so earnestly desire.' Therefore, Spence proposed an idea that many within political Loyalism had considered since 1974 and at one point acted on in 1974. Where much of the political thinking coming out of political Loyalism had called for bringing the paramilitaries to the table to work with all parties in Northern Ireland, Spence went further. Realising that the politicians could not or would not bring peace, Spence called,

upon all the paramilitaries – all the warring factions – to call a
universal ceasefire. To open dialogue with each other in order to
pursue ways and means of making such a ceasefire permanent.
Eventually Loyalist and republican must sit down together for
the good of our country if we claim to be patriots. There is no
obstacle that is insurmountable.

He asserted that, 'we have nothing to lose in such a summit' and
that the paramilitaries 'could learn something from one another.'[30]

Spence's speech reflected and complimented the thinking of the
other Loyalist documents studied to this point, especially the RHC's
Ten-Point plan in 1975. Building on the idea that there had to
be a breathing spell before there could be a settlement, Spence
argued, 'we must have peace with a modicum of trust to help bind
the wounds of ... three hundred years of strife, hatred, mistrust
and oppression.' Only then could the people of Northern Ireland
begin to build a new Northern Ireland, one in which they would
have decent homes, and employment. More importantly for his
audience, he stated that Loyalists would not 'suffer their deprivation
stoically lest their outcries be interpreted as disloyalty.' What Spence
proposed here was to bypass the politicians who were incapable of
bringing peace to Northern Ireland and putting that responsibility
squarely in the hands of those who had fought in this conflict.

Spence had anticipated the cries of 'traitor' from the 'usual
predictable quarters'.[31] Prepared for those attacks, he referred to
the meetings that took place in 1922 among Craig, Collins, and
DeValera. If the first Prime Minister of the Northern Ireland State
could meet with Republicans, so could Spence. This comparison
established his bona fides and buttressed his claim that no one could
call him a traitor for talking to the enemy. He also put his case
forcefully for talks in the strongest and clearest terms yet:

> dialogue will have to come sometime, so why not now? There is
> no victory in Ulster, not for the I.R.A. or the U.V.F., the police or
> the army. There is only victory for humanity and common sense.[32]

Spence's words echoed those of the 1975 article 'Futility of
Violence' with the call for a ceasefire and talks because 'In the midst
of the pounding clatter of the bombs and firearms, can we not take
time to consider that violence is not the mid-wife of freedom-but
its assassin?'[33] Like the 1975 article, Spence in 1977 pled, 'Surely

the time has come for all patriots to make a declaration of intent to forsake the gun (at least for a spell) in favour of dialogue.'[34]

He concluded the speech by calling on all those listening to it or reading it to 'not be hasty and dismiss my proposal out of hand.' Spence asked that people 'discuss among your membership the realities of the situation.' He stressed that in any talks or proposals, no one had to concede any principles. An example of how this could work and was working came on 25 January 1977 when the five paramilitary leaders in Long Kesh issued a joint statement in the Belfast *News Letter*. They stated clearly 'In Long Kesh we, Republicans and Loyalists, have attempted to bridge the gap by engaging in constructive dialogue without conceding principles.'[35]

This speech clearly differentiated the Loyalist political thinkers and their vision for ending the conflict with those of the Unionist establishment and those inside the UVF who had not moved to the position of people like Spence and those around him. Hence, one must ask, what sort of reaction did this speech elicit?

In July 1977, *Combat* published both the full text of Spence's speech and an analysis of it entitled 'Think or Perish', which laid out a strong challenge to the larger Loyalist community.[36] Examining Spence's words the writers admitted they had similar thoughts, but were afraid to pursue those ideas and put them into political programmes. Fearing the 'super-prods' and those who would shout 'traitor', they opted for 'populism', which, after Spence's speech, they now realised was no substitute for the truth. Reacting to Spence's speech, they paraphrased American General Omar Bradley's 1948 Memorial Day Speech, adding their own twist to it, in the harshest criticism of the Loyalist people yet heard:

> We are stumbling blindly trapped by our own moral adolescence, through a political and spiritual darkness while toying with the precarious secrets of life or death. We are a land of 'patriotic giants (super-prods) and ethical infants. We know more about contention and strife than we do about contentment and love; more about tribalism and division than about unity and co-existence, more about killing than about living.[37]

Taking up the challenge from Spence, the authors proposed, 'that we must escape from the stereotyped dogmas of the past and open our minds to new ideas and radical thought ... . It is essential that we cease to cling to old cherished myths and traditions in the face of new realities.' Finally, they proposed what Loyalists and indeed all factions had to do to escape the cycle of violence:

> The human intellect must now be employed for the salvation of our fair Province. We must think our way out of our present critical dilemma. To continue in meaningless violence is far too dangerous. It is think or die. Since there will obviously be no victors in this bitter war of attrition the only possible battleground is in the mind and around the conference table.

The authors concluded by quoting Elmo Roper, the founder of the polling company, which made clear what they needed to do to end the conflict:

> In order to save what is precious and essential in civilisation, we must cut out ruthlessly those parts of our thoughts and behaviour which have ceased to be relevant to the circumstances in which we live ... . We must give up cherished habits and prejudices or we will find ourselves, at best out of step, at worst out of existence.[38]

In essence, those who had worked since 1974 to find a new way forward reiterated that there would be no victory for anyone in this conflict; only talks and compromise offered the way forward for the people in Northern Ireland. This was the most thoughtful response that appeared in print. However, how did those to whom Spence addressed his speech react? What if any impact did the speech and this response have?

One young prisoner remembers the speech, the lead up to it, and the impact it had on him personally:

> It was around this time that many discussions were taking place amongst people who were starting to change their outlook on how things were going on the outside and we eagerly awaited Gusty's Twelfth day speech. There was much debate of what he would say and we spoke about it leading right up to the Twelfth – and invariably dissecting it afterwards. Gusty was also a great orator and it was inspiring to hear him deliver. He inspired me to read and latterly to write. I had a decent Grammar School education before incarceration but never learned half the things I learned while in Compounds 18 and 21.[39]

Hutchinson believes 'that Gusty's speeches on each 12th of July ... remain today essential reading and reflect what a visionary he was.'[40] Reading it today one cannot help but see how radical Spence's words were and still are. However, in the context of 1977, it had a limited effect. In assessing the impact of the speech, Hutchinson says, 'Well I think it was disregarded in the main, but in Long Kesh I think it resonated with the political figures.' He continued saying, 'It was missed by people except people who were in anoraks who listened to what was being said in Long Kesh, and you people [researchers] who would sit in the Linen Hall library and look at these things.' He believes that it 'drew attention to the UVF in Long Kesh at that time', and that it had 'some significance'. However, when reflecting on its failure to reach a broader audience, Hutchinson said, 'I suppose in many ways it was lost on people.'[41]

In a 2006 interview, Ervine agreed with Hutchinson's analysis characterising the reaction to the speech outside of Long Kesh as a 'mixed bag'.[42] When assessing the speech's impact on those in Long Kesh, he said,

> I think many of the Compound people would've been confused because they perceived Spence to be on a different level from them anyway. They would've accepted, I suppose the facts. I remember thinking it was good for us. I also remember being ridiculous and thinking naively, this could make a difference. Not a chance of it. [43]

Winkie Rea, Spence's son-in-law, who was in Long Kesh at the time, remembers the speech and its limited effect. In a 2009 interview, Rea said,

> It would've had an impact on a small number of people only. Some of them would've digested them all right or wouldn't. Not simply because they didn't want to, but just weren't in that way of thinking.

Rea made the point that it was one thing to be inside Long Kesh thinking politically and writing articles for *Combat*, it was another for those on the outside embroiled in the conflict.[44] Therefore, the speech did not have the impact on the outside in the way Spence and others hoped.

The response of the paramilitaries on the outside of Long Kesh provides stark evidence of the limited influence of Spence's speech. Despite Spence's call for talks, the Republican and Loyalist violence continued, albeit at a lower level, and the paramilitaries did not officially get around the table for another 20 years, after the second IRA ceasefire in 1997. The IRA was still 15 years away from publically accepting that the conflict would have to end in a compromise peace. In this period, Unionism itself never accepted the proposals nor any of the thinking coming from Loyalist paramilitaries. Finally, resistance or apathy within the UVF and the RHC towards this type of thinking was still too strong. The leadership, while attempting to move towards politics, had to find a way to bring its base with it, and in this period that failed.

## REMEMBRANCE DAY SPEECH 1977

Spence fired one more salvo in his attempt to prod the UVF towards politics. That came during his Remembrance Day 1977 speech. Suiting the occasion, Spence repeatedly referenced World War I and the lessons that he had personally learned from it. Utilising the poetry of the Siegfried Sassoon and Wilfred Owen, he pointed out how Unionism used and treated Loyalists in the modern era in the same manner as the upper classes had used the original UVF as cannon fodder on the Somme in 1916.[45]

However, the real point of this speech was that 'The war situation in Northern Ireland has changed dramatically and requires serious and radical re-appreciation on the part of the paramilitaries.' The lesson that Spence tried to impart to the IRA, the UVF, the RHC, the UDA and anyone who would listen is that, 'Further violence is useless and counterproductive since the aim of self-determination has been achieved'. Consequently, it was incumbent on all, especially Loyalism, to respond to this situation: 'There is a need for reconciliation with our neighbours ... and dialogue can fill the vacuum of violence'. Spence denounced war, claiming that 'War is obscene' and that 'there is no glory in it'. As a result, he argued, 'The only true testimony to the dead is peace'. Therefore, to give purpose to those who died in this conflict, Spence believed that the 'rattle of the oratory and the volleys of words be heard instead of the bombs and the bullets'.

As he had done in July, Spence called on all sides to develop new thinking and new strategies to find a way forward. It is worth quoting Spence at length here as this speech makes clear the advanced level of political thinking coming from Spence and those around him in Long Kesh, and just how far ahead of the rest of the parties and paramilitary organisations in Northern Ireland he and they were:

> We need the strategy of political policies in place of battle plans and let us face one another across the negotiating table as opposed to no man's land. Let us reconcile and permit the grass and flowers to grow over the battlefields just as they have at the Somme and Passchendaele. And lastly let us forget past dissensions and resolve to pass on to our children the fruitful lessons which cost us so high a price in life and human misery, so they may never know the hell and barbarity through which we had to pass.[46]

Like the July speech for the most part, his appeals fell on deaf ears. The same problems still existed in getting his message out. Spence did have the support of some of the UVF in Long Kesh, but not the support of the majority on the outside nor those in the H-Blocks. Meanwhile, the IRA still believed it could achieve total victory, while Unionism wanted no truck with Loyalism of any kind.

## CONCLUSION

Spence's 12 July speech, along with the response in *Combat,* as well as his Remembrance Day speech illustrates how far the leadership of political Loyalism had travelled, and how far ahead it was, at this time, of all the paramilitary groups and political actors in Northern Ireland, including its own members. Yet, as we know, these men achieved little.

Although Spence failed, as did the RHC, to bring people to the negotiating table, there were two important results of this work. One was the impact that, in particular, Spence's thinking and his speeches had on the peace process in the 1990s. In fact, Dawn Purvis believes that his speeches and the political thinking coming out of the UVF compounds were crucial to the peace process:

> Billy Hutchinson, David Ervine, Eddie Kinner, Martin Snodden, Tom Roberts, Billy Giles, you know I could rattle off a whole list of them. All these people came through as Gusty's graduates from Long Kesh in the early, mid 70s. And so that leadership and that inspiration coming from Gusty and, and what those people went through at that time, they were the founders of the peace process.[47]

The second point was that Spence's speeches and the thinking he put forward inside Long Kesh, especially in 1977, along with work of those who created the Ten-Point Plan, helped lead to the most forward thinking document from any group during the conflict, a document entitled *Sharing Responsibility*. This document represented the most realistic and practical political solution to the conflict in Northern Ireland that came from the paramilitaries and indeed anyone in this period.

# 7
# Sharing Responsibility: 1977–87

Unionists are always able to say 'no.' You know and effectively block political institutions they don't like, but they're not very imaginative in coming up with pragmatic solutions to the political problems.

Tom Roberts[1]

As the previous chapters have argued, the political thinkers in the UVF and RHC from 1974 on, and possibly earlier believed, that the conflict had reached a stalemate. Therefore, unlike Unionism, they had begun to develop proposals to create the breathing space they believed necessary to let the politics of compromise work. Spence's speeches, the various proposals from the UVF and the RHC and those found in *Combat*, *Sunday News*, *Orange Cross* and *Loyalist News*, and the RHC's 1975 Ten-Point plan, all pointed out ways to accomplish this. Simultaneously, their work and Spence's speeches held that because the politicians could not give them the peace they desired, then it fell to them, the paramilitaries, to find a way to bring all parties, including all warring factions, to the negotiating table to hammer out an agreement that would create a just and peaceful society in Northern Ireland.

While maintaining Northern Ireland as a political entity, the political thinkers within the UVF and RHC had no intention of going back to the old Stormont regime or returning to the 'stinking, polluted politics' that they now believed had led to the conflict in the first place. They had rejected mandatory power sharing and the Council of Ireland, as the UWC strike and their limited participation in it made evident. Yet, except for *Within the Context of Northern Ireland* and the *Manifesto of the Volunteer Political Party*, they had not developed a practical political programme and/or blueprint for a new Assembly that could serve all sections of Northern Ireland. That proposal came in May 1977 with the publication of a document by the Independent Unionist Group, which later became the PUP, entitled 'Devolution: The Plan for Ulster.'[2] In 1979, this became the *Proposed Democratic Devolved Administration for Northern Ireland*.[3] As we will see below, both these documents clearly formed the basis of the 1985 PUP *Sharing Responsibility*[4] document that the PUP eventually took to all the major parties and which all parties largely ignored. At the same time, the principles outlined by the UVF during the 1974 secret talks with the IRA underpinned much of the thinking in each of these documents.[5]

The political leadership within the UVF/RHC consistently tried, even in the face of resistance at all levels to develop policies that would create the breathing space for the politicians to craft a political settlement. The development and publication of the 1977 document 'Devolution: The Plan for Ulster', and its further iterations, represented a further step forward in the development of those policies aimed at ending the conflict and creating a just and inclusive society in Northern Ireland.

Even though 'Devolution' failed to have an impact on politics, the forward political thinking in this document demonstrates once again how advanced these particular Loyalists were in their political development. In fact, Graham Spencer discerned the development of this new brand of Unionism for a new Northern Ireland when analysing both *Sharing Responsibility* and *Common Sense*, the 1987 UDA document that called for power sharing. Spencer argues,

> It is the development of such political thinking which underpinned the emergence of articulate and politically motivated Loyalist representatives and which provided the foundation for a new Loyalist discourse which sought to move beyond the reactive and insular psychology of mainstream constitutional unionism.[6]

Sinnerton, looking at the development and adoption of *Sharing Responsibility* concurs, stating,

> This political pedigree scotches once and for all the notion that Spence, Ervine, Hutchinson and others are simply ventriloquist dummies manipulated by Loyalist paramilitaries.[7]

There is some argument as to when the discussions began that led to *Sharing Responsibility*. Both Hutchinson and Sinnerton agree that, under Spence's influence, *Sharing Responsibility* first saw 'the light of day' in the UVF Compounds in 1972.[8] Spence himself told Garland that, 'as far back as 1973 the U.V.F. suggested that there should be "shared responsibility" in any settlement.'[9] Spence may be referring to internal discussions, rather than specifically work on *Sharing Responsibility*. Two other sources claim that the discussions on this proposal began in 1974 and that was when the serious work took place on it.[10] What is interesting about the concept of 'sharing responsibility' is that in the secret talks with the PIRA in 1974, 'the UVF generally accepted the principle of "Equal Responsibility" in Government.'[11] Although, it is a different term, it illustrates that the UVF and RHC had debated this idea and principle before they met with the PIRA. This means they had engaged in discussions on this before 1974.

Billy Hutchinson remembers that the Rev. Stewart, David Overend and Jim McDonald 'were the three main people who actually influenced that', and they eventually brought in Hugh Smyth, the former member of the ULF and future PUP member.[12] After Rev. Stewart's death in 1977, the heavy political work fell to the remaining three.

In their political work, these men engaged with those inside Long Kesh, Spence, Hutchinson, Ervine, Flint McCullough, Plum Smith, Martin Snodden and Eddie Kinner, among others. After going through the documents smuggled into Long Kesh, they then held discussions on the proposals and provided feedback to the three outside. Hugh Smyth reports that,

> What we did was mostly done on the outside. But, it was sent in for comments and changes to the inside and there would have been comments coming out, which we would have looked at and implemented. But basically it was a joint document between those on the inside and those on the outside.[13]

This joint work went on for three to five years, during a period of political drift in Northern Ireland, and eventually resulted in 'Devolution: The Plan for Ulster' in 1977, which laid out plans for a new devolved government in Northern Ireland that included 'sharing responsibility' between the two communities in Northern Ireland.

What did the authors intend when they started this document? Unfortunately, Jim McDonald died almost immediately after agreeing to an interview for this book, and a great deal of knowledge went with him. Therefore, we must depend on the memories of those who could do interviews for this study and the work of Henry Sinnerton who did the only extensive work on this document, for an indication of what they intended.

Plum Smith, who worked on this and other documents inside Long Kesh says, we were 'talking about ... sharing responsibility. Because it's not about sharing power it's about sharing responsibility.'[14]

Spence concurs telling Garland that, 'sharing of responsibility must become our aim' in order to create a society in which everyone can realise their aspirations and 'walk forward in dignity, in pride and equality.'[15] Spence believed that only the sharing of responsibility could bring peace but he realised that, 'one has to be prepared to take that extra step – it's known as compromise',[16] in order to make sharing responsibility and peace work. He viewed 'sharing responsibility' as the 'politics of the fishbowl'.[17]

Billy Hutchinson, who was involved in developing *Sharing Responsibility* in Long Kesh beginning in 1975, argues that they,

> didn't construct a vision, but what we did do was construct some principles on what society would be based and the first one was society would have to be a pluralist society. It would have to be free from paramilitarism, and human rights for all and a political system that was fair and just for all and would have to have a police service that was fair for all, not just one section. So from that point of view we definitely had a set of principles ... we were definitely going to have a society with all those things.[18]

In an interview with Graham Spencer, Ervine went further concerning what underpinned their thinking:

> The concept of responsibility rather than referring to power, from our point of view as about not having to sign up to each other ... . From the very start our intent was underpinned by the idea that you can't enjoy this society unless everybody enjoys it. The only way ahead then, is to share it and to deal with responsibility or power in a shared sense.[19]

Sinnerton points out that Spence's goal was to establish an 'alternative unionism' and that dovetailed with Hugh Smyth's vision for the Loyalist working class. Sinnerton correctly argues that the people who developed this thinking and eventually created the PUP saw themselves as left of centre and took a very strong unionist and British Labour position. They believed that their thinking in this period as found in the PUP and *Sharing Responsibility* offered a 'realistic alternative' to the traditional parties and their intransigent positions, which they believed had led to nothing but one defeat after another for unionism.[20]

Finally, in 1977 the Independent Unionist Group published 'Devolution: The Plan for Ulster'.[21] Its publication came against the backdrop of the Paisley led United Unionist Action Coalition strike that demanded more stringent security measures and a return to majority rule based on the 1975 convention report. This strike supported by the UWC and the UDA failed miserably because the majority of unionists did not support it and the British government, in contrast to 1974, acted decisively in dealing with strikers and the intimidation that was so successful in the 1974 UWC Strike.[22]

This strike made clear that Paisley and his cohorts remained intransigent, as they did until 2007, in contemplating sharing power. They demanded a return to purely majority rule, and ran for elections on programmes such as 'This We Will Maintain'.[23] Essentially, the Unionist politicians, as the Rev. Roy Magee put it, created a situation where the electorate 'didn't have to think.'[24] Dawn Purvis explains how mainstream Unionism played on this 'populism' at the time:

> What was popular at that time was conflict, conflict was popular, being different from the other tribe was popular. The need to fit in with your own tribe was popular. And politicians ... they got returned to electoral office time and again for being part of the tribe, not for being the same as the "Other".[25]

In contrast, 20 years before the UUP and 30 years before Paisley embraced power sharing, the IUG put forward proposals that, while not going as far as mandatory power sharing or including an Irish dimension, went very far. To a certain extent, their plan resembled the 1975 Convention proposal of Bill Craig's 'voluntary coalition' for sharing power with the SDLP and eventually the GFA.[26]

In the introduction to the proposal, the IUG claimed that it was not a solution to the problems in Northern Ireland and that they did not believe it was a final document: 'the Independent Unionist Group do not claim to have the answer to Ulster's political stagnation.' Instead, they intended this proposal to serve as a 'discussion' piece to get people and parties engaged in politics that would work for everyone. What the IUG wanted was to find 'common ground' with 'different parties so they could air their views and eventually reach a level of agreement on which to go forward.' Acknowledging that not all shared the same aspirations for the future, their opening statement recognised that they could not resolve all the problems in Northern Ireland. Recognising that the principle of consent did exist and that 'the status of Northern Ireland can only be changed with the consent of its people', meant that the solution to the problem had to come within the context of Northern Ireland.[27]

The IUG believed that the only way to begin the process of resolving the problems internally was to create a devolved government. However, unlike the United Unionist Action Council and the mainstream Unionist parties, their solution included 'A system ... in which elected representation from both sides of the community would be willing to participate.' Echoing the confidence that many Loyalist thinkers had gained in Long Kesh and the confidence of the thinkers outside, in contrast to those like Paisley and other mainstream Unionists who refused to negotiate, they called for those who did not agree with them to come forward and put their ideas in the public forum. They wrote,

> We do not expect all sides to agree completely with our document, but we would hope that those who disagree with us would be willing to come forward with their ideas in order to present a basis for discussion.[28]

This represented a major step forward for Loyalism. Finally, a group of self-confident and capable political leaders emerged from within the Loyalist working class prepared to engage with their enemies across the negotiating table. Two months later, as we know, Spence reiterated this thinking in his 12 July Oration when he said, 'Eventually Loyalist and republican must sit down together.'[29]

The IUG dealt with the failure of Sunningdale and what that failure meant for both the British government and Northern Ireland. For the authors it meant that the British government could not enforce power sharing nor, as they saw it, the 'institutionalised sectarianism' of mandatory power-sharing, on the people of Northern Ireland. They learned two other lessons, from the Sunningdale and post-Sunningdale period: the paramilitaries had to be part of any solution, and the British could not impose a military solution. Citing the Rhodesian (Zimbabwe) situation, they pointed out the absurdity of the British talking to Mugabe and Nkomo, (revolutionary leaders) to end that conflict there, while 'in the top left corner [Northern Ireland] they are opting for the Military Solution' and refusing to engage politically with the paramilitaries. From these followed the final lesson they learned was that 'the problem must be worked out by the people of Northern Ireland.'

Having learned those lessons, the IUG wrote, 'our objectives are honourable and intended to secure for the People of Northern

Ireland better representation at a local level and ultimately a better future.' As they did in their Introduction, they welcomed comments 'of a constructive nature' from any and all sources. Finally, they hoped, in offering their proposals that, 'the form of Devolved Administration ... may be acceptable to a very large majority of people irrespective of Religious belief.'[30]

This proposal called for a 153-member assembly, elected by proportional representation. In a fashion similar to the appointment of the first minister and deputy first minister under the GFA, the House would elect a deputy leader from a minority party or group within the administration and the House would select the leader much the same as they choose the lord mayor of Belfast. Once they did this, the remaining 150 members would then sit on ten committees of 15 members, which they would elect by proportional representation.[31] They then would set up a central council made up of the chairs of the ten committees. Each committee would then 'co-opt' trade unionists, educators and so on, but they would not have voting rights. The non-voting members could then represent special interests and put forward ideas to the elected representatives. Anticipating the 'Civic Forum'[32] that came out of the GFA, the goal was to engage every member of society in the governance of Northern Ireland. The IUG made this clear when it wrote, 'We are in effect, offering to every single person in Northern Ireland the opportunity to share RESPONSIBILITY for our State'[33] (emphasis in original).

The last two sections of this document dealt with security issues and the issues of the political prisoners. Their initial proposal was vague on how they would formulate security policy, putting it under the Ways and Means Committee and stating only that, 'the Final Security Policy would have to have Major support within the full Congress.' They also put forward the vague hope 'that some agreement may be reached on the withdrawal of Troops to Barracks and the acceptance of the Police Authorities for a brief period.' It is not clear what they meant here. However, that is not surprising given that this was a proposal for discussion.

The IUG argued that it 'would be essential to take courage and open discussion on the question of a Phased Amnesty for persons convicted or detained for CLEAR POLITICAL OFFENCES' (emphasis in the original). Citing other colonial conflicts and their settlements, the IUG argued, 'the people of Northern Ireland are capable of forging a much better future for our future Generations.'[34]

When looking back on how the concept of sharing responsibility would work, Hugh Smyth explains,

> We have two communities in this society that needs to come together, and what our philosophy was in the sharing of responsibility was exactly that. That we come together in a voluntary basis and that would be done rather than power sharing that had been done in d'Hondt form.[35] That it would have been done on a proportionality basis which meant that if people go to the polls, if the unionist community got 60% of the vote and the Catholic community got 40%, come what may, that they would form a government that would represent both sections of the community. Something similar to what was forced on the people. But when we did this, we really thought this could work.[36]

Billy Hutchinson believes that, especially after the Hunger Strikes in 1981, sharing responsibility was the 'only way we were going to move forward.' The proposal for sharing responsibility, to him, meant an 'end to all political violence, the release of all political prisoners, re-forming the police ... the political analysis was that unless we do all those things then we can't get to the next step.'[37]

As is clear from this document they hoped that this new devolved government would bring in all sections of society to participate and share the responsibility for governing, while providing the breathing space to end the military campaign of all the paramilitary groups. Hugh Smyth argues that the UVF even bought into this, seeing it as,

> a way of ending the violence in Northern Ireland ... a way of keeping Northern Ireland within the UK, but at the same time offering a hand of friendship to those who we would have lost ... to bring them in from the cold.[38]

By using proportional representation for the elections, instead of a sectarian head count that would exist under a mandatory coalition, a true opposition could develop as the smaller parties worked together. They also felt it would bring in all shades of opinion from every segment of society. However, in the atmosphere of 1977, nothing came of this, even though they took the document to Roy Mason and others from the British government year after year.[39]

The IUG, along with Mario Biaggi, a member of the US (United States) Congress, did try to bring together a 'peace forum' to take place in Washington, DC. They met with him and both sides agreed that, 'WITHOUT DIALOGUE NOTHING CAN BE ACHIEVED' (emphasis in original). They also called for all parties to 'bury petty differences and talk with one aim in mind, THE WELFARE OF ULSTER'.[40]

The article on the Peace Forum appeared on the front page of *Combat* along with an interview with senior members of the UVF about such a peace forum. While protesting that they had never met with the PIRA, a patently untrue statement, the UVF leadership said they would participate in any forum like this, as long as there was a 'complete cessation of violence from the Provisionals for a period leading up to the talks.'[41] These senior UVF men argued that their June 1976 ceasefire was proof of the positive role they could play in reducing the violence. When questioned about what the British could do to create stability in Northern Ireland, they answered that the British should introduce a 'Democratic Devolved Administration for Northern Ireland'.[42] In a policy that the UVF has attempted to adhere to since this period, albeit with mixed results, the UVF made clear that in the case of any political settlement acceptable to the majority of people in Northern Ireland, it would stand down and would then direct its energies towards local community work and welfare work.[43]

Although the Peace Forum initiative went nowhere, this did not end the political thinking coming out of the UVF and its political representatives. In 1979, the UVF continued to call on the IRA to end its armed struggle and get around the table for talks. The leadership argued that, 'the climate is ripe for a new political initiative such as a Devolved Administration.'[44] Part of the reason that they believed the time was right for a political initiative was clearly wishful thinking on the UVF's part concerning the PIRA. The UVF leadership believed that 'The Provisionals are not naïve enough not to realise the futility of their aims and complete rejection of their methods by the people they claim to represent.'[45] This statement attacked the Provisionals' continued justification for the war:

Their excuse is that the roots of the present troubles go back into history, but have in the last decades, their source in the social and economic deprivation, suffered by Nationalist people. We would ask 'Have the Protestant people suffered no social or economic deprivation?'[46]

In the same year, the Progressive Unionist Group (PUG) published the second version of *Sharing Responsibility,* called *Proposed*

*Democratic Devolved Administration for Northern Ireland.* This document eventually became the political platform of the PUP once the Party changed its name in 1979. While much of what appeared in the 1977 document remained in the 1979 version, the PUG added a few more sections and ideas to the document, adding a foreword, and adding sections on aspirations, border poll, a bill of rights, and the building of an 'Israeli-type border'.

In the foreword, the PUG made sure to differentiate itself from other parties in Northern Ireland and feared that by using 'Independent' in the title the public would associate it with the UDA, who at the time flirted with independence, which came out clearly in the UDA's *Common Sense* document. Hugh Smyth explained,

> We worked together as Independent Unionists. But ... the UDA at that time, they were flirting with Independence. Glenny Barr [and the UDA] wanted an independent Ulster. We were scared of people misunderstanding where we were coming from.[47]

The PUG also made it clear that it stood for a new, democratic, devolved administration and that it 'agreed unanimously' to build a better future 'for all the people of Northern Ireland.' The PUG stated that it had three main aims and objectives in promulgating this document:

1. To form a group to deal with political issues and to attempt to formulate a political sense of purpose.
2. To pursue objectives of the group throughout all the parts of Northern Ireland.
3. To pursue policies favourable to working people throughout N. Ireland independent of any other political party or group.

The PUG then went through section-by-section with suggestions on how to do that.

While this document did contain some progressive additions, in particular the bill of rights, it also contained backward thinking as well. The proposal on an Israeli-type border is one example of this. The PUG used the examples of the violence and killing along the border to justify building a wall along the border, but this point had little or no support in any party in Great Britain.

Where the PUG moved forward was on 'Aspirations' and the 'Bill of Rights.' The PUG argued that the border poll showed the vast majority of those in Northern Ireland favoured maintenance of the link with Great Britain. While most observers do not accept the poll as legitimate because of the Nationalist boycott of it, for the PUG it was enough to say that the 'BORDER POLL GAVE US THAT MANDATE' (emphasis in original). However, what this allowed them to do was argue that,

> No person can be denied Political Aspirations. Our attitude on that matter is quite clear. Equally, no minority group should feel entitled to violently change the political aspiration of a Majority in N. Ireland and in so doing plunge the Community into civil strife.

Although, not explicitly stated here, this section, like the earlier UVF and RHC work examined here, points to an acceptance of competing national aspirations as long as those who hold those aspirations work inside the political arena and avoid the use of violence. The PUG did admit that a reversal of the border poll would necessitate a rethink of their positions, but this was a step forward in finding a way to move towards peaceful resolution of the conflict.

Where the PUG and eventually the PUP distinguished itself in this period was in its call for a bill of rights. The fight for a bill of rights in Northern Ireland continues today and is no closer now than in 1979. Yet, in 1979, the PUG called for,

> A BILL OF RIGHTS FOR ALL UNITED KINGDOM CITIZENS SHOULD BE DRAWN AND RATIFIED BY THE WESTMINSTER PARLIAMENT, GUARANTEED BY THE EUROPEAN COURT OF HUMAN RIGHTS AND THE UNITED NATIONS COMMISSION FOR HUMAN RIGHTS. [Emphasis in original]

It believed that the bill of rights would enhance the progressive democratisation of Northern Ireland and would force the politicians to 'commit themselves now to the politics of the mind and reject the politics of emotions'.

The PUG also inserted some minor changes in other areas of the document. In 1977, under the section on political prisoners, it wrote, 'It would be essential to take courage and open discussions on a phased amnesty' for convicted or detained political prisoners. The 1979 version read, 'It is essential that the British Government takes courage and opens discussion on the question of a Phased Amnesty.' Now, reading this closely, it appears that the PUG is putting the onus on the government for the amnesty. More likely, the authors had corrected language that, in the 1977 version was not clear.

Both Smyth and Hutchinson claim that the 'Three' (Smyth, McDonald, Overend) as Hutchinson calls them, delivered a draft to the Northern Ireland Secretary of State, Roy Mason, and a number of MPs at Westminster. Hutchinson claims that Mason thought the 'proposal was brilliant, A-One, the most forward thinking document, etc. and so forth',[48] but that it was up to the party itself to sell it to the other parties. Hugh Smyth said that the Secretary of State, 'made the statement that he said ... it was the best document. He said, if you can sell it to the political parties ... I believe that you are so far ahead in your thinking that ... you're blowing them [other political parties] out of the water.'[49]

At about the same time as it tried to sell this document the Progressive Unionist Group renamed itself the PUP. After consultations with the prisoners in Long Kesh, those on the outside chose the name. As Hutchinson explains, 'A UVF commander did some research and discovered that there had been a Progressive Unionist Party back around ... . 1938'[50] (see Chapter 2). As outlined earlier this Party stood in the 1938 elections and finished second with 12 per cent of the overall vote.[51] The real name was 'Ulster Progressive Unionist Association', but the politics were similar to those of the modern PUP. Smyth agrees with Hutchinson on this point, making it clear that the PUP went back to their past to find a name of a political party that interested itself in social and working class issues.[52] The Party took on the socialist labour mantle, even incorporating Clause IV of the British Labour Party's constitution, which reads,

> To secure for the workers by hand or by brain the full fruits of their industry and the most equitable distribution thereof that may be possible upon the basis of the common ownership of the means of production, distribution, and exchange, and the best obtainable system of popular administration and control of each industry or service.[53]

Sinnerton argues that, 'the PUP's agenda, as well as being conciliatory, was unapologetically left-wing Labour.'[54] The PUP, even today describes itself as,

> a labour orientated party, committed to achieving a new Northern Ireland, free from the ... stale politics of the past. The

PUP are committed to develop an anti-sectarian and pluralist Northern Ireland.[55]

Aaron Edwards argues that the PUP's discourse was a 'coherent analysis of the class structure of traditional Unionism' which challenges 'the old Stormont system of privilege and patronage.'[56] The PUP's analysis, like the VPP's, pointed out that traditional Unionism had failed the Protestant working class by not making the Union 'pay socio-economic dividends; thereby abandoning Protestant workers to the "same pattern of social deprivation that affects their counterparts in Nationalist areas."'[57]

The first task of the new party was to 'sell' the new document to the other political parties. Hutchinson claims that, 'Every year from [19]77 on, every political party in Northern Ireland got a copy of *Sharing Responsibility*, as did the press and Her Majesty's Government.'[58] He also claims that the PUP distributed, 'Over 700 copies ... to the House of Commons.' Smyth said, 'We went to the British government with it and [they] said "it's great, it's wonderful ... yes, that's what we want."'[59]

Hutchinson recounts how 'The PUP even sent a delegation to Washington, DC, for five weeks late in 1979. They hand-delivered copies to senior US government officials' and 'met individually with Senators Howard H. Baker, Daniel K. Inouye and Edmund S. Muskie, and the then Congressman J. Danforth Quayle.[60] One of the people on this trip, Hugh Smyth, remembers, 'The Americans told us "that we were, maybe ten years, 20 years before our time".'[61] Smyth also remembers that the PUP received a positive reception both in the USA and in England.[62] However, at every turn, nothing came of their initiatives in this period.

The PUP made further attempts to get its message heard. In 1979 and 1980, it attempted to put its ideas on the table with the British government and the other parties, but that failed also. Then on 6 October 1981, the PUP submitted another document called *Movement Towards a Devolved Democratic Administration for Northern Ireland*.[63] This submission was a supplement to its initial policy document and it laid out the thinking of the PUP in regards to bringing the paramilitaries to the table. It also appeared in *Combat* in 1981 entitled 'Constitutional Matters: The Way Ahead.'[64] In the 'Summary', the PUP wrote,

Our submission is generally intended to pave the way towards a Democratic Administration working for all the Community and at the same time giving military organisations the opportunity to pursue their aims through political persuasion and not through force of arms.[65]

The PUP repeated what the UVF and RHC had argued since 1973–74, 'Two factors are emerging. The Provisionals cannot win and attain their main objective. The British Government can never achieve 100 per cent military defeat of the Provisional IRA and their support groups.'

It therefore put forth the following four-point programme to bring about the breathing space necessary for the ceasefires and then the all-party talks.

1. Ceasefire of all Paramilitary Organisations
2. Troops withdrawn to barracks
3. Acceptance by all people of the RUC
4. All-Party conference after completion of above 3 points.[66]

Hugh Smyth recalls that James Prior, the then Northern Ireland Secretary, 'made a statement ... "This is the best I've ever seen, coming from anyone." He said "If this was coming from a major party, the people would be jumping on the bandwagon with it."'[67] Spence also claimed that 'Jim Prior [the Northern Ireland Secretary of State from 1981–84] himself said the only constructive proposals he got in Northern Ireland was from the Worker's Party [OIRA] and the Progressive Unionist Party.'[68] David Ervine remembers taking this document to James Prior:

> The party presented *Sharing Responsibility* to the Secretary of State at the time, Jim Prior, and he told them that he was very interested in it, but they were twenty years ahead of their time.[69]

Yet, for all their hard work and all the progressive proposals for 'sharing responsibility', the PUP could make no progress. The year 1981, in particular, was a difficult time for any type of conciliatory political thinking. The hunger strikes had poisoned the atmosphere for the contemplation of any sort of progressive, political thinking coming from Loyalist paramilitaries. As a direct result of the hunger strikes, Sinn Féin began to emerge as a political force and as the political wing of an armed movement, focused totally on victory. Finally, as we will see, the entrenched forces of Unionism refused to countenance any proposals from the working class Loyalists.

## SHARING RESPONSIBILITY, 1985

The 'drift' in Northern Ireland politics, particularly Unionist and Loyalist politics, continued after the failure of the talks with James Prior. This was an initiative aimed at restoring a devolved government in the aftermath of the hunger strikes and the rise of Sinn Féin. In this period, the Republic of Ireland's government published the *New Ireland Forum* on 2 May 1984, which called for either a federal solution or joint sovereignty, which the British government rejected in October of that year. Once again, the situation in Northern Ireland appeared to have reached a stalemate.

Despite this, the PUP continued to work on finding a way out of the stasis. It once more refined its proposals. In September 1985, the PUP published the full version of *Sharing Responsibility*.[70] In the conclusion of this document, the PUP writes,

> These legitimate proposals are presented by the Progressive Unionist Party to draw support from all political parties and groups who genuinely desire an end to the present round of political violence in Northern Ireland.[71]

As in its document on a devolved administration, the PUP stressed that, 'the Union is also of paramount importance' but accepted, unlike the mainstream Unionist parties, that 'there are two legitimate aspirations.' The PUP also recognised that while focusing on these aspirations, the political parties and society itself ignored, with catastrophic results, the other more basic aspirations, 'freedom from fear and violence, social deprivation in all areas' as well as violations of 'basic human rights'.[72]

To address and solve these social and political problems, and the competing aspirations in Northern Ireland, the PUP stated, 'We have concentrated on the sharing of responsibility rather than the sharing of Power', as 'The task of everyone in this region is to bring a halt to the violence and ensure that power politics is not allowed ever again to breed communal violence.'[73]

Recognising the deep divide in society, the PUP argued, 'clearly there will have to be radical change.'[74] Consequently, the PUP once more laid out what society needed to do to ensure the violence would end: that there could be no return to that violence, that power politics would not return, and that people would have their needs addressed. This is where its concept of sharing responsibility would play an important role.

As its earlier iterations had, *Sharing Responsibility* envisioned a regional devolved government in Northern Ireland made up of 153 members sitting atop a much broader local government structure, whose structure was vague in this document. In fact, it did not differ from the earlier proposals in this regards, except for the expansion of local government structures. Again, the electorate would choose the 153 members by proportional representation. In this version, the PUP laid out the option of having either ten committees of 15 members each or 15 committees of ten each and the principles of proportionality would determine the makeup of these committees. The new legislature would also have a Speaker, a Leader and a Deputy Leader appointed from the 153 members. A central committee would 'focus the opinions of political parties both large and small' and be responsible for 'assessing the likely success or failure of any matters put before the full Administration.' Even with this power, all 'issues would have to be put before the full assembly for approval.'[75]

The Central Committee would consist 'of all the Chairmen and Deputy Chairmen of all the Committees.' In thinking that anticipated the GFA, the PUP stated: 'This Central Committee should be chaired by the Leader of any Constitutional minority party, with the usual committee voting rights.' The PUP laid out other responsibilities, but then made clear that the rules governing the operation of the Central Committee would 'require careful consideration'.[76]

The PUP expanded on its idea for a bill of rights, arguing that the new bill of rights for Northern Ireland should follow the European Convention on Human Rights, with special emphasis on eliminating discrimination. To guarantee fairness and address the worries of the majority about Northern Ireland's constitutional position, it called for a committee of eight judges, 'two from the United Kingdom, two from the Republic of Ireland, two from Northern Ireland and two from the European Courts to oversee any bill of rights.' Anticipating the creation of the Northern Ireland Human Rights Commission, the PUP called for the creation of a 'local office in Belfast where Rights issues could be discussed with some urgency with a view to local conciliation.'[77]

The PUP, while rejecting 'the need for any grandiose Anglo–Irish pacts or agreements',[78] did envision an Irish Dimension in *Sharing Responsibility*, albeit on a restricted basis. Acknowledging there were many areas where the North and the South already cooperated, such as sport, banking, telecommunications, the PUP accepted that cross-border cooperation was necessary and beneficial to Northern

Ireland. Consequently, the PUP called for a 'properly constituted North/South Committee' to discuss all matters beneficial to all parts of Ireland, provided the issue of Northern Ireland's constitutional position was not subject to discussion. It also intended to have the work of this committee open and transparent and consist of an equal number of representatives from the North and the South, with each delegate holding veto power.[79]

When examining *Sharing Responsibility* in its various iterations, it is obvious how much thought and work went into creating this document. The potential in this proposal is obvious. It not only could have ended the violence, it could have addressed the needs and concerns of both communities in Northern Ireland, while at the same time including an Irish dimension, a bill of rights and a guarantee against discrimination. At this point, no Unionist party had developed any proposals remotely close to this or even considered sharing power or responsibility in any form.[80] Meanwhile, Sinn Féin and the IRA still focused on victory and a united Ireland as the solution to the conflict. What this demonstrates is that, in reality, the PUP, as Prior had said, was 20 years ahead of its time. It is also evident that his document, if accepted as a basis for discussion and negotiation would have accomplished what the GFA did twelve years later and in the process saved many lives.

## THE ANGLO–IRISH ACCORD

The most momentous event of this period occurred on 15 November 1985 when the British and Irish governments signed the Anglo–Irish Accord (AIA), which gave an 'Irish Dimension' to the political situation in the North. The real goal of the Thatcher government was to undercut Sinn Féin's increasing popularity and prop up the SDLP, because she 'was not prepared to tolerate a situation of continuing violence.'[81] However, the Accord caused her many problems with the unionist community. Even though, the agreement set up 'consultative' bodies and the secretariat of London and Dublin ministers had no real power, the acknowledgement by the British government that unification could take place with the consent of the people of Northern Ireland 'sent a shudder of horror through the Unionist Community.'[82]

Fearing a sell out by the British, over 100,000 unionists staged an 'Ulster Says No' rally at Belfast City Hall on 23 November 1985, and then on 17 December all the Unionist MPs resigned from parliament to fight by-elections based on their opposition to the Anglo–Irish

Accord.[83] At the same time, Loyalist violence increased. In 1985, the UDA and its 'military' wing, the Ulster Freedom Fighters UFF, had killed two people; that number jumped to seven in 1986 and to twelve in 1987. UVF/RHC killing followed the same pattern: they killed two people in 1985, eight in 1986, and seven in 1987.[84] Republican violence stayed at a consistent level of approximately 50 killings a year. However, this was not the only response. There was also a positive political response and once again, it came from the Loyalist politicians and not the Unionist parties.

## WAR OR PEACE? CONFLICT OR CONFERENCE?

> The Unionists response to the Anglo–Irish Agreement indeed betrayed political naivety. They left themselves with no negotiating space and seemed to think that displays of defiance would bring Thatcher to her senses.
>
> Graham Walker[85]

In response to the AIA, the Unionist Party under Molyneaux provided little practical or ideological leadership. In fact, as Graham Walker, quoting another observer, points out, there was a 'lack of ideological coherence within Unionism' to the Agreement.[86] While the traditional Unionist parties resigned their seats and forced by-elections that they then turned into a referendum on the Anglo–Irish Accord and in contrast to Unionism's incoherence and displays of defiance, the PUP went back to work on *Sharing Responsibility*. It published all of its past proposals, with one addition that dealt with education in a document called *War or Peace? Conflict or Conference?*

In the foreword, the PUP immediately rejected the AIA arguing that the 'stony path to peace and reconciliation lies mainly in our small community.'[87] Then in the section 'Anglo–Irish Agreement', after analysing Thatcher's shifts in policy from 1981–85, the PUP attacked the agreement as counter-productive, arguing that Thatcher overrode the democratic demands of the Ulster people and imposed joint-authority without the consent of the people of Northern Ireland.[88]

The PUP also sharply attacked US attitudes to the conflict in Northern Ireland; viewing the US attitude as unhelpful and cynical. It criticised the US for what it saw as an attempt to 'buy peace.' In fact, it found that there was 'something bizarre about a nation that can offer monetary settlements to political problems.' The PUP went on to criticise the gross inequalities that exist in US society, while the US leaders told those in Northern Ireland how to solve their problems by pushing for unification.[89]

By repeating much of what was in all of its earlier policy documents, including an appendix that laid out their proposals for a devolved government, *War or Peace?* reinforced the PUP's notion that only the people of Northern Ireland could solve the problems that existed there. It also fit with its long-standing belief that its philosophy and proposal for sharing responsibility was the way forward. Governance of a super-national body was unacceptable.

For the PUP, education would play a role here in terms of creating an internal solution, where all in Northern Ireland would learn to share the space and normalise their society. In educational policy, the PUP, once again placed itself ahead of the traditional Unionist and nationalist parties. Reflecting the RHC documents concerning education from 1973, the PUP called for integrated education at the junior level, writing,

> We believe that education of children should be on a totally integrated non-sectarian comprehensive schooling basis ... and should not be influenced by dogmatic church attitudes that foster and maintain division.[90]

Beyond calling for integration, what is interesting here is the implicit rejection of the system of grammar schools, and the eleven-plus exams, where children were separated into schools that prepared them for university if they passed the eleven plus or schools that prepared them for trades if they failed the exam. The PUP's vision of education would serve the purpose of creating an integrated society where people would learn to live with their differences and provide all children, regardless of their backgrounds, the chance to excel in school and move on to a third level education.

Although this document did not have a great impact at this time, it became part of the discussion when Unionism itself finally realised that it was not enough to say 'NO!' It had to develop a viable alternative political system.

## THE UNIONIST TASK FORCE

Finally, Unionism attempted to respond to the AIA in a responsible way by trying to develop alternatives to the AIA. The UUP and DUP set up a 'Joint Task Force' to try and impose Unionist control over events, instead of reacting to them. The task force consisted of Harold McCusker (UUP), Peter Robinson (DUP) and Frank Millar, Jr (UUP). Commissioned into action on 23 February 1987, its remit was:

1. To secure support for the continuing campaign against the Anglo–Irish Agreement, and
2. To ascertain what consensus, if any, exists about alternatives to the Agreement.[91]

This body was to meet and consult with various parties and civic organisations[92] to discuss and examine the various ideas and proposals, and then to present its findings on the way forward for Unionism.[93]

The PUP participated in these discussions and submitted *Sharing Responsibility*. In fact, Smyth reports that when they put *Sharing Responsibility* forward 'the like[s] of Peter Robinson, Frank Millar, Jr, Harold McCusker[94] ... actually said "That's the way forward. That's the best document we have read."'[95] Not coincidentally or surprisingly, when the Joint Task Force report did come out on June 16, 1987, it envisaged some sort of power sharing.[96]

The report noted that, 'Since the late 1960s Unionism has lost a series of vital rounds in the battle to preserve Northern Ireland's position within the United Kingdom.'[97] Those involved realised that if Unionism did nothing in this period, it would lose another round. After going through the many submissions, the Task Force attempted to offer alternatives to the Anglo–Irish Accord that would end the continued drift in Northern Ireland.

Although not laying out a structured plan, the Task Force endorsed a plan in which both Unionist parties abandoned pure majority rule as the price for Devolution.[98] In other words, it envisaged some sort of power-sharing with *Sharing Responsibility* and the UDA's *Common Sense* as the most likely models for that power sharing.

The task force report reached out to, but also warned the SDLP that,

In our opinion this emphasis on Unionist flexibility must be balanced by clear and repeated warning that the expedient of compromise and barter can only succeed if it is a two way process.[99]

Interestingly, the report indicated that, 'only one group invited us to consider as a serious proposition the return of majority rule devolution within the United Kingdom.' The Task Force responded negatively to this idea and commented, 'Our expressed incredulity prompted them in turn to speculate as to the viability of independence and repartition.'[100] This was not a serious thought as no other group even suggested independence or repartition, although the Task Force made it clear that independence was not off the table.

Finally, the Task Force examined and commented on the various proposals for independence, integration, devolution, and power sharing. This and issues around the Anglo–Irish Agreement, led the Task Force to call for strategic rethinking of the situation in Northern Ireland. They stated that,

> We offer no precise or definite suggestion as to what that alternative [to the AIA] might be. But we are convinced that ... membership of the United Kingdom or membership of an Irish Republic are *not* the only options available to the people of Northern Ireland.[101] [Emphasis in original]

The Task Force then proposed,

> the appointment of a Special Commission to consider and advise upon those alternative constitutional models, their implications viz a viz [sic] future relationships with Britain and the Irish Republic, and the steps by which an alternative constitutional arrangement might be secured and sustained.[102]

In other words, the Task Force urged flexibility, was prepared to share power, and more importantly rejected a return to majority rule as an alternative to the AIA. However, when this report went to the leaders of the DUP and the UUP, in Hugh Smyth's words, they, 'for their own selfish reasons, Paisley and Jim Molyneaux, just binned it ... they binned it.'[103] Graham Walker believes they did this because 'the report ... proved too radical for the party leaders in its willingness to consider power-sharing and ... in its willingness to consider devolved government "outside" the UK.'[104]

Even though Spence believed that the leadership of Unionism would ignore any recommendations from the Task Force he engaged with it anyway.[105] The results proved he had good reason not to trust the Unionist leadership again. Spence tells what happened:

> Jim Molyneaux who put it [the report] in his inside pocket. He never read it... Frankie Millar resigned, not only from the Ulster

Unionist Council, he resigned from the heap. Peter Robinson resigned from the deputy leadership [of the DUP] and McCusker says, 'I'm ill, Gusty', that was all.[106]

This rejection essentially destroyed the option of a negotiated and voluntary 'sharing of power' or 'sharing responsibility.' In reality, Unionism found itself, in McCusker's words 'punch drunk', leaderless and with no policies except 'wait and hope for some favourable turn of events'.[107] The failure of this initiative in 1987 meant that unionist community, as a whole would not provide the leadership in any agreement that would come in the future and would, for the most part find themselves reacting to events and policies. This failure on the part of Molyneaux and Paisley to provide leadership and accept a voluntary power sharing arrangement also meant that any likely settlement would now include a mandatory power-sharing component, which in Smyth's opinion is a 'system ... 20 times worse than what we were offering them.'[108] Furthermore, the delay in creating a political settlement then led to 'about another 1000 people killed as a result of the armed struggle.'[109]

## CONCLUSION

Why could the PUP and its allies not get their ideas through to the political parties and even their own community in Northern Ireland? The reasons are not that much different than from what the VPP and political leaders of the UVF experienced in the first era of Loyalist politics in 1973–75. The PUP faced attacks on itself and its thinking with the familiar epithet of 'communist' from the more reactionary elements in society. In fact, Sinnerton points out that people like Ervine and Hutchinson earned the title the 'Red Brigade' inside Long Kesh.[110] Although not seen as a derogatory term by some of the prisoners, some of the more reactionary elements inside and outside their organisation viewed them with suspicion. Smyth recalls the 'red-baiting' and the whispering campaign against any who dared to step out of their assigned role. He tells how behind his back those attacking him would say, 'Hugh's a good guy, but I would watch him. He's inclined to [socialism], you have to watch him.'[111]

For Unionism, what was even worse was that this thinking originated from working class paramilitaries and the PUP. Consequently, elements within Unionism attacked the PUP and those associated with it because they had, stepped outside of that [old sectarianism] and talked about uniting the tribes, or trying to bring people together. Looking at a peaceful way forward. Looking at structural injustices within our society. Looking at the social economic injustices within our society.[112]

Garland concurs with this analysis and argues, 'The fact that the new thinking entailed an acceptance of the legitimacy of alternative viewpoints, including Irish nationalism, made it a threat to right-wing Unionist politicians.'[113] Purvis goes even further arguing that,

An articulate political Loyalism posed the biggest threat to the Unionist elite. They didn't want Loyalism about the place. They were happy to manipulate them. They were happy to keep them barefoot tied to the kitchen sink. But they weren't happy to have them as political equals in any negotiation process. And I know from my conversations with both Gusty Spence and David Ervine and others that some Unionist political leaders went out of their way to try to ensure political Loyalism was excluded from processes.[114]

Ervine has opined,

I find it absolutely fascinating that those who had the time and space to evaluate and offer leadership chose not to do so, [while] those who were often spurned ... because of their paramilitary origins ... but maybe more because they were working class were beavering away through a thought process by themselves.[115]

An excellent example of this Unionist attitude towards and manipulation of Loyalism came in 1986. In this case, Molyneaux and Paisley called a 'secret' meeting with a committee 'of shop stewards, trade unionists and industrial workers' to plan a strike against the Anglo–Irish Accord.[116] Ervine and others were downstairs while the meeting took place. When it was over, Molyneaux told him that they would strike. Ervine then picks up the story:

It was supposed to be a private meeting, some would say a secret meeting, and when the door of Glengall Street [Unionist Party Headquarters] opened and we were leaving, we were met by banks of cameras, and the headlines in the *News Letter* the next morning was "Hard men change minds", and it was a total fucking fabrication to ... give the impression that our politicians were trying to do a deal with Mrs. Thatcher, but look, these hard men wouldn't let them.[117]

Sinnerton reports that 'Ervine was furious', as he realised that the meeting was a bluff so that Paisley could present himself as a 'reasonable man', who would do a deal with the government, except he had all these 'bad people' who would cause trouble if the government did not deal with him.[118]

Within the larger Protestant community, as in the VPP in 1974, the PUP, as a representative of the UVF and RHC, and self-professed representatives of the Protestant working class as well, could never gain support from what should have been its own base. In fact, as the VPP's experience showed, it could not even depend on the membership of the UVF and RHC to vote for it and support its policies, even though the party itself had its roots in those organisations.

Tom Roberts traces these problems to Unionist control, 'The [political] education amongst the working class was not very sophisticated', and maintains that Unionism 'used the fear factor to preserve their vote. They were always holding up the threat of a Republican invasion taking over the country.'[119] Liz Rea, Gusty Spence's daughter, agrees with Roberts and believes that the PUP could not get support among the Protestant working class because of the 'fear of the unknown.' She elaborates arguing,

> It always goes back to who they [the Protestant working class] see as the "big people" out there. I would say probably the ones who voted DUP probably put maybe a third, fourth vote in for the PUP. They're frightened going with that 'cause it's [PUP] a small party. They're frightened with going with a small Party ... if we do that and don't vote the DUP in, then Sinn Féin is going to take over government.[120]

Perhaps one of the most obvious reasons for the failure of the PUP to grow and get its policies taken seriously, as it was for the VPP, is internal to the Protestant community as a whole. That is, the aversion that many in the Protestant working class have of voting for anyone who committed a crime or had blood on their hands. Although many working class Protestants supported the UVF, RHC and UDA in defending their community, they remained conflicted as to the use of violence and breaking the law, and then giving their vote to those who broke the law. Roberts argues,

Protestants and Unionists seem to be, or they are people who are obsessed with law and order. They [Protestants] have great difficulty in lending their vote to people who have a past in terms of violence. ... And there is a degree of hypocrisy there, as well, because a lot of these Protestants/Unionists were happy with what the UVF were doing, but they wanted to keep a convenient distance between themselves and that element of Unionism.[121]

Within the Protestant community, if one wanted to defend the state, then one joined the police, the army, the UDR, and not the paramilitaries. Roberts relates the story of his brother who joined the B-Specials:

My family had no real difficulty with him [Roberts' brother] slaughtering people because he had the legitimacy of the state uniform. But they had great difficulty with me because I went outside the law.[122]

Plum Smith contends that Loyalist paramilitaries who took the political path, unlike the IRA, 'were not accepted by our own because ... [to them] we were criminals.[123] Smith noted that, 'Because Unionism supports law and order ... we are seen as criminals and just as bad as the IRA.'[124] Martin Snodden, a former UVF life prisoner, argues: 'Protestants will vote for the law and order and constitutional parties before they vote for the PUP, who is associated with the UVF.'[125]

Spence recounts a humorous, yet telling story of this attitude, when the authorities arrested him in 1972, after he had been on the run for four months:

When the paratroopers captured me on 4 November 1972 on the Glencairn Road, people found it outrageous that I should be in a stolen car. Here's us up to all types of hank-panky defending Ulster to the best of our ability, and that meant in a physical way, yet people were outraged by this.[126]

So although Spence and his comrades carried out essentially illegal acts in 'defence of Ulster' many Protestants felt,

it was a terrible thing that I was in a stolen car. "He was actually caught in a stolen motor", they would have said. "We'll shoot and kill and bomb and do all those dastardly things as long as it's within the law."[127]

Another factor internal to the Protestant community that prevented them from voting or supporting the PUP is that 'within the Protestant working class there has been a tradition that politicians are born to lead and Loyalists have always been subservient to this point of view.'[128] Tom Roberts claims,

> There is this innate subservience about them that they always think that there is somebody better that has to be their political master. There is this "begrudgery", where people who rise from the working class ... to become politicians. There is this "Who does he think he is?" attitude. Politics is for somebody else.[129]

Roberts then focused on the ramifications of this thinking. He claimed it was 'like turkeys voting for Christmas' because, as he put it, 'some of the people we put into power, haven't our best interests at heart.'[130] Jim McDonald, in an interview with Aaron Edwards agreed with Roberts. McDonald said, 'What the logic of people here is I don't know. It's beyond my comprehension ... they don't seem to want to vote for working class politics.'[131]

Hutchinson also contends that, 'Loyalists had been indoctrinated from birth that they must vote unionist or they would end up in a united Ireland.'[132] He believed that people would vote for the UUP as long as they 'brought a flute band and waved the Union Jack.'[133] Hutchinson also believes that people could vote for the UUP, but not for the people like Jim McDonald, because he was from the neighbourhood and not from the 'big country house.'[134]

Discussing the difficulty of getting Protestant working class support when he ran for election in the PUP, Hutchinson argues that, 'They [the Protestant working class] felt they couldn't trust me because I was an ex-prisoner, they couldn't put their trust in me to do politics because I was an ex-UVF prisoner.'[135] Even though Hutchinson has an advanced degree and a better education than most mainstream politicians do, many voters, because of his background, believe that he is not educated enough to be a politician. He tells of a meeting at an Orange Lodge before a particular election. One of his campaign workers,

> asked them why they wouldn't go to the PUP and she said they'd vote for Fred Cobain because he was more educated than Billy

Hutchinson. The woman in the lodge pointed out that I was much more educated than Fred Cobain, Fred doesn't have a degree to his name, I have a degree and a postgraduate diploma.[136]

Clearly, a great many factors worked against the PUP and those around it, as they tried to find a way forward politically, while at the same time trying to create the breathing space necessary to end the conflict. Yet, political Loyalism, as small as it was, worked tirelessly, in developing sophisticated and forward thinking documents and political ideas. We also know that if anyone, especially the main Unionist parties, and even the Republican movement, had taken their ideas seriously and attempted to implement them, a peaceful solution with a 'voluntary coalition' involving all shades of opinion in Northern Ireland, who shared in the responsibility for the running of Northern Ireland, may have come many years earlier.

Regardless of the factors that held the PUP back, the work and initiative around *Sharing Responsibility* and the Task Force should destroy the stereotype of all Loyalists as 'knuckle dragging' thugs who are incapable of thinking outside the 'binary logic'. The political leaders of Loyalism, as represented by the political thinkers in the PUP, the UVF, RHC and their supporters had developed a way forward, pointed a way forward and tried to lead the way forward. Here was a document and a Party, which emerged from the UVF and the RHC, prepared to break from the past, share responsibility with its 'traditional' enemy, represent all sections of Northern Ireland society, and build a Northern Ireland that would not be a 'cold house for Catholics' and the Protestant working class.

# Conclusion
# The Lost Opportunity

This story of the U.V.F is not a tale of protestant terrorism. It is the story of how the protestant working class was forced in extremes to take off on a voyage of self-discovery. It is a voyage that is not yet over – indeed, it is barely begun. But that it *has* begun, and that there can be no going back, is the light shining in Ulster's present darkness.

David Boulton[1]

It is fitting that we start this final chapter with the same quote that began this book. Fitting because this is the end of the study of this part of Loyalism's journey in 1987, a journey that was, at times, the darkness and at other times the light in the darkness. Yet, this study faces the same problem as Roy Garland did when he wrote *UVF: A Negotiating History*. At the end, one of his UVF subjects asked him 'will it [Garland's account] be believed?'[2] Garland writes,

My response was to point to the hard data available in the pages of *the Sunday News* and other sources. I also pointed out that the joint nature of the account, to which he and I and Gusty had contributed, had helped to authenticate the findings.[3]

This work faces the same question and problem. Who will believe this account of the origins and evolution of progressive political thinking within the UVF, the RHC and their political allies, and why it failed? Like Garland's work, the evidence from the *Sunday News*, *Loyalist News*, *Orange Cross* and *Combat*, as well as manifestos, secondary material and interviews, both primary and secondary, 'authenticate the findings'. There is no doubt that these men broke away from the traditional railway lines of Unionism and attempted to find a new way forward for Northern Ireland.

Their move away from traditional Unionism began with the breakdown of the 'Big House' Unionism between 1969 and 1972, when elements within the UVF, the RHC and their allies embarked on a 'voyage of self-discovery', a voyage that took them into 'unchartered waters'.[4] These unchartered waters were very rough and many times these men found themselves pounded on all sides by forces that they could not control and could not overcome. Regardless, they did embark on this voyage and against all odds attempted to find a way to end the conflict. At the same time, they attempted to create a Northern Ireland that would have a place for everyone and give everyone the opportunity to 'share responsibility' for the running of that new society.

There is no denying this occurred. The evidence is there in this work focusing on 1973–87, and Spencer's work on the 1980s and 1990s. It is now up to the reader to ponder this analysis and re-examine his/her long-held notions about Loyalism. This is necessary because for too long most analysts have ignored or downplayed Loyalism's role in developing political ideas and programmes to bring peace to Northern Ireland. Most people simply accepted the popular and negative stereotype of Loyalism. While ignoring what really happened in this period may be good politics, it is 'fantasy politics and poor history'.[5] This work has challenged this 'poor history' and has called into question the many accepted truths about Loyalism and, in the end, it has shown that these stereotypes do not hold in all cases.

In the first instance, this work throws the narrative of a totally Republican driven peace process in Northern Ireland into question. As illustrated in the previous chapters, once the IRA and Sinn Féin realised that they had to accept a compromise peace that would fall far short of their goals, the Republican agenda has dominated the peace process. This is nowhere more evident than the emergence and domination of Sinn Féin, within the nationalist/republican electorate. However, this ignores a peace process that evolved out of Loyalism, in particular, the UVF and the RHC, 20 years earlier. In essence, what is missing in the narrative of this period is how Loyalism actually realised what it took others 20 years to accept; that the conflict would have to end in a compromise political settlement within the context of Northern Ireland.

When asked what he what wanted people to take away from this study, Billy Hutchinson said,

I want people to understand that Loyalism isn't about Neanderthals trailing knuckles on the ground. It's about people who were real people, who had fears, who had aspirations, and that's why they were involved in this, rather than just seeing Loyalists as criminals. I just want people to understand that, you know, there was a strategy. It may not have worked on every occasion, but people changed their strategies when their strategies didn't work.[6]

The analysis presented here makes clear that these Loyalists were not all Neanderthals trailing knuckles on the ground. Contrary to all expectations and stereotypes, they stepped beyond their predictable and accepted roles. We now know that it was not the Unionist parties, nor the IRA and Sinn Féin, who rethought the nature of the struggle, how it was going to end, and what form the new society would take in the period under study. That came from within Loyalism.

These Loyalists began to think about and propose ways of creating a breathing space to bring everyone together in talks. It was this group of men, inside and outside the prisons, who began to formulate proposals for a new assembly; an assembly, which would serve, and benefit, all in Northern Ireland, as well as bringing everyone into the running and sharing of society. Furthermore, after each of their attempts and failures, they changed strategies and tried again to find a way to put their ideas into the public square for discussion and to find a way to end the terrible violence even while carrying out that violence.

This leads us to ask, 'If these proposals were so good and, they were serious about what they were doing, why did their ideas not work or why did no one really listen to them?' One further question hangs out there, 'Did they ever have a chance?'

Answering the first question will also answer the second one. This study has shown the many obstacles that the UVF, RHC, VPP and the PUP encountered throughout their political evolution. Chief among these was that the leadership had moved too far and too fast and did not even have the support of its own membership when moving into politics. The failure of the VPP in 1974 is proof of that.

At the same time, on a very basic level, a number of interviewees echoed Frank Steele's (MI6) famous statement of why it took so long to get peace. When asked this question, Steele responded, 'I don't think either community suffered enough to want peace.'[7] Twelve years later, Billy Hutchinson, agreed, arguing that 'I still think no matter what happened in the 70s I don't think we'd suffered enough yet, I think there was a bit more suffering to go before people were going to draw back.'[8] When asked the same question, Tom Roberts concurred: 'the crude answer to that question is that people hadn't suffered enough.'[9]

This study has also established how difficult it was for these groups to get support within their own communities. Protestants would not and, in many cases, could not support those who had broken the law, or stepped beyond their station in life and challenged those who had ruled Northern Ireland for 50 years. As Plum Smith has pointed out, there was and is still no real history of the Protestant community voting for or supporting paramilitaries in the way that exists in the Republican community. Furthermore, within the larger Protestant community, as illustrated when Billy Hutchinson stood for election, many people did not support him, even though he has a degree and a post-degree certification. They did not believe he was qualified because of his background; he was working class, a former paramilitary and a former prisoner.

The relationship with Unionism was also very difficult. Unionism itself, as many studies, and documents have shown, and those interviewed for this project argued, would not tolerate any challenge coming from its own working class, let alone from the paramilitaries. Whenever it did face a challenge from working class Protestants or the paramilitaries, it played the 'sectarian card', and/or the 'red card' and inflamed the fears of ordinary Protestants. This occurred throughout Northern Ireland's history and has always stymied the development of class-based politics. In the modern era, it has prevented the development of these politics and kept ordinary Protestants from supporting the progressive and political thinking coming from the paramilitary thinkers in the UVF, the RHC and the VPP, as well as the PUP.

When considering the inability to develop normal politics, Tom Roberts made a keen observation about both Unionism and Republicanism and why the class-based politics coming out the UVF, RHC, VPP, and PUP could never take hold. He argues that the border and the relationship with either Britain or Ireland would always dominate voters' minds. Roberts maintains that, 'There will always be the constitutional question here and that will always be primary focus in people's minds ... That's primary in people's minds, rather than social issues.'[10] Roberts argues that Unionism and Republicanism need the border issue and that this has served to prevent normal politics:

Because, when people start to think about their social conditions and vote in that manner and elevate parties, the traditional parties will try to wreck that. You see it here. It's ironic. Sinn Féin needs Northern Ireland because it's the only environment, it's the only place they can get an established vote. Both extreme ends of Unionism and nationalism need each other. That's what feeds their vote here.[11]

Tied to the issue of preventing the development of normal politics, for some elements of Unionism, as this study clearly demonstrated, those in the paramilitaries were there to do Unionism's dirty work, such as subverting O'Neill, or used as a threat whenever Unionism found itself at loggerheads with the British government. The paramilitaries were not there to formulate policies and to lead the way forward in politics. The paramilitaries and the working class were there to do as they always had done, follow orders, fight the wars, and then go back to their homes, work, and lives. Then the Unionist politicians, not the paramilitaries and the working class, would make the peace and then go back to running Northern Ireland.

This study has also argued that beyond the problems within the Protestant/Unionist community, other factors conspired to undercut the Loyalist political vision and consequently prolonged the conflict. As Garland puts it,

> when they sought to find a new way forward. Many vested interests and not all on the Unionist side preferred the Volunteers to conform as far as possible to the traditional stereotype.[12]

This is correct, especially when talking about the IRA. The IRA's reaction to political Loyalism damaged the prospects of ending this conflict much earlier than 1994. When Spence and elements of the UVF and the RHC and their allies outside the paramilitaries reached out to the Provisional IRA, the Provisionals, for their own reasons, except for a brief period in 1974, were unable to engage with them. There were a number of reasons for this.

One can understand why Republicans would reject the restoration of what they saw as a sectarian state and more importantly, which left the dream of a united Ireland unfulfilled. At the same time, the Provisionals preferred that Loyalism adhere to the base stereotype. The narrative of Loyalists as nothing more than thugs or agents of the British state suited the PIRA narrative of this conflict as an anti-imperialist struggle between Republicans and the British Empire, and served it well in its propaganda war. As Purvis has pointed out the emergence of a politically aware and progressive Loyalism that demanded to be included in any settlement, complicated matters for Republicanism because 'it fed into this notion of two warring tribes and left the government out of it.'[13]

Furthermore, in the Republican narrative, Loyalists were deluded Irishmen and/or an arm of the British state, instead of an independent actor with their own political analysis. Even in the 1987 'Scenario for Peace', Sinn Féin argued, 'We believe that Loyalism derives an artificial psychological strength from the British presence.'[14] This analysis and narrative served to marginalise Loyalism, as that meant the IRA could then talk to the British government over the heads of Loyalists and not have to compromise with them.

One of the more contentious arguments of this study is that the reason that the PIRA could not engage with the political elements of Loyalism, unlike the OIRA, was the PIRA's lack of political sophistication in this period. The story that David Ervine related earlier about meeting the PIRA volunteer, for whom the war had become a way of life, as well as the ascension of the militarist minded leadership in the Provisionals after the split in 1970 is indicative of this. At the time, 1973 to 1975, when people like Spence, Mitchell, Hugh Smyth, and Plum Smith, and others in the UVF and RHC realised that no one would or could win in this conflict, again the PIRA, even though it engaged with the UVF briefly, still believed it could achieve a united Ireland through the armed struggle. Therefore, for the IRA there was no need to talk about a compromise peace with Loyalism within a Northern Ireland context. *Abandoning Historical Conflict?*, Alonso's work in *The IRA and the Armed Struggle*, Bowyer Bell's and Peter Taylor's work, and the other secondary works cited here, as well as those interviewed for this study, all reinforce this argument.

Another factor that played a role in preventing the Loyalist paramilitaries and working class Loyalism from finding its own voice was the impact of shifting British policies and the actions that elements of the British security forces had on the evolution of political Loyalism. On one level, the evidence suggests that some elements of the British establishment did not want an independent Loyalist voice, as that would complicate the government's own agenda. Crawford, in particular, argues that when Loyalism began to develop an independent voice, it threatened Britain's desire to withdraw from Northern Ireland. It also complicated any peace talks for them because the British government would not only have to deal with the Republican movement, but would also have to engage with Loyalism. That limited what the government could do to achieve peace. Therefore, instead of encouraging cooperation and the development of politics, officials and/or groups within the British security establishment and even higher echelons of the British civil service focused on defeating the paramilitaries instead of talking to them.

This relates to the confused and sometimes contradictory nature of British policy. Chapter 5 pointed this out when it argued that the British government did not always engage in 'joined up' thinking and its policies tended to shift based on the circumstances. This was evident when the government granted special category status to paramilitary prisoners in 1972, then criminalised all paramilitary activities in 1976, then shifted from engagement to disengagement with the paramilitaries, legalisation and proscription, and Ulsterisation. Making this claim does not diminish Paul Dixon's argument that successive British governments wanted,

> to achieve a stable settlement to the conflict and contain its impact, whether this was within the Union or in a United Ireland or some compromise between the two. There was a range of options before successive British governments but only power-sharing, with some kind of Irish dimension, was perceived as likely to win wide-spread nationalist and unionist support and therefore provide stability.[15]

What the argument here does is point out that when the government attempted to find a compromise solution acceptable to all parties to the conflict and to manage the conflict, it made 'tactical adjustments', such as special category status and then its antithesis, criminalisation. While their overall goal and overarching policy was consistent, these policies did not always work the way the government wanted and they had negative ramifications.

While many parties and people in Northern Ireland and the United Kingdom could not stomach the idea of granting special category status to paramilitary gunmen, killers and bombers, ending special category status proved in the long run to be counterproductive. As we have seen, criminalisation broke down the already fragile relationships among the various groups in Long Kesh, and it destroyed the cooperation schemes that had developed in the prisons. It ended the process of mentoring that had developed inside Long Kesh where the older prisoners helped the younger prisoners adapt to life, as well as exposing them to politics, history and education. It also led to the blanket and dirty protests, which culminated in the 1981 Hunger Strikes.

Although Dixon argues that there was a consistent overall government policy, these policy shifts actually convey the image of an uncertain government trying to cope with a situation that was in constant flux, while facing pressures from many sides. However, while the government itself may have acted according to a set of principles to end the conflict, the evidence presented here about other policies and actions that emanated from some elements of MI5 and the security establishment raises disturbing questions about the role that some within these agencies may have played in this period. The evidence presented here strongly suggests that elements of the security forces were involved in a 'dirty tricks' campaign in Northern Ireland. As is well documented, they did this in terms of collusion, where elements of the security forces used Loyalist and Republican paramilitaries to do their dirty work for them. However, beyond collusion, there is more to this story.

The anti-Communist campaign, the unexplained sectarian killings, the role of Tara and William McGrath, combined with the evidence presented in many published works referenced in this study,[16] as well as the testimony of those on the ground in this period, all point to malevolent forces operating within the intelligence services. Based on the evidence presented here, rogue elements within MI5 and the military may have enacted their own agenda with the purpose of undercutting any political movement towards understanding or compromise among the paramilitaries. If this evidence is correct, and future research bears these findings out, then these elements of MI5 and the security forces subverted the movement of Loyalism towards politics and prevented a possible rapprochement among the paramilitaries.

In the same period, the evidence suggests that the security forces worked to sabotage the emergence of progressive political thought coming from the Loyalist paramilitaries, and any cooperation developing among the paramilitary groups, while undermining British government policy in Northern Ireland. If we accept Colin Wallace's word, then elements of the security forces carried out sectarian murders to sabotage the nascent understanding developing among the paramilitary groups. According to Wallace, elements of the security forces also worked to remove the emerging political thinkers within Loyalism. Because of these actions, the Loyalist political initiative failed in this period and it took 20 more years before the Republican, and Loyalist ceasefires took place. While the evidence presented here points to this conclusion, it will take much more work to verify the validity of this argument.

Despite all the forces arrayed against them and even after the collapse of their political initiatives, those within the UVF, RHC and their allies continued to work on ways to end the conflict, develop a political programme and keep their politics alive. Spence's two speeches and the response in *Combat* to the 12 July speech, along with the RHC's 'Ten Point Plan For Peace with Honour and Justice', illustrated that even after the collapse of the UVF and RHC's active engagement with politics, they continued to try to find a way out of the darkness.

Outside the prisons and the paramilitary organisations, men like Hugh Smyth, Jim McDonald and David Overend continued to work in conjunction with those in Long Kesh and they eventually created the *Sharing Responsibility* document. This visionary document had the potential to end the conflict 20 years earlier, and on terms very similar to those under which Northern Ireland operated after the GFA. In talking about this, the exasperation and frustration comes through unmistakably in Hugh Smyth's voice when he says,

> I mean what they did [with the GFA] they stole our clothes and decorated it up ... but if you looked at the whole setup of what we have ... that's our document. I mean, we brought that into the fold. No one can ever take that away from us. So what we're working now is basically founded within a *Sharing of Responsibility* document that we produced so many years ago.[17]

It is beyond the ability of this work to validate Smyth's claim and compare the GFA and *Sharing Responsibility*. What is important here is that, unlike the GFA, *Sharing Responsibility* did not receive the opportunity to work. The PUP and those who tried to sell it as a solution to the conflict in Northern Ireland ran head on into nearly the same resistance as those who tried to move the UVF and the RHC towards politics in the 1970s.

What is also evident throughout this study is that a number of the accepted myths and inherited histories of this particular period of Northern Ireland and Loyalist history do not hold. Clearly, those people studied, both here and in the secondary materials, and those interviewed for this study do not fit the stereotype of either Loyalism as a whole or the image of the individual Loyalist. Yes, there was mindless thuggery, killings, bombings and terrible violence committed by these organisations and even by some of the men cited here, but these men represented a new breed of Loyalist and Loyalism who sought a compromise political solution to the conflict.

They also do not fit the accepted wisdom that Republicans led and Loyalists followed. That may be true somewhat after 1992, but it is definitely not true in the period studied here. From the earliest days of the conflict, Loyalism, in particular, those coming from the UVF, the RHC and their allies, worked to find a way to create the 'breathing space' necessary to allow politics to work. At the same time, they were at work creating the *Sharing Responsibility* document that they hoped would make politics take precedence over armed conflict.

Another conclusion from this study is there was not just one lost opportunity, there were many lost opportunities. For Hugh Smyth, the failure of the Unionist Task Force to move forward using *Sharing Responsibility* represented the real lost opportunity. Smyth believes that the 'party [UUP and DUP] leaders, for their own selfish reasons, Paisley and Jim Molyneaux, just binned it.'[18] The result, in Smyth's words, was that 'we had about another 1000 people killed' when 'so many lives could have been saved.'[19]

Seamus Mallon, formerly Deputy First Minister in Northern Ireland, once famously said that the GFA was 'Sunningdale for slow learners',[20] believing with some justification, that what was on offer in 1974, is essentially, what the IRA and Sinn Féin settled for in 1998 and then 2007. Harry Donaghy agrees with Mallon. When asked what he thought was the 'lost opportunity', he said, 'I do believe it was the power-sharing Executive ... it was ... Sunningdale.'[21]

According to David Ervine, Unionism's failure to acknowledge and deal with the legitimate demands of the civil rights movement was a lost opportunity as this failure led directly to the outbreak of violence in 1969. Tom Roberts agrees. He claims that the 'right wing' of Unionism prevented reform in the 1960s and this then led to the violence.[22] Bobby Cosgrove concurs, arguing that, '1968 was unneeded, if it had have been handled properly',[23] the violence would never have occurred. He also contends that, 'the Big House didn't want that [reform] at that stage.'[24] Consequently, in a period, where Unionism could have avoided the violence by instituting reform, that reform did not take place and the result was a terrible and bloody 25-year conflict.

Tom Roberts also views the period of criminalisation and Ulsterisation as another lost opportunity to wind down or end the conflict because,

the British Prison policy was absurd and it gave a whole impetus both to the IRA's violent campaign and plus it gave Sinn Féin a platform to build the political machine they are today, on the backs of the hunger strikes.[25]

Roberts argues that the conflict 'would've been in the winding down process by 1979 onwards. But, you had a blanket protest in [19]76 ... and then ultimately the hunger strike.'[26]

Although, not pinpointing any one episode as a lost opportunity, Billy Hutchinson had an interesting take on this question. He cites the 1973 Bodenstown speech by the OIRA as a critical moment for Republicans and the conflict as whole. Hutchinson argues,

> Well, I think that speech actually defined the struggle. It also ended the struggle as well in terms of that the war was over. I suppose in many ways there was a term for people who didn't sign up to the Sunningdale agreement in 1974. You know people who were slow learners in terms of Unionism. I think that "slow learners" needs to be attached to the Republicans who didn't buy into the Bodenstown stuff in 1973. I mean, it was quite clear that it [the speech] defined that the war was over; that it was defined how do we move forward and the way to move forward was through working class politics.[27]

Hugh Smyth's interview with Sean McKee supports Hutchinson's observation as well as Loyalism's mistake about giving power back to the politicians after the UWC strike. Smyth told McKee,

> The Official IRA realised early on that the bomb and bullet was dividing the people. They were great believers that sectarianism breeds sectarianism, violence breeds violence. I looked at their theory and said: "Yeah, I agree with much of what these boys are saying", and it had a great bearing upon me when we were forming the Progressive Unionists ... I still believe, had we went a stage further than the Workers' Party and formed an Ulster Workers' Party, that eventually, those two parties would have united.[28]

Harry Donaghy argues that another lost opportunity was the IRA's 'all or nothing' attitude at a time when Loyalism was reaching out to the IRA. He believes this was a serious mistake. In fact, Donaghy argues,

What was going on then, between those [Loyalist] position papers and view points and critiques of things, if more ... room for manoeuvre had been in existence at the time where the thoughts of ... Loyalism or representatives of it, saying [we] would have to find better ways ... .The Provos had [said] "Look, we're not settling. All we want is, a declaration from Britain of its intent to withdraw, simple." That was it ... Loyalism, especially working class Loyalism assumed "this is a Dublin, Fenian conspiracy to do us in, to take everything that we stand for away from us. They're [PIRA] not satisfied with proroguing the parliament in [19]72, the next thing it'll be ... it'll be Dublin Ministers sitting in Stormont administering the country."[29]

For these observers, this period represented a series of lost opportunities for the paramilitaries to come together. If the PIRA had made a realistic assessment of the situation, it might have engaged more constructively with the OIRA, the UVF, and the RHC in this period. However, it would take the PIRA 20 or more years to accept a compromise solution within the context of Northern Ireland.

In response to the question about the lost opportunity, Purvis said,

I look back and I read about the stuff that was written by Gusty and Hugh Smyth, Jim McDonald, Davey ... Gibson ... The stuff that they wrote ... I am thinking look, look at this resource that was on offer at that time in order to resolve the conflict; in order to bring people together, to build. Look at all those opportunities. That came from Loyalism. That came from working class communities ... . it was ignored by political leaders.[30]

Hutchinson himself believes that no matter what was on offer at the time, it had no chance of working or ending the conflict. He claims that there were just too many factors preventing political Loyalism from making an impact: 'it's a number of things, one was its disinformation. There's no question of that. And the DUP and the Unionists were behind it.' He continues arguing that what prevented them from succeeding and caused this lost opportunity was,

Fear of communism and misunderstanding as well of what people [had] done. Then on top of that you had this notion, I suppose ... where in the Unionist community there was a very structured way of things being done. So before there was the DUP, there was the

Ulster Unionists, and they had their people that you went to. So if you needed advice this person gave you advice. If you wanted a house you paid them and they got you a key to a house. So they had this very strong structure. And back then in the 70s even though that structure was dissipating, it hadn't gone completely. There was still this notion of that these people [Loyalists] are corner boys, they're not educated and what would they know about politics and this notion that people are born to lead. So you were fighting against that whole culture of perception and that fed into people misunderstanding what was being done.[31]

Each of those interviewed for this book, in one way or another, views this period or different times and events within the period under study as a 'lost opportunity' for Loyalism and those who tried to bring peace to Northern Ireland. These opinions range from the belief that it was one event or policy change to those like Hutchinson, who perceives too many forces arrayed against the UVF, RHC and their allies preventing them from creating the breathing space to implement a political solution.

Clearly many factors came together to undercut political Loyalism and made the failure of political Loyalism a 'lost opportunity' for Northern Ireland. As mentioned above, for Loyalism to have had any impact on the politics of Northern Ireland would have been nothing short of miraculous and as we know, that miracle did not occur. In reality, if anyone would have accepted the Loyalist vision for peace, including those within its own community, then possibly 2,000 more people would still be alive; all the hatred, anger, hurt, and level of bitterness that we see today in Northern Ireland would not be as acute. When viewed in this light, this entire period truly was a lost opportunity.

There is one more lost opportunity that, to this point, this study has not addressed. That is the 'lost opportunity' of engaging working class Loyalism in the guise of the paramilitaries and Protestant working class communities with politics. Although not part of this study, nor even a consideration when this study began, it is clear that the failure and at times deliberate destruction of Loyalist working class politics has left the Protestant working class and the Loyalist paramilitaries feeling alienated from the larger society. While many of the problems leading to this alienation are external to the Protestant working class, as this study has illustrated, there are problems originating within the Protestant working class community itself that have led to its alienation and marginalisation.

Failure by the Protestant working class to grasp opportunities presented by its own leadership throughout the conflict and create class-based politics, represents a terrible lost opportunity for Loyalism, the Protestant working class communities, as well as Northern Ireland as whole. With this failure, they lost the opportunity to develop a viable class-based alternative to traditional Unionism, and now find themselves with little or no political voice.

One final point is crucial here. With the combination of this work focusing on progressive Loyalist politics between 1973–87 and Graham Spencer's work on progressive Loyalism in the 1980s and 1990s, we now have an alternative history of political/progressive Loyalism. Still, even with this and Spencer's work and the fact that more studies, mainly academic, are now coming out that focus on Loyalism, Loyalist identity, Loyalism after the ceasefires and so on, Loyalism has a history that few really know about. Consequently, the author hopes that this book, although somewhat limited in its scope, along with Spencer's work, will open the door to further studies, in both academic and non-academic circles, of the history and politics of not just the UVF, the RHC and its allies, but of Loyalism as a whole. If this does happen, hopefully, we will abandon our inherited histories of the conflict and gain a deeper and richer understanding of what really happened in Northern Ireland in this period. Furthermore, we will begin to understand Loyalism's role in all aspects of the conflict as well as the political promise that it offered to the Protestant working class and everyone in Northern Ireland.

# Notes

## PREFACE AND OVERVIEW

1. David Boulton, *UVF 1966–73: An Anatomy of a Loyalist Rebellion* (Dublin: Torc Books, 1973), 6.
2. Progressive Unionist Party, *War or Peace? Conflict or Conference?* (Belfast: Progressive Unionist Party, 1986), 3.
3. New Ulster Political Research Group, *Beyond the Religious Divide* (report, Belfast, 1979).
4. Ulster Political Research Group, *Common Sense* (Belfast, 1979).
5. New Ulster Political Research Group, *The People and the State: A Proposed Constitution and Political Structures* (Belfast, 1979).

## INTRODUCTION

1. Dawn Purvis, interview with author, PUP Office, East Belfast, 10 July 2009.
2. Tim Pat Coogan, *The Troubles: Ireland's Ordeal and the Search for Peace* (London: Palgrave and Macmillan, 2002).
3. Ed Moloney, *The Secret History of the IRA* (New York, NY: W.W. Norton & Co., 2003).
4. Gerry Adams, 'A united Ireland is possible', *Comment is Free, guardian.co.uk*, 15 July 2009, www.guardian.co.uk/commentisfree/2009/jul/15/united-ireland-gerry-adams (4 August 2009). The IRA Ceasefire statement made this obvious also. See 'Irish Republican Army (IRA) Ceasefire Statement, 31 August 1994', *CAIN Web Service*, cain.ulst.ac.uk/events/peace/docs/ira31894.htm (4 August 2011).
5. This is referenced in most histories of the peace process. For a brief outline of this position, see Paul Dixon, *Northern Ireland: The Politics of War and Peace* (Basingstoke: Palgrave, 2001), 215–25. See also Tim Pat Coogan, *The Troubles*, 397–401; Peter Taylor, *Provos: The IRA and Sinn Fein* (London: Bloomsbury, 1997), 304–8, 325–7; Jonathan Tonge, *Northern Ireland* (Polity: Cambridge, 2006), 18–121.
6. Moloney, *The Secret History of the IRA*, 392–427. This notion of a 'mutually hurting stalemate' is called into question in a recent book: Peter Shirlow, et al., *Abandoning Historical Conflict? Former Political Prisoners and Reconciliation in Northern Ireland* (Manchester: Manchester University Press, 2010), 6.
7. Republicans come to Bodenstown every year to commemorate Wolfe Tone, the leader of the United Irishmen executed by the British in 1798 after the United Irishmen uprising. Republicans use this occasion to reaffirm republican ideals and indications of current republican thinking.
8. Sinn Féin, 'Annual Bodenstown Speech 1992 Address by Jim Gibney June 1992', 18 June 1992, www.sinnfein.ie/files/Speech_Bodenstown92.pdf (7 May 2011).
9. Ibid.

10. Christopher Farrington, *Ulster Unionism and the Northern Ireland Peace Process* (Basingstoke: Palgrave, 2006).

11. Catherine O'Donnell, 'The Evolution of Irish Republicanism and the Peace Process in Northern Ireland', in *Transforming the Peace Process: From Terrorism to Democratic Politics*, eds Aaron Edwards and Stephen Bloomer (Dublin: Irish Academic Press, 2008), 44.

12. The term 'Loyalist' refers to those from the Protestant working class who took up arms to defend the Union with Great Britain. Loyalism was and is exclusively working class in makeup and character.

13. David Lister and Hugh Jordan, *Mad Dog: The Rise and Fall of Johnny Adair and 'C' Company* (Edinburgh: Mainstream Publishing, 2004).

14. Michael Stone, *None Shall Divide Us* (London: Blake Publishing, 2004).

15. Graham Spencer, *The State of Loyalism in Northern Ireland* (Basingstoke: Palgrave Macmillan, 2008).

16. Ibid., 1.

17. Lyndsey Harris, 'The Power of Perception – Duck or Rabbit?: The Strategic Tradition of Loyalist Paramilitaries in Northern Ireland', Lecture, 45th Anniversary Biennial International Conference of the Inter-University Seminar on Armed Forces and Society, Chicago, Illinois, 21–3 October 2005.

18. Carolyn Gallaher, *After the Peace: Loyalist Paramilitaries in Post-Accord Northern Ireland* (New York, NY: Cornell University Press, 2007).

19. Peter Shirlow and Mark McGovern, eds, *'Who are the People?': Unionism, Protestantism and Loyalism in Northern Ireland* (Chicago, IL: Pluto Press, 1997).

20. Peter Shirlow and Kieran McEvoy, *Beyond the Wire: Former Prisoners and Conflict Transformation in Northern Ireland* (Ann Arbor, MI: Pluto Press, 2008).

21. For an example of his output, visit the Northern Ireland Political Collection at the Linen Hall Library or perform a search at prism.talis.com/linenhall/.

22. Shirlow, et al., *Abandoning Historical Conflict?*.

23. Private conversation, June 2007,

24. David McKittrick and David McVea, *Making Sense of the Troubles: A History of the Northern Ireland Conflict* (Chicago, IL: New Amendment Press, 2002), 329. See also David McKittrick, et al., *Lost Lives: The Stories of the Men, Women and Children who Died as a Result of the Northern Ireland Troubles* (Edinburgh: Mainstream Publishing Company, 2004), 1528.

25. BBC News, 'Man arrested in Belfast over Shankill UVF shooting', 29 May 2010, www.bbc.co.uk/news/10183941 (23 May 2011).

26. Stephen Howe, 'Mad dogs and Ulstermen: The crisis of Loyalism (part one)', *Open Democracy*, 27 September 2005, www.opendemocracy.net/globalization-protest/Loyalism_2876.jsp (19 July 2010).

27. This was a no-warning bombing of a Catholic bar by the UVF that killed 15 innocent people. It still stands as one of the worst atrocities in Northern Ireland.

28. Martin Dillon, *Shankill Butchers: A Case Study of Mass Murder* (London: Arrow Press, 1990); Jim Cusack and Henry McDonald, *UVF* (Dublin: Poolbeg Press, 1977), 173–94.

29. Cusack and McDonald, *UVF*, 161–4.

30. James W. McAuley, *Ulster's Last Stand? Reconstructing Unionism after the Peace Process* (Dublin: Irish Academic Press, 2010), 108.

31. Spencer, *State of Loyalism*, 48.
32. Steve Bruce, *The Edge of the Union: The Ulster Loyalist Political Vision* (Oxford: Oxford University Press, 1994), 37–71.
33. Ibid., 99–100.
34. Steve Bruce, *The Red Hand: Protestant Paramilitaries in Northern Ireland* (New York, NY Oxford University Press, 1992), 123.
35. Ibid., 122–3.
36. Sarah Nelson, *Ulster's Uncertain Defenders: Protestant Political, Paramilitary, and Community Groups, and the Northern Ireland Conflict* (Belfast: Appletree Press, Ltd., 1985).
37. Bruce, *The Edge of the Union*, 99.
38. Discussion with individual political analyst, June 2009.
39. Jennifer Todd, 'Two Traditions in Unionist Political Culture', *Irish Political Studies*, Vol. 2, No. 1 (1987): 1–26.
40. Brian Hanley and Scott Millar, *The Lost Revolution: The Story of the Official IRA and the Workers Party* (Dublin: Penguin, 2009), 80. See also 'History of Eire Nua', *Indymedia*, 11 April 1998, www.indymedia.ie/article/87142 (8 May 2011).
41. Moloney, *The Secret History of the IRA*, 181.
42. Sinn Féin, 'ÉIRE NUA, THE SINN FÉIN POLICY: The Social, Economic and Political Dimensions', *CAIN Web Service*, 14 May 2011, cain.ulst.ac.uk/issues/politics/docs/sf/sinnfein79.htm (8 May 2011).
43. J. Bowyer Bell, *The Secret Army: The IRA* (New Brunswick, NJ: Transaction Publishers, 1997), 519.
44. Moloney, *The Secret History of the IRA*, 184–7.
45. Sinn Féin, 'Annual Bodenstown Speech 1992 Address by Jim Gibney June 1992', 18 June 1992.
46. n.a., 'Background Paper B: Paramilitary Organisations in Northern Ireland,' paper presented to the Working Party on Law and Order in Northern Ireland (PRONI Public Records CENT/1/5/5; Belfast: PRONI, 1976).
47. Tom Roberts, interview with author, EPIC Office, Shankill Road, 16 June 2009.
48. Rogelio Alonso, *The IRA and the Armed Struggle* (New York, NY: Routledge, 2006), 5.
49. Ibid., 1–23.
50. McIntyre is a former life prisoner. He has earned a Ph.D. and writes extensively on the conflict and its aftermath. He also published an online forum called 'The Blanket'. He has broken with Sinn Féin and stands as a leading Republican critic of Sinn Féin and its policies.
51. Alonso, *The IRA and the Armed Struggle*, 13.
52. Billy Hutchinson, interview with author, Mt Vernon Community Centre, North Belfast, 2 June 2009.
53. Cusack and McDonald, *UVF*, 1.
54. Shirlow, et al., *Abandoning Historical Conflict?*, 18.
55. Ibid.
56. Nelson, *Ulster's Uncertain Defenders*, 170.
57. Dawn Purvis, interview with author, PUP Office, East Belfast, 10 July 2009.
58. Bruce, *The Red Hand*, 123.
59. Dawn Purvis, interview with author, PUP Office, East Belfast, 10 July 2009.
60. Ibid.

61. This phrase comes from an anonymous reviewer's comment of the first draft proposal for this work.
62. Hugh Smyth, follow-up interview with author, PUP Office, Shankill Road, 19 June 2009.

## 1: THE ULSTER VOLUNTEER FORCE AND O'NEILL

1. In its declared war on the IRA, the UVF attempted to find and kill known IRA men. When they could not find one, they targeted innocent Catholics. In this case, Spence and two others were involved in the killing of Peter Ward, a young Catholic barman having an after-work drink in a bar on the Shankill Road.
2. Roy Garland, *Gusty Spence* (Belfast: Blackstaff Press, 2001), 10. The actual quote reads, 'People do not wish to know that their government hired gunmen at ten bob a day to shoot Catholics and to ignite sectarianism in order to break the fleeting unity between Prods and Taigs.'
3. Garland, *Gusty Spence*, 53–5; Tim Pat Coogan, *The Troubles: Ireland's Ordeal 1966–1996* (Boulder, CO: Roberts Rinehart Publishers, 1997), 48–9; Peter Taylor, *Loyalists: War and Peace in Northern Ireland* (New York, NY: TV Books, L.L.C., 1999), 33.
4. Boulton, *UVF 1966–73*, 25.
5. John Spain, 'Pass the Paisley sick bag', *IrishAbroad*, 12 March 2008, www.irishabroad.com/news/irish-voice/spain/Articles/Pass-the-Paisley-Sickbag150308.aspx (23 July 2011).
6. 'Northern Ireland Troubles – The Beginning: Introduction to the Northern Ireland Conflict', *Northern Ireland History*, 23 January 2011, northern-ireland-history.blogspot.com/2011/01/northern-ireland-troubles-beginning.html (28 July 2011).
7. Taylor, *Loyalists*, 33.
8. Garland, *Gusty Spence*, 54.
9. Roy Garland, 'The Ulster Volunteer Force: Negotiating History' (Masters thesis, Queen's University Belfast, 1991), 16.
10. Boulton, *UVF 1966–73*, 23–36.
11. Ibid., 36.
12. Cusack and McDonald, *UVF*, 20.
13. Ibid., *UVF*, 20–1.
14. Bruce, *The Red Hand*, 26.
15. Ibid., 26.
16. Ian Wood, *God Guns and Ulster: A History of Loyalist Paramilitaries* (London: Caxton Editions, 2003), 43.
17. Dawn Purvis, interview with author, PUP Office, East Belfast, 10 July 2009.
18. Sinnnerton, *David Ervine: Unchartered Waters* (Dingle: Brandon, 2002), 77.
19. Taylor, *Loyalists*, 34.
20. Garland, *Gusty Spence*, 75.
21. Chris Moore, *The Kincora Scandal: Political Cover-up and Intrigue in Northern Ireland* (Cork: Mercier Press, 1996), 45–6.
22. Ibid., 46.
23. Ibid.
24. Billy Mitchell, 'Principles of Loyalism', Progressive Unionist Party, 2002, progressiveunionistparty.org/articles/principles-of-Loyalism/ (20 May 2011).

25. Ibid.
26. Billy Hutchinson, follow-up interview with author, Mt Vernon Community Centre, North Belfast, July 7, 2009.
27. Ibid.
28. Ibid.
29. Garland, *Gusty Spence,* 75.
30. Moore, *Kincora Scandal,* 46.
31. Kate Fearon, *The Conflict's Fifth Business: A Brief Biography of Billy Mitchell* (Belfast: LINC [Local Initiatives for Needy Communities] Resource Centre, 2002), 20.
32. Ed Moloney, *Paisley: From Demagogue to Democrat* (Dublin: Poolbeg, 2008), 75–80.
33. Ibid., 79–88, 95–6.
34. Ibid., 96.
35. Ibid., 129–30.
36. Ibid., 129.
37. Hugh Jordan, *Milestones in Murder: Defining Moments in Ulster's Terror War* (London: Mainstream Publishing, 2002).
38. Ibid., 47.
39. Ibid. Jordan is not specific on who did the swearing-in to the UVF.
40. Ibid., 51.
41. Ibid.
42. Brian Rowan, '"New information" may clear Gusty Spence of 1966 gun killing', *The Belfast Telegraph,* 24 January 2011, www.belfasttelegraph.co.uk/news/local-national/northern-ireland/lsquonew-informationrsquo-may-clear-gusty-spence-of-1966-gun-killing-15062647.html (24 January 2011).
43. Ibid.
44. Garland, *Gusty Spence,* 56. See also Nelson, *Ulster's Uncertain Defenders,* 61.
45. Taylor, *Loyalists,* 41.
46. Ibid., 35.
47. Boulton, *UVF 1966–73,* 48–59.
48. Tom Hayden, *Trial* (New York, NY: Holt, Rinehart and Winston, 1970), 91.
49. Brian Hanley and Scot Millar, *The Lost Revolution: The Story of the Official IRA and the Worker's Party* (Dublin, Penguin Group, 2009).
50. Hanley and Millar, *The Lost Revolution,* 66–107. This gives a very detailed analysis of this strategy.
51. Liam McMillen, 'The Role of the IRA: 1962–1967' (lecture, Official IRA Comhairle Ceeanntar, Tailor's Hall Dublin, June 1972).
52. Ibid.
53. Ibid.
54. Ibid.
55. David Ervine, video interview with University of Pittsburgh students, Pittsburgh and Belfast, 13 November 2004.
56. Ibid.
57. Tom Roberts, interview with author, EPIC Office, Shankill Road, 16 June 2009.
58. Ibid.
59. Ibid.

60. Henry Patterson, *Politics of Illusion* (London: Serif, 1997), 96–121. Patterson lays out a detailed analysis of the politics of the republican movement in the 1960s.

61. Bobby Cosgrove, interview with author, PUP Office, East Belfast, 16 June 2009.

62. There are many good studies of the rising tensions and the role Paisley and others played in this. See Boulton, *UVF 1966–73*; Nelson, *Ulster's Uncertain Defenders*; and Bruce, *The Red Hand*, among others.

63. Bruce, *The Red Hand*, 21.

64. Taylor, *Loyalists*, 35.

65. Ibid., 35.

66. Boulton, *UVF 1966–73*, 44.

67. Bruce, *The Red Hand*, 22.

68. Taylor, *Loyalists*, 39.

69. This reference is to a children's nursery rhyme 'Oh, the grand old Duke of York, / He had ten thousand men; / He marched them up to the top of the hill, / And he marched them down again. / And when they were up, they were up, / And when they were down, they were down, / And when they were only halfway up, / They were neither up nor down.'

70. Bruce, *The Red Hand*, 22.

71. McKittrick and McVea, *Making Sense of the Troubles*, 46–7. See also 'Sir Kenneth Bloomfield Long Play interview', *BBC Radio Ulster*, n.d., www.bbc.co.uk/northernireland/radioulster/historylessons/features145043.shtml (23 May 2011). Sir Ken Bloomfield was former Head of the Northern Ireland Civil Service, Cabinet Secretary to three Northern Ireland Prime Ministers between 1963 and 1972, and to the power-sharing executive in 1974. In this interview, he talks about the 'Ulster at the Crossroads' speech.

72. Coogan, *The Troubles*, 68–70. McKittrick and McVea, *Making Sense of the Troubles*, 48–9.

73. Boulton, *UVF 1966–73*, 91.

74. Coogan, *The Troubles*, 71–2. Taylor, *Loyalists*, 59–61.

75. Moloney, *Paisley*, 174.

76. Government of Northern Ireland, *Violence and Civil Disturbances in Northern Ireland in 1969 Report of Tribunal of Inquiry Chairman: The Hon. Mr Justice Scarman Presented to Parliament by Command of His Excellency the Governor of Northern Ireland April, 1972*. Cmnd. 566. Paragraph 1.13. n.d., *CAIN Web Service*, cain.ulst.ac.uk/hmso/scarman.htm#3 (14 December 2011).

77. Ibid., 129.

78. 'A Chronology of the Conflict – 1969', 14 March 2011, *CAIN Web Service*, cain.ulst.ac.uk/othelem/chron/ch69.htm (13 August 2010).

79. McKittrick and McVea, *Making Sense of the Troubles*, 329.

80. 'Sutton Index of Deaths', 14 March 2011, *CAIN Web Service*, cain.ulst.ac.uk/sutton/chron/1972.html (14 August 2010).

81. W. H Van Voris, 'The Provisional IRA and the Limits of Terrorism', *The Massachusetts Review*, Vol. 16, No. 3 (Summer 1975): 420.

82. David Ervine, interview with author, PUP Headquarters East Belfast, 27 June 2006.

83. Former RHC, email message to author, 3 August 2010.

84. Paul Bew and Gordon Gillespie, *Northern Ireland: A Chronology of the Troubles, 1968–1999* (Dublin: Gill and Macmillan, 2009), 28.
85. Garland, *Gusty Spence*, 151–2.
86. Boulton, *UVF 1966–73*, 172.
87. Bew and Gillespie, *Chronology of the Troubles*, 44–57.
88. *Orange Cross*, 29 July 1972.
89. Garland, *Gusty Spence*, 146.
90. Hutchinson, interview with author, Mt Vernon Community Centre, North Belfast, 2 June 2009.
91. Boulton, *UVF 1966–73*, 173.
92. Hutchinson, interview with author, Mt Vernon Community Centre, North Belfast, 2 June 2009.
93. Ibid.
94. Garland, *Gusty Spence*, 151–2.
95. *Orange Cross*, 12 August, 1972.
96. Boulton, *UVF 1966–73*, 172.
97. Ibid., 172.
98. Hutchinson, interview with author, Mt Vernon Community Centre, North Belfast, 2 June 2009.
99. Garland, *Gusty Spence*, 143.
100. Boulton, *UVF 1966–73*, 174.
101. Billy Hutchinson, interview with author, Mt Vernon Community Centre, North Belfast, 2 June 2009.
102. Boulton, *UVF 1966–73*, 174–5.
103. Boulton, *UVF 1966–73*, 6.

## 2: MANIPULATION, ACQUIESCENCE AND AWAKENING

1. Bobby Cosgrove, interview with author, PUP Office, East Belfast, 16 June 2009.
2. Peter Taylor, Andrew Williams and BBC, *Provos: The IRA and Sinn Fein* (BBC Documentaries, 1997), *Watch Documentary*, 21 December 2010, watchdocumentary.com/watch/provos-Loyalists-and-brits-provos-episode-01-born-again-video_cc806d71f.html.
3. Robert Lynch, 'The People's Protectors? The Irish Republican Army and the "Belfast Pogrom," 1920–1922', *Journal of British Studies*, Vol. 47, No. 2 (2008): 375–91.
4. Paddy Devlin, *Yes, We Have No Bananas: Outdoor Relief in Belfast: 1920–1939* (Belfast: Blackstaff Press, 1981), 7.
5. Maurice Goldring, *Belfast: From Loyalty to Rebellion* (London: Lawrence and Wishart, 1991), 135.
6. McKittrick and McVea, *Making Sense of the Troubles*, 13.
7. For an excellent analysis of the breakdown in the cross-class alliance see Graham Walker, *A History of the Unionist Party: Protest, Pragmatism and Pessimism* (Manchester: Manchester University Press, 2004), 139–57.
8. As stated earlier, Loyalism is now associated exclusively with the Protestant working class and those who took up the gun to 'defend Ulster'. 'Middle unionism' or simply unionism refers mainly to the constitutional unionist parties that tend to reflect middle class or rural interests in the case of the DUP and upper class and business interests in the case of the UUP.

9. McKittrick and McVea, *Making Sense of the Troubles*, 4–5.
10. Jonathan Bardon, *A History of Ulster* (Belfast: Blackstaff Press, 1992), 501. McKittrick and McVea, *Making Sense of the Troubles*, 7–8. Michael Farrell, *Northern Ireland: The Orange State* (London: Pluto Press, 1980), 82–3.
11. Bardon, *A History of Ulster*, 499.
12. McKittrick and McVea, *Making Sense of the Troubles*, 8.
13. Ibid. Bardon *A History of Ulster*, 499–501. Farrell, *Orange State*, 83–5.
14. Bardon, *A History of Ulster*, 501.
15. Ibid.
16. Coogan, *The Troubles*, 30.
17. 'Introduction to the Electoral System in Northern Ireland', 14 March 2011, *CAIN Web Service*, cain.ulst.ac.uk/issues/politics/election/electoralsystem.htm (30 May 2011).
18. Coogan, *The Troubles*, 30.
19. Farrell, *Orange State*, 84–5.
20. Ibid., 85.
21. McKittrick and McVea, *Making Sense of the Troubles*, 9.
22. D. G. Pringle, 'Electoral Systems and Political Manipulation: A Case Study of Northern Ireland in the 20s', *Economic a and Social Review*, Vol. 11, No. 3 (April 1980): 204, quoted in Aaron Edwards, *A History of the Northern Ireland Labour Party: Democratic Socialism and Sectarianism* (Manchester: Manchester University Press, 2009), 3.
23. Edwards, *A History of the Northern Ireland Labour Party*, 14.
24. Farrell, *Orange State*, 114.
25. Bardon, *History of Ulster*, 511.
26. Edwards, *A History of the Northern Ireland Labour Party*, 15.
27. Bardon, *History of Ulster*, 511.
28. Edwards, *A History of the Northern Ireland Labour Party*, 15.
29. This mentality persists today. In the 2009 European Elections, the DUP ran on a platform of 'Smash Sinn Féin', even though the DUP was in a power-sharing arrangement with Sinn Féin.
30. 'Northern Ireland Parliamentary Election Results', n.d., www.election.demon.co.uk/stormont/totals.html (30 May 2011).
31. Bardon, *History of Ulster*, 490.
32. 'Civil Authorities (Special Powers) Act (Northern Ireland), 1922', *CAIN Web Service*, 14 March 2011, cain.ulst.ac.uk/hmso/spa1922.htm (30 May 2011).
33. Michael Farrell, *Arming the Protestants* (London: Pluto Press Ltd., 1983), 30–54.
34. Ibid., 30.
35. The Black and Tans were former soldiers brought to Ireland during the War of Independence to aid the Police. The RIC was the all-Ireland Police Service. The A, B and C branches of the USC each had different levels of responsibility. The A was eventually absorbed into the RUC, the C was disbanded and the B-Specials existed until October 1969.
36. Bardon, *History of Ulster*, 490.
37. Ibid.
38. McKittrick and McVea, *Making Sense of the Troubles*, 11.
39. Devlin, *Yes, We Have No Bananas*, 73ff.
40. McKittrick and McVea, *Making Sense of the Troubles*, 15. Tim Pat Coogan, *Ireland in the Twentieth Century* (Huddersfield: Arrow, 2006), 299–300.

41. McKittrick and McVea, *Making Sense of the Troubles*, 15.
42. Ibid., 12.
43. Peter Taylor, *Provos: The IRA and Sinn Fein* (London: Bloomsbury, 1999), 31.
44. Brendan O'Neill, 'How the Peace Process Divided Ireland', 25 July 2002, indiamond6.ulib.iupui.edu:81/peaceprocessdivide.html (31 May 2011).
45. Peter Taylor, Andrew Williams and BBC, *Provos: The IRA and Sinn Fein*, BBC Documentary, 1997. BBC, *Watch Documentary*, 21 December 2010, watchdocumentary.com/watch/provos-Loyalists-and-brits-provos-episode-01-born-again-video_cc806d71f.html.
46. McKittrick and McVea, *Making Sense of the Troubles*, 6.
47. Ibid., 1–25.
48. Michael Hall, *Ulster's Protestant Working Class* (Newtonabbey: Island Pamphlets, 1994), 13.
49. Hugh Smyth, interview with author, PUP Office, Shankill Road, 26 May 2009.
50. Nelson, *Ulster's Uncertain Defender*, 135.
51. Boulton, *UVF 1966–73*, 6.
52. Graham Spencer, *State of Loyalism*, 6.
53. Ibid., 6.
54. Garland, '*The Ulster Volunteer Force*', 30.
55. Hall, *Ulster's Protestant Working Class*, 9.
56. William, 'Plum' Smith, interview with author, EPIC Office, Shankill Road, 10 June 2009.
57. Ibid.
58. William 'Plum' Smith, interview with author, EPIC Office, Shankill Road, 10 June 2009.
59. Ibid.
60. Ibid.
61. Goldring, *Belfast: From Loyalty to Rebellion*, 103–7.
62. Henry Patterson and Eric Kaufmann, *Unionism and Orangeism in Northern Ireland Since 1945: The Decline of the Loyal Family* (Manchester: Manchester University Press, 2007), 14, 17–21.
63. Ibid., 17.
64. Edwards, *A History of the Northern Ireland Labour Party*, 10.
65. Devlin, *Yes, We Have No Bananas*, 47.
66. Farrell, *Orange State*, 103–6. Bardon, *History of Ulster*, 462–4.
67. Farrell, *Orange State*, 105. Bardon, *History of Ulster*, 463.
68. See also Goldring, *Loyalty to Rebellion*, 130–1, for more on the UULA and its ineffectiveness in this strike.
69. Farrell, *Orange State*, 28.
70. Devlin, *Yes, We Have No Bananas*, 50.
71. Ibid., 28.
72. Farrell, *Orange State*, 27–36.
73. Devlin, *Yes, We Have No Bananas*, 49.
74. Farrell, *Orange State*, 29.
75. Nelson, *Ulster's Uncertain Defenders*, 44.
76. Devlin, *Yes, We Have No Bananas*, 51. Farrell, *Orange State*, 33.
77. Devlin, *Yes, We Have No Bananas*, 51.
78. Ibid., 40.
79. Ibid., 52.

80. Billy Hutchinson, *Hard Man Honourable Man: My Loyalist Life* (unpublished manuscript), 68.
81. Bardon, *History of Ulster*, 509.
82. Devlin, *Yes, We Have No Bananas*, 53, 57.
83. Farrell, *Orange State*, 29.
84. Goldring, *Loyalty to Rebellion*, 48–9.
85. Devlin, *Yes, We Have No Bananas*, 125.
86. Ibid., 134–6.
87. Ronnie Munck and Bill Rolston, *Belfast in the Thirties* (Belfast: Blackstaff Press, 1987), 30–1.
88. Devlin, *Yes, We Have No Bananas*, 130.
89. Graham Walker, 'POTESTANTISM BEFORE PARTY!': THE ULSTER PROTESTANT LEAGUE IN THE 1930s, *The Historical Journal*, Vol. 28, No. 4 (1985): 961–7.
90. Devlin, *Yes, We Have No Bananas*, 138–41; Farrell, *Orange State*, 135–40; Munck and Rolston, *Oral History*, 44–5.
91. Graham Walker, *A History of the Unionist Party*, 72.
92. Devlin, *Yes, We Have No Bananas*, 140; Bardon, *History of Ulster*, 538–9.
93. Devlin, *Yes, We Have No Bananas*, 137–45. For more detailed analysis see Munck and Rolston, *Oral History*, 46–56. Bardon, *History of Ulster*, 539–42.
94. Garland, *Gusty Spence*, 10.
95. Bobby Cosgrove, interview with author, PUP Office, East Belfast, 16 June 2009.
96. Ibid.
97. Billy Hutchinson, interview with author, Mt Vernon Community Centre, North Belfast, 2 June 2009.
98. Hutchinson, *Hard Man Honourable Man*, 14.
99. Billy Hutchinson, interview with author, Mt Vernon Community Centre, North Belfast, 2 June 2009.
100. Hugh Smyth, interview with author, PUP Office, Shankill Road, 19 June 2009.
101. Jim McDonald, interview with Aaron Edwards, PUP Head Office, Shankill Road, 4 May 2005.
102. Former UVF volunteer, conversation with author, June 2008.
103. Nelson, *Ulster's Uncertain Defenders*, 135.
104. Taylor, *Loyalists*, 50.
105. Ibid., 49.
106. Ibid., 48.
107. Ron Weiner, *The Rape and Plunder of the Shankill Community Action: The Belfast Experience* (Belfast: Nothems Press, 1976), 24.
108. Hugh Smyth, interview with author, PUP Office, Shankill Road, 26 May 2009.
109. Ibid.
110. Ibid.
111. Ibid., See also Sean McKee, 'The Real Voice of Ulster Loyalism? – the Progressive Unionist Party' (BA (Hon), University of Ulster, 1995). In particular see his interview with Spence. (a)–(k).
112. Hugh Smyth, interview with author, PUP Office, Shankill Road, 26 May 2009.
113. Bobby Cosgrove, interview with author, PUP Office, East Belfast, 16 June 2009.
114. Craig was a prominent right-wing Unionist politician at the time, and founder and leader of the extremist VUP.

115. McKeague was one of the founders and leaders of the RHC.
116. Winston 'Winkie' Rea, interview with author, home, Shankill Road, 9 July 2009.
117. Liz Rea, interview with author, home, Shankill Road, 6 June 2009.
118. Ibid.
119. Winston 'Winkie' Rea, interview with author, home, Shankill Road, 9 July 2009.
120. Tom Roberts, interview with author, EPIC Office, Shankill Road, 16 June 2009.
121. Ibid.
122. Garland, 'The Ulster Volunteer Force', 45.
123. Hutchinson, Hard Man Honourable Man, 47. Goldring, Loyalty to Rebellion, 105.
124. Nelson, Ulster's Uncertain Defenders, 128.
125. Ibid., 136.
126. Ibid., 128.

## 3: THE PRISON EXPERIENCE AND LOYALIST POLITICS

1. Shirlow, et al., Abandoning Historical Conflict?, 69.
2. Ibid., 69.
3. Anthony McIntyre, Of Myths and Men: Dissent within Republicanism and Loyalism, 115, in Transforming the Peace Process in Northern Ireland: From Terrorism to Democratic Politics, eds Aaron Edwards and Stephen Bloomer (Dublin: Irish Academic Press, 2008).
4. Shirlow, et al., Abandoning Historical Conflict?, 69–90.
5. They do not mention the RHC, but the RHC and UVF worked together in Long Kesh and as we will see one of the education officers in Long Kesh was from the RHC.
6. There were a number of journals called Loyalist News, at least three, two of which the UDA published.
7. Marion Green, The Prison Experience – A Loyalist Perspective (Belfast: EPIC Print, 1998).
8. The title of this section is taken from an article written by an RHC prisoner in Cage 19. Red Hand Commando Student, 'The Long Kesh University', Combat, Vol., No. 22 (1974).
9. Liam Clarke, 'Maze Tale: The Killing of King Rat and The True Story of the Maze Prison', IrelandsOWN, 30 December 2006, irelandsown.net/RatStory. html (9 May 2011).
10. Moloney, The Secret History of the IRA, 149.
11. Shirlow, et al., Abandoning Historical Conflict?, 75–80. Taylor, Provos, 210–26.
12. Peter Taylor, Andrew Williams and BBC, Provos: The IRA and Sinn Fein (BBC Documentaries, 1997), Watch Documentary, 21 December 2010, watchdocumentary.com/watch/provos-Loyalists-and-brits-provos-episode-01-born-again-video_cc806d71f.html. See also Shirlow, et al., Abandoning Historical Conflict?, 80; Moloney, The Secret History of the IRA, 149–61.
13. Kirsty Scott, 'Men of letters, men of arms', Guardian, 2 December 2000, www.guardian.co.uk/books/2000/dec/02/society.politics (24 May 2011).
14. Taylor, Loyalists, 141.

15. Shirlow, et al., *Abandoning Historical Conflict?*, 59–60.
16. Hutchinson, *Hard Man Honourable Man*, 108.
17. Dawn Purvis, interview with author, PUP Office, East Belfast, 10 July 2009.
18. Tony Catney, interview with author, Suffolk, 1 June 2009.
19. Billy Hutchinson, interview with author, Mt Vernon Community Centre, North Belfast, 2 June 2009.
20. Ibid.
21. Hutchinson, *Hard Man Honourable Man*, 105.
22. Ibid., 107.
23. Sinnerton, *David Ervine*, 50.
24. Hutchinson, *Hard Man Honourable Man*, 106.
25. 'Gusty' video file excerpt 0.33, *YouTube*, 2007, www.youtube.com/watch?v=-DGU_FPN2ac&playnext=1&list=PL0891ABD33614B48E (3 August 2011), originally found in Peter Taylor, Sam Collyns, BBC, *Loyalists* (BBC Documentaries, 1999), *Watch Documentary*, 21 December 2010, watchdocumentary.com/watch/provos-Loyalists-and-brits-Loyalists-episode-01-no-surrender-video_10a660cb6.html.
26. Garland, 'The Ulster Volunteer Force', 33.
27. Hutchinson, *Hard Man Honourable Man*, 107.
28. 'THE FUTILITY OF VIOLENCE', *Combat* (December 1975).
29. Garland, 'The Ulster Volunteer Force', 53.
30. Taylor, *Loyalists*, 142.
31. Peter Taylor, Andrew Williams and BBC, *Provos: The IRA and Sinn Fein* (BBC Documentary, 1997) *Watch Documentary*, 21 December 2010, watchdocumentary.com/watch/provos-Loyalists-and-brits-provos-episode-01-born-again-video_cc806d71f.html.
32. Ed Moloney, *Voices from the Grave: Two Men's War in Ireland* (London: Faber and Faber Ltd., 2010), 366.
33. Ibid., 366–7.
34. Taylor, *Loyalists*, 142.
35. Billy Hutchinson, interview with author, Mt Vernon Community Centre, North Belfast, 2 June 2009.
36. Sinnerton, *David Ervine*, 44.
37. Ibid., 44.
38. William 'Plum' Smith, interview with author, EPIC Office, Shankill Road, 10 June 2009.
39. Moloney, *Voices from the Grave*, 364.
40. Ibid., 363–4.
41. Green, *The Prison Experience – A Loyalist Perspective*, 11.
42. Green, *The Prison Experience – A Loyalist Perspective*, 12–13. See also Colin Crawford, 'Long Kesh: an alternative perspective' (M.Sc., Cranfield Institute of Technology, 1979).
43. Green, *The Prison Experience – A Loyalist Perspective*, 19.
44. Green, 19. For an expanded discussion on the use of handicrafts and arts in Long Kesh. See also Billy Hutchinson, 'Transcendental Art' (unpublished manuscript, Belfast, 2010)
45. Hutchinson, 'Transcendental Art', 4.
46. Green, *The Prison Experience*, 19. William 'Plum' Smith, interview with author, EPIC Office, Shankill Road, 10 June 2009.

47. William 'Plum' Smith, interview with author, EPIC Office, Shankill Road, 10 June 2009.
48. An 'O' level is a standard qualification in the UK, usually taken at the age of 15/16 years. An 'A' level is an Advanced level GCE ('O' level) qualification. This exam is normally taken after two years of 'A' level study and leads to University study if completed successfully. Open University is university-level adult education.
49. Garland, *Gusty Spence*, 169–71.
50. Moloney, *Voices from the Grave*, 366–77; Garland, *Gusty Spence*, 173.
51. Garland, *Gusty Spence*, 173.
52. Garland, 'The Ulster Volunteer Force', 42–3.
53. Hutchinson, *Hard Man Honourable Man*, 115.
54. Garland, 'The Ulster Volunteer Force', 42.
55. Bill Rolston, *Children of the Revolution: The lives of sons and daughters of activists in Northern Ireland* (Derry: Guildhall Press, 2011), 183–4.
56. William Mitchell, 'Priorities in Prison Education', *Combat*, No. 26 (1979).
57. Hutchinson, 'Transcendental Art', 5.
58. Sinnerton, *David Ervine*, 72–3.
59. Boulton, *UVF 1966–73*, 139.
60. Cusack and McDonald, *UVF*, 144–6; Hanley and Millar, *Lost Revolution*, 226–8. See also Billy Mitchell, 'Discussions with the Provisional I.R.A.' (1977), for more on this.
61. Garland, *Gusty Spence*, 130–6; Green, *The Prison Experience*, 9–10; Boulton, *UVF 1966–1973*, 168–9.
62. Private discussion with individual who was at the funeral.
63. Garland, *Gusty Spence*, 125.
64. Ibid., 120.
65. Hanley, *Lost Revolution*, 70–107.
66. Garland, *Gusty Spence*, 127–8.
67. Sinnerton, *David Ervine*, 66.
68. Moloney, *Voices from the Grave*, 369.
69. Ibid.
70. 'The Long Kesh Visits', *Orange Cross* 51 (March 1974).
71. Colin Crawford, *Long Kesh: An Alternative Perspective*. M.A. thesis.
72. Crawford, Colin, *Defenders or Criminals? Loyalist Prisoners and Criminalization* (Belfast: Blackstaff Press, 1999).
73. Crawford, *Defenders or Criminals?*, 35.
74. William 'Plum' Smith, interview with author, EPIC Office, Shankill Road, 10 June 2009; Crawford, *Defenders or Criminals?*, 36–8.
75. Crawford, *Defenders or Criminals?*, 39.
76. Garland, *Gusty Spence*, 167.
77. Winston 'Winkie' Rea, interview with author, home, Shankill Road, 9 July 2009.
78. Moloney, *Voices from the Grave*, 367.
79. Ibid., 367.
80. 'The Long Kesh Visits', *Orange Cross* 51 (March 1974).
81. Crawford, *Defenders or Criminals?*, 40.
82. Garland, *Gusty Spence*, 168–9; Clarke, *Defenders or Criminals?*, 40–1.
83. Garland, *Gusty Spence*, 183.

84. Ibid., 183–7; Crawford, *Defenders or Criminals?*, 41–4. See also 'Prison Riots Logged', *Combat*, Vol. 1, No. 31 (October 1974).

85. Garland, *Gusty Spence*, 186–7; Crawford, *Defenders or Criminals?*, 42; Green, *The Prison Experience*, 17.

86. 'Prison Riots Logged', *Combat*, Vol. 1, No. 31 (October 1974).

87. Garland, *Gusty Spence*, 187.

88. This insight came in a private conversation with a former PIRA volunteer in summer 2007.

89. 'Call for a review of the "COMPASSIONATE PAROLE" system', *Combat* (October 1975). This is a good example of the thinking going on in the UVF and in the Camp Council on the topic of Compassionate Parole.

90. 'The Long Kesh Visits', *Orange Cross*, 51 (March 1974).

91. Garland, *Gusty Spence*, 213–14.

92. Crawford, *Defenders or Criminals?*, 50.

93. Ibid., 51.

94. Ibid., 50.

95. Bobby Cosgrove, interview with author, PUP Office, East Belfast, 16 June 2009.

96. William 'Plum' Smith, interview with author, EPIC Office, Shankill Road, 10 June 2009.

97. Green, *The Prison Experience*, 18.

98. Billy Hutchinson, follow-up interview with author, Mt Vernon Community Centre, North Belfast, 7 July 2009.

99. Moloney, *Voices from the Grave*, 367.

100. Tony Catney, interview with author, Suffolk, 1 June 2009.

101. Harry Donaghy, interview with author, Belfast Unemployed Resource Centre (BURC), Belfast, 6 June 2009.

102. Ibid.

103. The Northern Ireland Office. This body essentially had responsibility for running Northern Ireland.

104. Tony Catney, interview with author, Suffolk, 1 June 2009.

105. William 'Plum' Smith, interview with author, PUP Office, Shankill Road, 10 June 2009.

106. *The Third Force* (Co. Antrim: Hand to Mouth Press, 1986), 4. See also Garland, *Gusty Spence*, 194.

107. Crawford, *Defenders or Criminals?*, 45.

108. UVF, 'Proposals for Re-Settlement Programme for Special Category Prisoners', *Combat* (October 1975).

109. Crawford, 'Long Kesh: an alternative perspective', 134–7.

110. UVF, Proposals for Re-Settlement Programme for Special Category Prisoners'.

111. Ibid.

112. Crawford, *Defenders or Criminals?*, 47.

113. Garland, *Gusty Spence*, 194.

114. Crawford, *Defenders or Criminals?*, 48.

115. Ibid.

116. Ibid., 47.

117. Ibid., 48–9.

118. Ibid.

119. Ibid., 49.

120. Ibid., 48.

121. Tony Catney, interview with author, Suffolk, 1 June 2009.
122. Garland, *Gusty Spence*, 196.
123. Shirlow and McEvoy, *Beyond the Wire*, 59.
124. The British Government introduced this in 1975 in the Gardiner Report. However, it did not take effect until 1 March 1976, when anyone convicted of a crime would then be sentenced as an 'ordinary' criminal.
125. Shirlow and McEvoy, *Beyond the Wire*, 59.
126. Hutchinson, *Hard Man Honourable Man*, 123.
127. Crawford, *Defenders or Criminals?*, 61.
128. David Ervine, interview with author, PUP Headquarters, East Belfast, 27 June 2006.
129. Mitchell, 'Principles of Loyalism Document Principles of Loyalism An Internal Discussion Paper', *Progressive Unionist Party*, 1 November 2002, progressiveunionistparty.org/articles/principles-of-Loyalism/ (9 May 2011).
130. Billy Hutchinson, follow-up interview with author, Mt Vernon Community Centre, North Belfast, 7 July 2009.
131. Ibid.

## 4: THE EMERGING LIGHT: POLITICAL LOYALISM, 1973–75

1. Gusty Spence, 'The Oration Delivered by the Commanding Officer in Long Kesh' (speech, Cage Twenty One Long Kesh Prison Camp, 12 July 1977).
2. Taylor, *Loyalists*, 46.
3. David Ervine, video interview with University of Pittsburgh students, Pittsburgh and Belfast, 13 November 2004.
4. Berghahn, Volker R., *Europe in the Era of Two World Wars* (Princeton, NJ: Princeton University Press, 2006), 141.
5. Ibid., 141.
6. Garland, 'The Ulster Volunteer Force', 4.
7. David Ervine, video interview with University of Pittsburgh students, Pittsburgh and Belfast, 13 November 2004.
8. Berghahn, *Europe in the Era of the Two World Wars*, 141.
9. Fearon, *The Conflict's Fifth Business*, 24.
10. 'Annual Orange Parade at Long Kesh P.O.W. Camp', *Combat* (July 1975).
11. UVF, 'U.V.F. PEACE CHALLENGE TO THE PROVOS', *Combat*, Vol. 6., No. 27 (1979). There was justification for thinking this was the PIRA's campaigns around criminalisation and the blanket protests had not attracted mass support and the PIRA appeared, even with its reorganisation, to be a spent force. See Richard O'Rawe, *BLANKETMEN: An Untold Story of the H-Block Hunger Strike* (Dublin: New Island, 2005).
12. I have found two dates for this. Some sources say that this work began in 1972 and others in 1974. Evidence presented later in this study indicates this work began before 1974.
13. McKittrick and McVea, *Making Sense of the Troubles*, 329.
14. Garland, *Gusty Spence*, 160.
15. William 'Plum' Smith, interview with author, PUP Office, Shankill Road, 10 June 2009.
16. Brian MacIntyre, 'David Ervine: Both Sides Need to Give Up Violence', *Salt Lake Tribune*, 27 July 1997.
17. Garland, *Gusty Spence*, 160.

18. Moloney, *Voices from the Grave*, 378.
19. Hutchinson, 'Hard Man, Honourable Man', 120.
20. Private conversation, summer 2009.
21. Hugh Smyth, follow-up interview, PUP Office, Shankill Road, 19 June 2009.
22. Jim McDonald, interview with Aaron Edwards, PUP Head Office, Shankill Road, 4 May 2005.
23. Fearon, *The Conflict's Fifth Business*, 65–6.
24. Ibid., 66.
25. Billy Mitchell, interview with Aaron Edwards, LINC Recourse Centre, 27 September 2005.
26. For more on the NILP's influence on the UVF, RHC and PUP see Edwards, 'The Northern Ireland Labour Party and Paramilitary Politics in the 1970s'; Edwards, 'Democratic Socialism and Sectarianism: The Northern Ireland Labour Party and Progressive Unionist Party Compared', *Politics*, Vol. 27, No. 1 (2007): 24–31. For detailed information on the NILP and its thinking, see Edwards, *A History of the Northern Ireland Labour Party*.
27. Tom Roberts, interview with author, EPIC Office, Shankill Road, 16 June 2009.
28. McKittrick and McVea, *Making Sense of the Troubles*, 327.
29. Nelson, *Ulster's Uncertain Defenders*, 171.
30. Hugh Smyth, interview with author, PUP Office, Shankill Road, 26 May 2009.
31. Fearon, *The Conflict's Fifth Business*, 66. Taylor, *Loyalists*, 123.
32. Fearon, *The Conflict's Fifth Business*, 67. See also Taylor, *Loyalists*, 122.
33. Fearon, *The Conflict's Fifth Business*, 67. See also Cusack and McDonald, *UVF*, 144–7. Taylor, *Loyalists*, 123–4.
34. Mitchell, 'Discussions with the Provisional I.R.A.' (1977). These were the notes, plus analysis of the secret meetings held in early 1974 between the PIRA and the UVF. According to two sources familiar with this document, Billy Mitchell wrote this in late 1976 or early 1977 when he was in Long Kesh. While Mitchell's notes appear accurate concerning the 1974 meetings, one must approach this document with caution because of the three-year gap between the meetings and the recording of them.
35. Taylor, *Loyalists*, 122.
36. Ulster Volunteer Force, 'Pure Frustration', *Loyalist News*, 6th Edn, Vol. 5 (2 March 1974).
37. 'The UVF Answers', *Orange Cross* (16 December 1972).
38. 'Strictly Confidential: Assistant Governor Robert Gibson and Vivian Simpson, MP – Approach to Secretary of State for NI, RE: Continuing discussions at Crumlin Road Prison with Political Prisoners', May 1972, PRONI, D3233/2/1/1, 8.
39. Garland, *Gusty Spence*, 126–74.
40. Boulton, *UVF 1966–73*, 168–9; Green, *The Prison Experience*, 9; Taylor, *Loyalists*, 131–4.
41. Aaron Edwards, 'The NILP and Loyalist Paramilitary Politics in the 1970s' (lecture, PSAI conference, Cork, 2006), 8.
42. 'Proposals for the Assembly', *Loyalist News*, 27th Edn, Vol. 4 (28 July 1973).
43. 'Northern Ireland Constitutional Proposals Presented to Parliament by the Secretary of State for Northern Ireland by Command of Her Majesty', *CAIN Web Service*, 14 March 2011, cain.ulst.ac.uk/hmso/cmd5259.htm (25 July 2011).

44. 'Proposals for the Assembly', *Loyalist News*, 27th Edn, Vol. 4 (28 July 1973).
45. Ibid.
46. Ibid.
47. Ibid.
48. Ibid.
49. UVF, 'THE MYTH EXPLODED: THE TRUTH ABOUT THE U.V.F.: (The Organization with a social Conscience)', *Loyalist News*, 23rd Edn, Vol. 4 (June 1973).
50. 'Proposals for the Assembly', *Loyalist News*, 29th Edn, Vol. 4 (August 1973).
51. 'Unemployment', *Loyalist News*, 30th Edn (September 1973).
52. Ibid.
53. Ibid.
54. Ibid.
55. 'New Loyalist Front Political Voice of Banned UVF', *Sunday News*, 14 October 1973.
56. Ibid.
57. Ibid.
58. Hugh Smyth, interview with author, PUP Office, Shankill Road, 26 May 2009.
59. Cusack and McDonald, *UVF*, 126–7; Bruce, *The Red Hand*, 119. Bruce, *The Edge of the Union*, 99.
60. 'New Loyalist Front Political Voice for Banned UVF', *Sunday News*, 14 October 1973.
61. Cusack and McDonald, *UVF*, 126.
62. 'New Loyalist Front Political Voice for Banned UVF', *Sunday News*, 14 October 1973.
63. 'How the U.V.F. Think!', *Loyalist News*, 40th Edn, Vol. 4 (October 27, 1973).
64. Nelson, *Ulster's Uncertain Defenders*, 172.
65. Ibid.
66. Bruce, *The Red Hand*, 132.
67. Cusack and McDonald, *UVF*, 130.
68. Taylor, *Loyalists*, 126. This was the phrase used by David Ervine when Taylor asked him why the UVF bombed Dublin.
69. 'A letter from Colin Wallace to Tony Stoughton, the Chief Information Officer of the British Army Information Service at Lisburn, 14 August 1975', *Colin Wallace – Biography,* biographicon.com/view/h13we/Colin_Wallace (19 August 2010). See also: Michael Browne, 'Death Squad Dossier', *Irish Mail*, 10 December 2006. For more on Colin Wallace and the possible role of intelligence services in the violence see the 'Barron Report', *CAIN Web Service*, December 2003, cain.ulst.ac.uk/events/dublin/barron03.pdf (3 August 2011).
70. 'UVF OFFERS HAND OF CONCILIATION "LET'S GET TOGETHER AND TALK PEACE"', *Sunday News*, 3 February 1974.
71. Ibid.
72. Ibid.
73. Ibid.
74. Ibid.
75. Ibid.
76. Ibid.
77. 'U.V.F. TAKES THE LEAD', *Loyalist News*, 3rd Edn, Vol. 5 (9 February 1974).
78. Ibid.

79. Cusack and McDonald, *UVF*, 144–7, 153. See Taylor, *Loyalists*, 124 for more on this. See also Mitchell, 'Discussions with the Provisional I.R.A.' (1977).

80. Patrick Riddell, 'Responses to UVF Statement 3 February 1974', *Sunday News*, 10 February 1974.

81. Ibid.

82. 'Sectarianism: Who Stands to Gain?', *Combat*, Vol. 1., No. 13 (April 1974).

83. East Antrim Workers' Council and East Antrim Volunteer, 'Combat Violence', *Combat*, Vol. 1, No. 13 (April 1974).

84. Bew and Gillespie, *Chronology of the Troubles*, 84.

85. For a detailed account of the strike, see Don Anderson, 14 *May Days: The Inside Story of the Loyalist Strike of 1974* (Dublin: Gill & Macmillian, Ltd., 1994). See also 'Ulster Workers' Council Strike – Chronology of the Strike', 14 March 2011, *CAIN Web Service*, cain.ulst.ac.uk/events/uwc/chr. htm (14 March 2011). See also 'Ulster Workers' Council Strike – Details of Source Materials', 14 March 2011, *CAIN Web Service*, cain.ulst.ac.uk/events/ uwc/soc.htm (2 August 2011).

86. Hugh Smyth, interview with author, PUP Office, Shankill Road, 26 May 2009.

87. McKee, 'The Real Voice of Ulster Loyalism?', (g).

88. Bruce, *The Red Hand*, 100. Bruce, *The Edge of the Union*, 99.

89. Coogan, *The Troubles: Ireland's Ordeal 1966–1996*, 179.

90. Bew and Gillespie, *Chronology of the Troubles*, 92–3.

91. Ibid., 91.

92. 'Wilson had NI "doomsday plan"', *BBC News*, 11 September 2008, news. bbc.co.uk/2/hi/uk_news/politics/7610750.stm (2 August 2010).

93. 'Volunteer Political Party Statement', *Combat*, Vol. 1 No 14 (June 1974).

94. The Volunteer Party, *Manifesto of the Volunteer Political Party (VPP)* (Belfast, Northern Ireland: Westminster Election, October 1974). This document was also published in *Combat*. Volunteer Political Party, 'For God and Ulster: A Progressive and Forward Thinking Unionist Party', Vol. 1 No. 26 (1974).

95. 'Volunteer Political Party Statement', *Combat*, Vol. 1 No 14 (June 1974).

96. Tom Roberts, interview with author, EPIC Office, Shankill Road, 16 June 2009.

97. 'UVF Ceasefire for Elections', *Loyalist News* (17 August 1974).

98. Volunteer Political Party, *Manifesto of the Volunteer Political Party*.

99. Ibid.

100. '"Let's hear from you" says VPP', *Sunday News*, 22 September 1974.

101. Volunteer Political Party, *Manifesto of the Volunteer Political Party*.

102. Ron Weiner, *The Rape and Plunder of the Shankill – Community Action*, 20–2, 27, 31.

103. Volunteer Political Party, *Manifesto of the Volunteer Political Party*.

104. 'View of a Volunteer', *Loyalist News*, 21st Edn, Vol. 5 (22 June 1974).

105. Red Hand Commando, *Within the Context of Northern Ireland* (Belfast, Northern Ireland, 1974).

106. 'Proposal for the Assembly', *Loyalist News*, 29th Edn, Vol. 4 (11 August 1973).

107. Former RHC, email to author, 3 August 2010.

108. There is some contention over who was involved in writing this document. In the Linen Hall Library, it is stamped 'Red Hand Commando'. However, the UVF also reportedly took part in writing this document.

109. Volunteer Political Party, *Manifesto of the Volunteer Political Party*.

110. Red Hand Commando, *Within the Context of Northern Ireland*.
111. Ibid.
112. Ibid., 1.
113. Ibid., 2.
114. Ibid.
115. Ibid.
116. Ibid., 3.
117. Ibid., 2.
118. Ibid., 3.
119. Ibid.
120. This description fit Ian Paisley, who many paramilitaries felt 'wound up' the people to fight for Ulster and then disowned them when they did just that.
121. Red Hand Commando, *Within the Context of Northern Ireland*, 4.
122. Ibid., 4.
123. Ibid., 6.
124. Alliance Party, 'Alliance Party Policy: Integrated Education Alliance Party Policy Document Approved By Party Council: March 2006', *Alliance Party*, n.d., allianceparty.org/pages/policy-integratededucation.html, 5 August 2010. Department of Employment and Leaning, 'Integrated Schools', *Department of Employment and Leaning*, n.d., deni.gov.uk/index/85-schools/10-types_of_school-nischools_pg/16-schools-integratedschools_pg.htm 2011 (26 July 2011).
125. Red Hand Commando, *Within the Context of Northern Ireland*, 7.
126. Ibid., 8.
127. Ibid.
128. Patterson and Kaufmann, *Unionism and Orangeism*, 57.
129. In this electoral system, if candidates did not garner enough votes they would not get their deposit back they paid to stand in the election.
130. 'Westminster General: 10 October 1974 Belfast West Borough Constituency Belfast Area (Ulster)', *ElectionsIreland.org*, n.d., electionsireland.org/result.cfm?election=1974octUK&cons=714 (26 July 2011).
131. 'Future Political Role of the UVF', *Combat*, No. 31 (1974).
132. Ibid.
133. Ibid.
134. W. Mitchell, 'Where does the UVF Stand Regarding Politics?', *Combat* (1974).
135. 'Future Political Role of the UVF', *Combat*, No. 31 (1974).
136. 'IRA Campaigns in England', *BBC News*, 4 March 2001, news.bbc.co.uk/2/hi/uk_news/1201738.stm (24 May 2011).
137. Mitchell, 'Discussions with the Provisional I.R.A.' (1977).
138. Nelson, *Ulster's Uncertain Defenders*, 178.
139. See Dillon, *Shankill Butchers*, 44–9, for a brief analysis of the coup and how people like Murphy viewed politics and the coup.
140. Cusack and McDonald, *UVF*, 151–3.
141. Billy Hutchinson, interview with author, Mt Vernon Community Centre, North Belfast, 2 June 2009.
142. Hanley and Millar, *The Lost Revolution*, 227.
143. Cusack and McDonald, *UVF*, 152.
144. Ibid., 150–1.
145. Hutchinson, interview with author, Mt Vernon Community Centre, North Belfast, 2 June 2009.

146. Cusack and McDonald, *UVF*, 185.
147. Nelson, *Ulster's Uncertain Defenders*, 189.
148. Ibid., 189.
149. Ibid., 188.
150. UVF, *U.V.F. Military Policy* (Belfast: UVF, 1974).
151. Ibid.
152. Ibid.
153. Ibid.
154. 'UVF Slam Killers' *United Irishmen* (December 1974).
155. 'Full Circle for the UVF', *Fortnight*, No. 112 (10 October 1975).
156. Hutchinson, *Hard Man Honourable Man*, 49.
157. McKittrick and McVea, *Making Sense of the Troubles*, 329.
158. Dillon, Martin, *The Shankill Butchers*, 44–60.
159. Cusack and McDonald, *UVF*, 166.
160. 'Ashamed of the UVF', *Loyalist News*, 39th Edn. (18 October 1975).
161. McKee, 'The Real Voice of Ulster Loyalism?', (h).
162. Nelson, *Ulster's Uncertain Defenders*, 191.
163. Ibid., 191.
164. Billy Hutchinson, interview with author, Mt Vernon Community Centre, North Belfast, 2 June 2009.
165. Aaron Edwards, 'Abandoning Armed Resistance? The Ulster Volunteer Force: The Ulster Volunteer Force as a Case Study of Strategic Terrorism in Northern Ireland', *Studies in Conflict and Terrorism*, Vol. 32, No. 21 (10 February 2009): 21.

## 5: DARKNESS AT THE END OF THE TUNNEL: THE FAILURE OF POLITICS

1. Hugh Smyth, follow-up interview with author. PUP Office, Shankill Road, 19 June 2009.
2. Mitchell, 'Discussions with the Provisional I.R.A.' (1977).
3. Bowyer Bell, *The Secret Army*, 404–5; Cusack and McDonald, *UVF*, 144–5.
4. Bowyer Bell, *The Secret Army*, 404–5. See also Bruce, *The Red Hand*, 132, for more on this. It should be noted here that even without the IRA's violence, these talks would have failed for other reasons, as we will see later in this chapter.
5. Ibid., 386.
6. Liam McMillen, 'Bodenstown Speech: Wolfe Tone Commemoration' (speech, Bodenstown, Ireland, 28 June 1973). You can also see this as part of a wall mural in West Belfast. For more on that go to, *CAIN Web Service*, 14 March 2011, cain.ulst.ac.uk/mccormick/album31.htm (24 May 2011).
7. Tomás MacGiolla, 'Where We Stand: The Republican Position' (speech, Republican Clubs Conference, Carrickmore, Co. Tyrone, July 1972).
8. Bowyer Bell, *The Secret Army*, 385–9.
9. Patterson, *Politics of Illusion*, 180–221.
10. See more of this in Shirlow, et al., *Abandoning Historical Conflict?*.
11. Hugh Smyth, interview with author, PUP Office, Shankill Road, 26 May 2009.
12. Bowyer Bell, *The Secret Army*, 525.
13. Shirlow, et al., *Abandoning Historical Conflict?*, 55.
14. Taylor, *Provos*, 204–5.
15. Alonso, *The IRA and the Armed Struggle*, 13.

16. Ibid., 13.

17. Ibid., 1–31.

18. Ibid., 9.

19. Tommy McKearney, *The Provisional IRA: From Insurrection to Parliament* (London: Pluto Press, 2011), 106.

20. Ibid., 107.

21. The National Irish Freedom Committee, 'The True Path to Irish Reunification, Éire Nua', *National Irish Freedom Committee*, 14 March 2011, irishfreedom. net/Eire%20Nua/Promotional%20Material/The%20True%20Path%20 %20Eire%20Nua.htm (8 May 2011). This article first appeared in the San Francisco based *Irish Herald* in July 2009.

22. Ibid.

23. Ibid.

24. Hugh Smyth, follow-up interview with author, PUP Office, Shankill Road, 19 June 2009.

25. Roy Garland, 'Progressive Loyalism continually undermined by "super-Prods"', *Irish News*, 20 April 2012, 21.

26. Mitchell, 'Discussions with the Provisional I.R.A.' (1977). In this document, the PIRA did not consider any solution that was strictly internal to Northern Ireland. That is also clear from actions and statements from 1972 onwards.

27. Bowyer Bell, *The Secret Army*, 404. Bruce, *The Red Hand*, 132.

28. McKearney, *The Provisional IRA*, 105. McKearney also blames the actions of Conor Cruise O'Brien and Ian Paisley who both played a role in undercutting the initiative around Boal's Federal Ireland proposal and Éire *Nua*.

29. Mitchell, 'Discussions with the Provisional I.R.A.' (1977).

30. Bowyer Bell, *The Secret Army*, 519.

31. Political analyst, email message to author, 29 May 2012. This analyst, who has interviewed many of the actors of this period, supports this argument. He points out that while some within the old Dublin leadership supported a federal solution, Gerry Adams rejected this and focused on victory over the British.

32. Bowyer Bell, *The Secret Army*, 519.

33. Moloney, *The Secret History of the IRA*, 181–3.

34. Patterson, *Politics of Illusion*, 187.

35. Ibid., 180–1.

36. Mitchell, 'Discussions with the Provisional I.R.A.', (1977).

37. Richard Davis, *Political Propaganda and the Ulster Troubles: A Mirror Image of Antagonism 1968–82* (University of Tasmania, 1983), 214–15, quoted in Henry Patterson, *The Politics of Illusion: A Political History of the IRA* (London: Serif. 1997), 186–7.

38. Patterson, *The Politics of Illusion*, 181.

39. 'History of Éire Nua', *Independent Media Centre Ireland*, 11 April 2008, www.indymedia.ie/article/87142 (16 May 2011).

40. Prior to the split of the IRA into the Provisional and Official wings in 1970, the IRA had accepted the need to develop a mass movement in the South, while unifying the Protestant and Catholic working class in the North before the armed struggle. The Provisionals rejected this and went back to the physical force tradition of Republicanism. See Hanley's *Lost Revolution* and Henry Patterson's *Politics of Illusion* for a complete explanation of the politics of the two wings of the republican movement.

41. Patterson, *Politics of Illusion*, 180–1.

42. Coogan, *The Troubles*, 208.

43. Ibid., 238. Taylor, *Provos*, 282.

44. Taylor, *Provos*, 200.

45. Shirlow, et al., *Abandoning Historical Conflict?*, 96.

46. Moloney, *The Secret History of the IRA*, 134–216, 392–427; Taylor *Provos*, 281–91.

47. Moloney, *The Secret History of the IRA*, 392–427.

48. Shirlow et al., *Abandoning Historical Conflict?*, 18.

49. Bowyer Bell, *The Secret Army*, 152.

50. Ibid., 481.

51. David Ervine, interview with author, PUP Headquarters, East Belfast, 27 June 2006.

52. G. O. Danachair, *Provos: Patriots or Terrorists?* (Dublin: Irish Book Bureau, 1974), 29–30, quoted in Alonso, *The IRA and the Armed Struggle*, 1.

53. Alonso, *The IRA and the Armed Struggle*, 1.

54. Jeffrey Sluka, 'For God and Ulster: The Culture of Terror and Loyalist Death Squads in Northern Ireland' in *Death Squad: The Anthropology of State Terror*, ed. Jeffrey Sluka (Philadelphia, PA: University of Pennsylvania, Press, 2000), 127–57.

55. Taylor, *Loyalists*, 206–10. 'What is Collusion?', BBC, 22 January 2007, news. bbc.co.uk/2/hi/uk_news/northern_ireland/6287049.stm (24 May 2011).

56. Taylor, *Loyalists*, 205–9.

57. BBC News, 'Stevens Inquiry: At a glance', *BBC*, 17 April 2003, news.bbc. co.uk/2/hi/uk_news/northern_ireland/2956337.stm (24 May 2011).

58. Dillon, *The Dirty War*, 211.

59. Liam Clarke, 'Claims of Provo infiltration of police are supported', Belfast Telegraph, 23 December 2011, accessed 28 December 2011, www. belfasttelegraph.co.uk/news/local-national/northern-ireland/claims-of-provo-infiltration-of-police-are-supported-16094761.html#ixzz1hqzKFQxb.

60. Tom Roberts, interview with author, EPIC Office, Shankill Road, 16 June 2009.

61. Private conversation, summer 2009.

62. Tom Roberts, interview with author, EPIC Office, Shankill Road, 16 June 2009.

63. Ibid.

64. Jordan, *Milestones in Murder*, 105–7. For other instances of the IRA being 'run' by the Special Branch and innocent people dying see Jordan, *Milestones in Murder*, 109. For more example of this, see Colin Crawford, *Inside the UDA*, 189–90.

65. Liam Clarke, 'Claims of Provo infiltration of police are supported', Belfast Telegraph, 23 December 2011, accessed 28 December 2011, www. belfasttelegraph.co.uk/news/local-national/northern-ireland/claims-of-provo-infiltration-of-police-are-supported-16094761.html#ixzz1hqzKFQxb.

66. Dawn Purvis, interview with author, PUP Office, East Belfast, 10 July 2009.

67. Alonso, *The IRA and the Armed Struggle*, 23.

68. Hugh Smyth, follow-up interview with author, PUP Office, Shankill Road, 19 June 2009.

69. Winston 'Winkie' Rea, interview with author, home, Shankill Road, 9 July 2009.

70. Shirlow, et al., *Abandoning Historical Conflict?*, 69–90.
71. Bruce, *The Red Hand*, 122–3.
72. Hanley, *The Lost Revolution*, 228.
73. Diana Rusk, '"Rules of war" set out during meetings', *Irish News*, 30 April 2012, 20.
74. Mitchell, 'Discussions with the Provisional I.R.A.' (1977).
75. Rusk, '"Rules of war" set out during meetings', 20. In this case, as Roy Garland regularly points out, this resistance came from within the UVF, the larger Loyalist community, and the Unionist establishment.
76. 'BRING BACK THE 'B' SPECIALS', *Loyalist News*, 19th Edn, Vol. 2 (29 May 1971).
77. 'NATIONAL FRONT PARTY COMES TO ULSTER', *Combat*, No. 5 (April 1974).
78. 'just "ned" a true story', *The Orange Cross*, No. 51 (March 1974).
79. 'Chinky Restaurant Theft', *Loyalist News*, 6th Edn, Vol. 6 (1 March 1975).
80. See *Loyalist News* between 1 March 1975 and August 1975 for this series of articles.
81. Hugh Smyth, interview with author, PUP Office, Shankill Road, 26 May 2009.
82. Ibid.
83. Cusack and McDonald, *UVF*, 149.
84. Fearon, *The Conflict's Fifth Business*, 24–5.
85. Nelson, *Ulster's Uncertain Defenders*, 183–4.
86. Ibid., 184. In particular, see her reference to *Fortnight* No. 77, 8 February 1974.
87. Ibid., 185.
88. Ibid., 186.
89. Ibid., 185.
90. Roy Garland, 'Progressive loyalism continually undermined by "super-Prods"', *Irish News*, 30 April 2012, 21.
91. Tom Roberts, interview with author, EPIC Office, Shankill Road, 16 June 2009.
92. Ibid.
93. T. K., Daniel, 'Myths and militants', *Political Studies* Volume 24, Issue 4 (December 1976): 455–61.
94. Ibid., 456–7.
95. Ibid., 457.
96. Daniel, 'Myths and militants', 461.
97. Nelson, *Ulster's Uncertain Defenders*, 183.
98. David Ervine, interview with author, PUP Headquarters, East Belfast, 27 June 2006.
99. Moloney, *Voices from the Grave*, 385–6.
100. Shirlow, et al., *Abandoning Historical Conflict?*, 75–9.
101. Tom Roberts, interview with author, EPIC Office, Shankill Road, 16 June 2009.
102. O'Rawe, *Blanketmen*, 74.
103. Ibid., 74.
104. Billy Hutchinson, interview with author, Mt Vernon Community Centre, North Belfast, 2 June 2009.
105. Tony Catney, interview with author, Suffolk, 1 June 2009.

106. Ibid. It is important to note here that criminalisation and the security solution began under a Labour government, well before the IRA killed Neave.

107. Billy Hutchinson, follow-up interview with author, Mt Vernon Community Centre, North Belfast, 7 July 2009.

108. Stephen Dorril and Robin Ramsay, *Smear!: Wilson and the Secret State* (London: Fourth Estate Ltd, 1991).

109. Ibid., 256.

110. Dawn Purvis, interview with author, PUP Office, East Belfast, 10 July 2009.

111. Garland, 'The Ulster Volunteer Force', 53.

112. William 'Plum' Smith, interview with author, EPIC Office, Shankill Road, 10 June 2009.

113. David Ervine, interview with author, PUP Headquarters, East Belfast, 27 June 2006.

114. Garland, 'The Ulster Volunteer Force', 53.

115. Nelson, *Ulster's Uncertain Defenders*, 17.

116. DailyPost.co.uk, 'Is it time to for Lodge marchers to call it a day?', *DailyPost. co.uk*, n.d., forums.dailypost.co.uk/viewtopic.php?p=502365 (19 August 2010).

117. Nelson, *Ulster's Uncertain Defenders*, 185–6.

118. *Sunday News*, 30 September 1973, quoted in Roy Garland, 'The Ulster Volunteer Force', 58.

119. Garland, 'The Ulster Volunteer Force', 58.

120. Nelson, *Ulster's Uncertain Defenders*, 162–3.

121. Ibid., 162.

122. Dawn Purvis, interview with author, PUP Office, East Belfast, 10 July 2009.

123. Ibid.

124. Hugh Smyth, interview with author, PUP Office, Shankill Road, 26 May 2009. See also McKee, 'The Real Voice of Ulster Loyalism?', (a)–(k).

125. *Loyalist News*, 31st Edn, Vol. 5 (31 August 1974).

126. Letter to the Editor, *Loyalist News*, 33rd Edn, Vol. 5 (14 September 1974).

127. *Loyalist News* (28 November 1970).

128. Nelson, *Ulster's Uncertain Defenders*, 162.

129. *Loyalist News*, 16th Edn, Vol. 6 (10 May 1975) through 20th Edn (June 1975) for these articles. This is just a sample. There were many articles of this nature that appeared in *Loyalist News* throughout 1974 and 1975.

130. RED GREEN OR ORANGE, *Loyalist News*, 30th Edn, Vol. 6 (16 August 1975).

131. Garland, 'The Ulster Volunteer Force', 68.

132. Billy Mitchell, interview with Aaron Edwards, LINC Resource Centre, 27 September 2005.

133. Reader of *Combat*, 'time to end this nonsense', *Combat*, No. 32 (December 1974).

134. 'To Mr Ken Gibson, for his very good vote in West Belfast Constituency', *Loyalist News*, 38th Edn, Vol. 5, No. 19 (October 1974).

135. 'Reds Under the bed', *Loyalist News*, Vol. 4, No. 29 (29 September 1973).

136. Ibid.

137. Ibid.

138. 'Communism and the Loyalist News', *Loyalist News*, 31st Edn (31 August 1974).

139. Andy McCann, 'Smear Allegations Answered!', *Loyalist News*, 33rd Edn, Vol. 5 (14 September 1974).
140. 'The Red Menace: UVF Supports Orange Order in its Stand Against Communism', *Combat*, Vol. 1, No. 30 (1974).
141. 'Communism – The Enemy of the Working Class', *Combat*, No. 11 (1974).
142. 'Jenx', 'Working Class Politics Not Communism', *Combat*, No. 13 (May 1974).
143. Nelson, *Ulster's Uncertain Defenders*, 186.
144. Garland, 'The Ulster Volunteer Force', 68.
145. Ibid., 68.
146. Billy Mitchell, interview with Aaron Edwards, LINC Resource Centre, 27 September 2005. Martin Dillon, *The Dirty War* (London: Arrow, 1992), 200.
147. Bruce, *Red Hand*, 23.
148. Moore, *The Kincora Scandal*, 29–30, 206–11. Dillon, *The Dirty War*, 200. Cusack and McDonald, *UVF: The Endgame* (Dublin: Poolbeg, 2008), 95, 379–80. Martin Dillon, *God and the Gun: The Church and Irish Terrorism* (New York, NY: Orion Books Ltd., 1998), 235–6.
149. Ed Moloney and Andy Pollak, *Paisley* (Dublin: Poolbeg, 1986), 285, quoted in Garland, 'The Ulster Volunteer Force', 59.
150. Garland, 'The Ulster Volunteer Force', 59. Foot, *Who Framed Colin Wallace*, 355.
151. Chris Moore, *The Kincora Scandal*, 29–30, 206–11. Dillon, *The Dirty War*, 200. Cusack and McDonald, *UVF: The Endgame*, 95, 379–80. Dillon, *God and the Gun*, 235–6.
152. Moore, *Kincora Scandal*, 217.
153. Ibid., 73.
154. This is a very murky episode that is too long to go into here. What we know is that McGrath, a known homosexual and paedophile, ran a boys' home for nearly nine years even though the police allegedly had knowledge of the sexual abuse taking place there. It is suspected that his 'handlers' protected him. See Moore, *Kincora Scandal* for the best analysis of this episode.
155. Cusack and McDonald, *UVF*, 94–7; Moore, *Kincora Scandal*, 78–9.
156. Cusack and McDonald, *UVF*, 67.
157. Ibid., 67.
158. 'Tara Proclamation, 1973', *CAIN Web Service*, 14 March 2011, cain.ulst. ac.uk/othelem/organ/docs/tara73.htm accessed (19 August 2010).
159. Ibid.
160. Ibid.
161. 'The present struggle is for the survival of evangelical Protestantism Tara: There is not the basis for peaceful co-existence', *Sunday News*, 24 March 1974.
162. Ibid.
163. Foot, *Who Framed Colin Wallace?*, 135–9, 148–51, 174–5.
164. Coogan, *The Troubles*, 251.
165. 'Attempt to form "Provo" UVF Bribery used in splinter group move', *Sunday News*, 24 March 1974. 'Ceasefire in Danger', *Combat*, Vol. 1, No. 1 (18 March 1974).
166. 'Attempt to form "Provo" UVF Bribery used in splinter group move', *Sunday News*, 24 March 1974.

167. 'Ceasefire in Danger', *Combat*, Vol. 1, No. 1 (18 March 1974).

168. 'Lynch is Guilty of Murder', *Orange Cross*, October 1972. *Orange Cross* reprinted an article that originally appeared in *the Sunday Times*. See also Hanley, *The Lost Revolution*, 136–48 and also the Official IRA, *Fianna Fail: The IRA Connection* (Dublin, 1971).

169. Peter Wright, *Spy Catcher: The Candid Autobiography of a Senior Intelligence Officer* (New York, NY: Viking, 1987).

170. Paul Foot, *Who Framed Colin Wallace?* (London: Macmillan, 1989).

171. Fred Holroyd with Nick Burbridge, *War Without Honour* (Hull: Medium, 1989).

172. Stephen Dorril and Robin Ramsay, *Smear!* (London: Fourth Estate Limited, 1991).

173. Foot, *Who Framed Colin Wallace?*, 342–3.

174. 'WHO WAS PLOTTING AN ARMY COUP TO GET RID OF WILSON', *The Daily Mirror*, 16 March 2006, www.mirror.co.uk/news/tm_objectid=168 19862&method=full&siteid=115875&headline=who-was-plotting-an-army-coup-to-get-rid-of-harold-wilson--name_page.html (19 August 2010).

175. Brian Wheeler, 'Wilson "plot": The Secret Tapes', *BBC*, 9 March 2006. news. bbc.co.uk/2/hi/uk_news/politics/4789060.stm (19 August 2010).

176. Foot, *Who Framed Colin Wallace?*, 47.

177. Christopher Andrews, *Defend the Realm: The Authorized History Of* (New York, NY: Alfred A. Knopf, 2009), 642.

178. Ibid., 640–3.

179. Ibid., see Sections D and E, 503–753.

180. Foot, *Who Framed Colin Wallace*, 47–61. Dorril and Ramsay, *Smear!*, 256–7.

181. Barrie Penrose, 'MI5 "plotted Ulster strikes"', *Sunday Times*, 22 March 1987. Foot, *Who Framed Colin Wallace?*, 104–5.

182. Foot, *Who Framed Colin Wallace?*, 109–11, 353.

183. Dillon, *The Dirty War*, 199.

184. Dorril and Ramsay, *Smear!*, 287.

185. Dillon, *The Dirty War*, 199.

186. Ibid., 200.

187. Foot, *Who Framed Colin Wallace?*, 82.

188. 'A letter from Colin Wallace to Tony Stoughton, the Chief Information Officer of the British Army Information Service at Lisburn, 14 August 1975', *Colin Wallace – Biography*, biographicon.com/view/h13we/Colin_Wallace (19 August 2010). See also: Michael Browne, 'Death Squad Dossier', *Irish Mail*, 10 December 2006. For more on Colin Wallace and the possible role of intelligence services in the violence see the 'Barron Report', *CAIN Web Service*, December 2003, cain.ulst.ac.uk/events/dublin/barron03.pdf (3 August 2011).

189. Holroyd, *War Without Honour*, 70.

190. Holroyd, *War Without Honour*, 70–88. See also Coogan, *The Troubles*, 254–7.

191. 'Sectarian Killings', *Combat*, Vol. 1, No. 1 (18 March 1974).

192. 'Sectarianism: Who Stands to Gain?', *Combat*, Vol. 1, No. 5 (April 1974).

193. This is an obvious reference to the secret talks that took place in early 1974 between the UVF and both the PIRA and the OIRA.

194. 'Sectarianism: Who Stands to Gain?', *Combat*, Vol. 1, No. 5 (April 1974).

195. Garland, 'The Ulster Volunteer Force', 67.

196. 'A letter from Colin Wallace to Tony Stoughton, the Chief Information Officer of the British Army Information Service at Lisburn, 14 August 1975', *Colin Wallace – Biography,* biographicon.com/view/h13we/Colin_Wallace (19 August 2010). See also: Michael Browne, 'Death Squad Dossier', *Irish Mail,* 10 December 2006. For more on Colin Wallace and the possible role of intelligence services in the violence see the 'Barron Report', *CAIN Web Service,* December 2003, cain.ulst.ac.uk/events/dublin/barron03.pdf (3 August 2011).
197. Garland 'The Ulster Volunteer Force', 68.
198. Ibid.

## 6: THE LIGHT IN THE DARKNESS: POLITICAL LOYALISM, 1975–77

1. Cusack and McDonald, *UVF,* 254.
2. McKittrick and McVea, *Making Sense of the Troubles,* 329.
3. McKee, 'The Real Voice of Ulster Loyalism?', (g).
4. Nelson, *Ulster's Uncertain Defenders,* 191.
5. Independent Unionist Group, 'Devolution: The Plan for Ulster', *Combat,* Vol. 4, No. 21 (1977).
6. 'THE FUTILITY OF VIOLENCE', *Combat* (December 1975).
7. 'Towards a United Ulster', *Combat* (July 1975).
8. 'Annual Orange Parade at Long Kesh P.O.W. Camp', *Combat* (July 1975).
9. 'A TEN POINT PLAN FOR PEACE WITH HONOUR AND JUSTICE', *Loyalist News,* 52nd Edn, Vol. 5 (18 January 1975).
10. Ibid.
11. Ibid.
12. Sinn Féin member, private discussion with author, 8 June 2009.
13. William 'Plum' Smith, interview with author, EPIC Office, Shankill Road, 10 June 2009.
14. Ibid.
15. Ibid.
16. Bew and Gillespie, *Chronology of the Troubles,* 99. See also Bew and Patterson, *The British State and the Ulster Crisis,* 66.
17. Nelson, *Ulster's Uncertain Defenders,* 188.
18. 'Bill of Rights', *Loyalist News,* 28th Edn, Vol. 6 (2 August 1975).
19. Garland, *Gusty Spence,* 202–13.
20. Ibid., 227.
21. Dillon, *The Shankill Butchers,* 41–3. See also Garland, *Gusty Spence,* 200–2.
22. McKittrick and McVea, *Making Sense of the Troubles,* 329.
23. Ibid. See Dillon *The Shankill Butchers,* 114–ff.
24. Spence, 'Oration'.
25. Ibid.
26. Bruce, *The Edge of the Union,* 99.
27. Harry Donaghy, interview with author, BURC, Belfast, 22 June 2009.
28. Spence, 'Oration'.
29. Spence, 'Oration'. To illustrate how important this section of the speech was and still is, Dawn Purvis, in the final decommissioning statement for the RHC and UVF in 2009, used this exact quote to link political and progressive Loyalism of the past to the present. See 'Statement by the UVF (UVF) on Decommissioning', *CAIN Web Service,* 14 March 2011, cain.ulst.ac.uk/othelem/organ/uvf/uvf270609.htm (26 July 2011).

30. Spence, 'Oration'.
31. See previous chapter for more on this.
32. Spence, 'Oration'.
33. 'THE FUTILITY OF VIOLENCE', *Combat* (December 1975).
34. Ibid.
35. Garland, *Gusty Spence*, 213–14.
36. 'Think or Perish', *Combat* (July 1977). There is speculation that Billy Mitchell and Billy Hutchinson wrote this article. Garland, *Gusty Spence*, 217–18.
37. 'Think or Perish', *Combat* (July 1977). For the original speech see 'General Omar Bradley's Memorial Day Address', *Guideposts*, May 1948, www.guideposts.org/other/memorial-day-address (3 August 2011).
38. The authors used this quote without attribution and the author of this work has been unable to track its original source.
39. Hutchinson, 'Transcendental Art', 4.
40. Billy Hutchinson, interview with author, Mt Vernon Community Centre, North Belfast, 2 June 2009.
41. Ibid.
42. David Ervine, interview with author, PUP Headquarters, East Belfast, 27 June 2006.
43. Ibid.
44. Winston 'Winkie' Rea, interview with author, at home, Shankill Road, 9 July 2009.
45. In particular, he recited Sassoon's 'Suicide in the Trenches', a poem in which Sassoon bitterly criticises those who send young men to war.
46. Gusty Spence, 'Remembrance Day Oration', *Combat* (November 1977).
47. Dawn Purvis, interview with author, PUP Office, East Belfast, 10 July 2009.

## 7: SHARING RESPONSIBILITY, 1977–87

1. Tom Roberts, interview with author, EPIC Office, Shankill Road, 16 June 2009.
2. Independent Unionist Group, 'Devolution: The Plan for Ulster', *Combat*, Vol. 4, Issue 21 (1977).
3. Progressive Unionist Group, *Proposed Democratic Devolved Administration for Northern Ireland* (Belfast: Northern Ireland, 1979).
4. Progressive Unionist Party, *Sharing Responsibility* (Belfast: PUP, 1985).
5. These were the protection of the Protestant way of life, rejection of the 'fur coat brigade' and satisfying the aspirations of Irish nationalism.
6. Spencer, *State of Loyalism*, 73.
7. Sinnerton, *David Ervine*, 119.
8. Ibid., 116.
9. Garland, 'The Ulster Volunteer Force', 54.
10. These were discussions with two of those involved in developing *Sharing Responsibility*, June and October 2009. One was private and one was in an email.
11. Mitchell, 'Discussions with the Provisional I.R.A.' (1977).
12. Billy Hutchinson, interview with author, Mt Vernon Community Centre, North Belfast, 2 June 2009.
13. Hugh Smyth, interview with author, PUP Office, Shankill Road, 26 May 2009.

14. William 'Plum' Smith, interview with author, EPIC Office, Shankill Road, 10 June 2009.
15. Garland, *Gusty Spence*, 198.
16. Ibid.,198.
17. Garland, *Gusty Spence*, 198. Moloney, *Voices from the Grave*, 366–7.
18. Billy Hutchinson, interview with author, Mt Vernon Community Centre, North Belfast, 2 June 2009.
19. Spencer, *State of Loyalism*, 70.
20. Sinnerton, *David Ervine*, 118–99.
21. Independent Unionist Group, 'Devolution: The Plan for Ulster', Vol. 1, Issue 21 (1977).
22. Bew and Gillespie, *Chronology of the Troubles*, 121–3.
23. Sinnerton, *David Ervine*, 123.
24. Ibid., 123.
25. Dawn Purvis, interview with author, PUP Office, East Belfast, 10 July 2009.
26. McKittrick and McVea, *Making Sense of the Troubles*, 113. Moloney, *The Troubles*, 179. Aaron Edwards and Cillian McGrattan, *The Northern Ireland Conflict: A Beginners Guide* (Oxford: OneWorld Publishers, 2010), 36–7.
27. Independent Unionist Group, 'Devolution'.
28. Ibid.
29. Spence, 'Oration'.
30. Independent Unionist Group, 'Devolution'.
31. They did not lay out this process clearly until the 1985 version of 'Sharing Responsibility', but they had in 1977 and 1979 clearly laid out what the House or Assembly would look like. This did not differ between the two proposals. What differed was the clarity.
32. OFMDFM',Structure and Operation of Civic Forum', *OFMDFM*, 2005, www.ofmdfmni.gov.uk/index/making-government-work/civic-forum-review/ background/civic-forum-structure-operation.htm (25 July 2011).
33. Independent Unionist Group, 'Devolution'.
34. Ibid.
35. 'The d'Hondt voting system for European Parliament', *BBC*, 21 July 2004, http://www.h2g2.com/approved_entry/A2757873 (26 July 2011). This provides explanation of how the system works for elections.
36. Hugh Smyth, interview with author, PUP Office, Shankill Road, 26 May 2009.
37. Billy Hutchinson, interview with author, Mt Vernon Community Centre, North Belfast, 7 July 2009.
38. Hugh Smyth, interview with author, PUP Office, Shankill Road, 26 May 2009.
39. Hutchinson, *Hard Man Honourable Man*, 120.
40. 'PEACE FORUM?', *Combat*, Vol. 4, No. 19 (1977).
41. Ibid.
42. This is an interesting choice of words, because in 1979 the Progressive Unionist Group will use this title for its second version of *Sharing Responsibility*. This indicates a level of engagement between the UVF and the Loyalist politicians.
43. *Combat*, Vol. 4, No. 19 (1977). This is still a struggle for the UVF as it tries to demobilise 14 years after the Good Friday Agreement.
44. Ulster Volunteer Force, 'U.V.F. Peace Challenge to the Provos', *Combat*, Vol. 6, No. 27 (1979).
45. Ibid.
46. Ibid.

47. Hugh Smyth, follow-up interview, PUP Office, Shankill Road, 19 June 2009.
48. Hutchinson, *Hard Man Honourable Man*, 122.
49. Hugh Smyth, interview with author, PUP Office, Shankill Road, 26 May 2009.
50. Hutchinson, *Hard Man Honourable Man*, 119.
51. 'Northern Ireland Parliamentary Election Results', n. d., www.election.demon. co.uk/stormont/totals.html (10 August 2010).
52. Hutchinson, *Hard Man Honourable Man*, 119; Hugh Smyth, interview with author, PUP Office, Shankill Road, 26 May 2009.
53. 'Clause IV', The Citizen, n.d., www.thecitizen.org.uk/views/clause4.htm, 11 August 2010). The PUP still maintains this clause although 'New Labour' under Tony Blair jettisoned it.
54. Sinnerton, *David Ervine*, 119.
55. PUP, 'What is the Progressive Unionist Party?', n.d., www.pup-ni.org.uk/ home/whatisthepup.aspx (10 August 2010).
56. Aaron Edwards, 'Democratic Socialism and Sectarianism: The Northern Ireland Labour Party and Progressive Unionist Party Compared', *Politics*, 27, No. 1 (2007): 24–31.
57. Ibid.
58. Hutchinson, *Hard Man Honourable Man*, 160.
59. Hugh Smyth, follow-up interview with author, PUP Office, Shankill Road, 19 June 2009.
60. Hutchinson, *Hard Man Honourable Man*, 160.
61. Hugh Smyth, follow-up interview with author, PUP Office, Shankill Road, 19 June 2009.
62. Ibid.
63. Progressive Unionist Party, *Movement Towards a Devolved Democratic Administration for Northern Ireland: Presentation to the Secretary of State for Northern Ireland the Rt. Hon. James Prior, M.P.* (Belfast, 1981).
64. 'Constitutional Matters: The Way Ahead', *Combat* (1981).
65. Ibid.
66. Progressive Unionist Party, *Movement Towards a Devolved Democratic Administration for Northern Ireland*.
67. Hugh Smyth, interview with author, PUP Office, Shankill Road, 26 May 2009.
68. Garland, 'The Ulster Volunteer Force', 54.
69. Moloney, *Voices from the Grave*, 396–7.
70. Progressive Unionist Party, *Sharing Responsibility* (Belfast: PUP, 1985).
71. Ibid., 8.
72. Ibid., 1.
73. Ibid., 8.
74. Ibid., 1.
75. Ibid., 3–4.
76. Ibid., 4–5.
77. Ibid., 6.
78. Ibid., 2.
79. Ibid., 7.
80. In 1979 and 1987 the UDA published documents that envisioned some form of power sharing and a bill of rights. However, they tended to think in terms of a Ulster Independence. People like Glen Barr of the UDA also supported the idea of a 'voluntary coalition' in 1975.
81. Bew and Gillespie, *Chronology of the Troubles*, 189–90.

82. Ibid.
83. Ibid., 195.
84. McKittrick and McVea, *Making Sense of the Troubles*, 329.
85. Walker, *A History of the Ulster Unionist Party*, 236.
86. Ibid., 237.
87. Progressive Unionist Party, *War or Peace? Conflict or Conference?*, 2.
88. Ibid., 3.
89. Ibid., 7.
90. Progressive Unionist Party, *War or Peace? Conflict or Conference?*, 6.
91. Harold McCusker, Frank Millar Jr, and Peter Robinson, 'An End to Drift', *CAIN Web Service*, 16 June 1987, cain.ulst.ac.uk/events/aia/taskforcereport87.htm (25 May 2010).
92. The Archbishop of Armagh, Dr Robin Eames, The Moderator of the Presbyterian Church, Rev. Dr John Thompson, The New Ulster Political Research Group, The Charter Group, The Ulster Clubs, The Independent Orange Order, The Orange Order, The Royal Black Institution, The Campaign for Equal Citizenship, Mr Jim Smyth, Mr Roger Corry, Dr Clifford Smyth, The Progressive Unionist Party, The Ulster Young Unionist Council, The Chamber of Commerce and Industry, The Apprentice Boys of Derry, The Northern Consensus Group and The Confederation of British Industry participated in these discussions, as well as 'over 100 written submissions from concerned and interested individuals'.
93. Harold McCusker, Frank Millar Jr, and Peter Robinson, 'An End to Drift', *CAIN Web Service*, 16 June 1987, cain.ulst.ac.uk/events/aia/taskforcereport87.htm (25 May 2010).
94. Peter Robinson was deputy leader of the DUP and both Frank Millar Jr. and Harold McCusker were senior members of the Ulster Unionist Party.
95. Hugh Smyth, interview with author, PUP Office, Shankill Road, 26 May 2009.
96. Garland, *Gusty Spence*, 266.
97. Harold McCusker, Frank Millar Jr, and Peter Robinson, 'An End to Drift', *CAIN Web Service*, 16 June 1987, cain.ulst.ac.uk/events/aia/taskforcereport87.htm (25 May 2010).
98. Ibid.
99. Ibid.
100. Ibid.
101. Ibid.
102. Ibid.
103. Hugh Smyth, interview with author, PUP Office, Shankill Road, 26 May 2009.
104. Walker, *A History of the Unionist Party*, 239.
105. Sinnerton, *David Ervine*, 122.
106. Garland, *Gusty Spence*, 266–7.
107. Walker, *A History of the Ulster Unionist Party*, 240.
108. Hugh Smyth, interview with author, PUP Office, Shankill Road, 26 May 2009.
109. Ibid.
110. Sinnerton, *David Ervine*, 119.
111. Hugh Smyth, interview with author, PUP Office, Shankill Road, 26 May 2009.
112. Dawn Purvis, interview with author, PUP Office, East Belfast, 10 July 2009.
113. Garland, 'The Ulster Volunteer Force', 46.
114. Dawn Purvis, interview with author, PUP Office, East Belfast, 10 July 2009.
115. Moloney, *Voices from the Grave*, 397.

116. Sinnerton, *David Ervine*, 121.
117. Moloney, *Voices from the Grave*, 403–4.
118. Sinnerton, *David Ervine*, 121–2.
119. Tom Roberts, interview with author, EPIC Office, Shankill Road, 16 June 2009.
120. Liz Rea, interview with author, home, Shankill Road, 6 June 2009.
121. Tom Roberts, interview with author, EPIC Office, Shankill Road, 16 June 2009.
122. Spencer, *State of Loyalism*, 48.
123. William 'Plum' Smith, interview with author, EPIC Office, Shankill Road, 10 June 2009.
124. Spencer, *State of Loyalism*, 47.
125. Ibid., 46.
126. Garland, *Gusty Spence*, 153.
127. Ibid., 154.
128. Spencer, *State of Loyalism*, 48.
129. Tom Roberts, interview with author, EPIC Office, Shankill Road, 16 June 2009.
130. Ibid.
131. Jim McDonald, interview with Aaron Edwards, PUP Head Office, Shankill Road, 4th May 2005.
132. Hutchinson, *Hard Man Honourable Man*, 118.
133. Ibid.
134. Ibid.
135. Billy Hutchinson, interview with author, Mt Vernon Community Centre, North Belfast, 2 June 2009.
136. Ibid.

## CONCLUSION

1. Boulton, *UVF 1966–73*, 6.
2. Garland, 'The Ulster Volunteer Force', 76; quote from 'John', a member of the UVF who worked politically outside Long Kesh.
3. Ibid., 76.
4. This is the title used by Henry Sinnerton for his biography of David Ervine and is taken from a quote by Ervine.
5. Cusack and McDonald, *UVF*, 1.
6. Billy Hutchinson, follow-up interview, Mt Vernon Community Centre, North Belfast, 7 July 2009.
7. Taylor, *Provos*, 147.
8. Billy Hutchinson, interview with author, Mt Vernon Community Centre, 2 June 2009.
9. Tom Roberts, interview with author, EPIC Office, Shankill Road, 16 June 2009.
10. Ibid.
11. Ibid.
12. Garland, 'The Ulster Volunteer Force', 29.
13. Dawn Purvis, interview with author, PUP Office, East Belfast, 10 July 2009.
14. Sinn Féin, 'A Scenario for Peace', *CAIN Web Service*, 1 May 1987, cain.ulst. ac.uk/issues/politics/docs/sf/sf010587.htm (14 June, 2011).

15. Paul Dixon, 'A tragedy beyond words', in *Transforming the Peace Process in Northern Ireland: From Terrorism to Democratic Politics*, eds Aaron Edwards and Stephen Bloomer (Dublin: Irish Academic Press, 2008), 177.

16. See the work of by Crawford et al., as well as the documents in *Orange Cross, Combat* and *Loyalist News* referenced in this work.

17. Hugh Smyth, interview with author, PUP Office, Shankill Road, 26 May 2009.

18. Ibid.

19. Ibid.

20. James Downey, 'Sad to say, end of Paisley is no reason to chuckle', *Independent.ie*, 22 March 2008, www.independent.ie/opinion/analysis/sad-to-say-end-of-paisley-is-no-reason-to-chuckle-1324793.html (26 July 2011).

21. Harry Donaghy, interview with author, BURC, 22 June 2009.

22. Tom Roberts, interview with author, EPIC Office, Shankill Road, 16 June 2009.

23. Bobby Cosgrove, interview with author, PUP Office, East Belfast, 16 June 2009.

24. Ibid.

25. Tom Roberts, interview with author, EPIC Office, Shankill Road, 16 June 2009.

26. Ibid.

27. Billy Hutchinson, follow-up interview with author, Mt Vernon Community Centre, 7 July 2009.

28. McKee, 'The Real Voice of Ulster Loyalism?, (aa).

29. Harry Donaghy, interview with author, BURC, Belfast, 22 June 2009.

30. Dawn Purvis, interview with author, PUP Office, East Belfast, 10 July 2009.

31. Billy Hutchinson, interview with author, Mt Vernon Community Centre, North Belfast, 2 June 2009.

# Bibliography

## SECONDARY SOURCES

6th Connaught Rangers Research Project, *The 6th Connaught Rangers: Belfast Nationalists and the Great War* (Belfast: W & G Baird, 2011).

'A chronology of the conflict: 1969', *CAIN Web Service – Conflict and Politics in Northern Ireland*, last modified 14 March 2011, cain.ulst.ac.uk/othelem/chron/ch69.htm (accessed 13 August 2011).

Alonso, Rogelio, *The IRA and the Armed Struggle* (London: Routledge, 2007).

Anderson, Benedict, *Imagined Communities: Reflections on the Origin and Spread of Nationalism* (New York, NY: Verso, 1991).

Anderson, Don, *14 May Days: The Inside Story of the Loyalist Strike of 1974* (Dublin: Gill & Macmillan, 1994).

——, 'History lessons: Sir Kenneth Bloomfield long play interview', *BBC Radio Ulster*, last modified June 2007, www.bbc.co.uk/northernireland/radioulster/historylessons/features145043.shtml (accessed 23 May 2011).

Andrews, Christopher, *Defend the Realm: The Authorized History of MI5* (New York, NY: Alfred A. Knopf, 2009).

Bardon, Jonathan, *A History of Ulster* (Belfast: Blackstaff Press, 1992).

BBC News, 'Stevens Inquiry: At a glance: the key points from the publication of the Stevens Inquiry into collusion in Northern Ireland', *BBC*, last modified 17 April 2003, news.bbc.co.uk/2/hi/uk_news/northern_ireland/2956337.stm (accessed 24 May 2011).

——, 'The d'Hondt voting system for European Parliament', *BBC*, last modified 21 July 2004, www.h2g2.com/approved_entry/A2757873 (accessed 26 July 2011).

——, 'The IRA campaigns in England', *BBC*, last modified 4 March 2001, news.bbc.co.uk/2/hi/uk_news/1201738.stm (accessed 24 May 2011).

——, 'What is collusion?', *BBC*, last modified 22 January 2007, news.bbc.co.uk/2/hi/uk_news/northern_ireland/6287049.stm (accessed 24 May 2011).

——, 'Wilson had NI "doomsday" plan', *BBC*, last modified 11 September 2008, news.bbc.co.uk/2/hi/uk_news/politics/7610750.stm (accessed 2 August 2010).

Beattie, Geoffrey, *We Are the People: Journeys Through the Heart of Protestant Ulster* (London: Heinemann, 1992).

Beresford, David, *Ten Men Dead: The Story of the 1981 Irish Hunger Strike* (New York, NY: Atlantic Monthly Press, 1987).

Berghahn, Volker R., *Europe in the Era of the Two World Wars: From Militarism and Genocide to Civil Society 1900–1950* (Princeton, NJ: Princeton University Press, 2006).

Bew, Paul, and Gordon Gillespie, *Northern Ireland: A Chronology of the Troubles, 1968–1999* (Dublin: Gill and Macmillan, 1999).

Bew, Paul, Peter Gibbon and Henry Patterson, *Northern Ireland 1921–1994: Political Forces and Social Classes* (London: Serif, 1995).

Black, John, *Killing for Britain* (Edinburgh: Frontline Noir Publishing, 2008).

Bleakley, David, *Peace in Ireland: Two States One People* (London: Mowbray, 1995).

Boulton, David, *UVF 1966–73: An Anatomy of a Loyalist Rebellion* (Dublin: Torc Books, 1973).

Bowyer Bell, J., *The IRA: 1968–2000: Analysis of a Secret Army* (London: Frank Cass Publishers, 2000).

——, *The Secret Army: The IRA* (New Brunswick, NJ: Transaction Publishers, 1997).

Bruce, Steve, *God Save Ulster: The Religion and Politics of Paisleyism* (Oxford: Oxford University Press, 1986).

——, 'Loyalists in Northern Ireland: further thoughts on "pro-state terror"', *Terrorism and Political Violence*, Vol. 5, No. 4 (1993): 252–65.

——, *Paisley: Religion and Politics in Northern Ireland* (Oxford: Oxford University Press, 2009).

——, 'Paramilitaries, peace, and politics', *Studies in Conflict and Terrorism*, Vol. 18, No. 3 (1995): 187–202.

——, 'Terrorists and politics: the case of Northern Ireland's Loyalist paramilitaries', *Terrorism and Political Violence*, Vol. 13, No. 2 (2001): 27–48.

——, *The Edge of the Union: The Ulster Loyalist Political Vision* (Oxford: Oxford University Press, 1994).

——, *The Red Hand: Protestant Paramilitaries in Northern Ireland* (New York, NY: Oxford University Press, 1992).

Burbridge, Nick and Fred Holroyd, *War Without Honour: True Story of Military Intelligence in Northern Ireland* (Hull: Medium Publishing Co., 1989).

Clarke, Liam, *Maze Tale: The Killing of King Rat and The True Story of the Maze Prison*, last modified 30 December 2006, irelandsown.net/RatStory.html (accessed 9 May 2011).

'Colin Wallace – Biography', *Biographicon*, n.d., www.biographicon.com/view/h13we/Colin_Wallace (accessed 19 August 2011).

Collins, Peter, ed., *Nationalism and Unionism: 1885–1921* (Belfast: Institute of Irish Studies, 1994).

Coogan, Tim Pat, *The Troubles: Ireland's Ordeal 1966–1996 and the Search for Peace* (Boulder, CO: Roberts Rinehart Publishers, 1997).

——, *The Troubles: Ireland's Ordeal aand the Search for Peace* (London: Palgrave and Macmillan, 2002).

Cottrell, Roger, 'Parallel development: the Workers Party and the Progressive Unionist Party in Northern Ireland', *Lobster: Politics, Parapolitics, History*, last modified 1 December 2005, www.lobster-magazine.co.uk/IRA.html (accessed 11 May 2011).

Crawford, Colin, *Defenders or Criminals: Loyalist Prisoners and Criminalisation* (Belfast: Blackstaff Press, 1999).

——, *Inside the UDA: Volunteers and Violence* (London: Pluto Press, 2003).

——, *Long Kesh: An Alternative Perspective* (M.Sc. Thesis, Bedfordshire: Cranfield Institute of Technology, 1979).

Cusack, Jim, and Henry McDonald, *UDA: Inside the Heart of Loyalist Terror* (Dublin: Penquin Books, 2005).

——, *UVF* (Dublin: Poolbeg Press, 1997).

——, *UVF: The Endgame*, Dublin: Poolbeg, 2008.

Daniel, T. K., 'Myths and militants: a new look at the Ulster Loyalist', *Political Studies*, Vol. 2, Issue 4, No. 4 (1975): 455–61.

Darby, John, Nicholas Dodge and, A. C. Hepburn, eds, *Political Violence: Ireland in a Comparative Perspective* (Ottawa: Ottowa University Press, 1990).

Devlin, Paddy, *Yes, We Have No Bananas: Outdoor Relief in Belfast: 1920–1939* (Belfast: Blackstaff Press, 1981).

Dillon, Martin, *God and the Gun: The Church and Irish Terrorism* (New York, NY: Orion Books, Ltd., 1998).

——, *The Dirty War* (London: Arrow Books, 1991).

——, *The Shankill Butchers: A Case Study in Mass Murder* (London: Arrow Press, 1990).

Dillon, Martin, and Denis Lehane, *Political Murder in Northern Ireland* (Hammondsworth: Penquin, 1973).

Dixon, Paul, 'A tragedy beyond words', in *Transforming the Peace Process in Northern Ireland: From Terrorism to Democratic Politics*, eds Aaron Edwards and Stephen Bloomer (Dublin: Irish Academic Press, 2008), 175–94.

——, *Northern Ireland: The Politics of War and Peace* (Basingstoke: Palgrave, 2001).

Dorril, Stephen, and Robin Ramsay, *Smear!: Wilson and the Secret State* (London: Fourth Estate Limited, 1991).

Downey, James, 'Sad to say, end of Paisley is no reaston to chuckle', *Independent.ie*, last modified 22 March 2008, www.independent.ie/opinion/analysis/sad-to-say-end-of-paisley-is-no-reason-to-chuckle-1324793.html (accessed 26 July 2011).

Edwards, Aaron, *A Case for Class Politics?: The Origins, History, and Development of Political Thought Within the Progressive Unionist Party of Northern Ireland* (B.A. Thesis. Coleraine: Coleraine University, 2001).

——, *A History of the Northern Ireland Labour Party: Democratic Socialism and Sectarianism* (Manchester: Manchester University Press, 2009).

——, 'Abandoning armed resistance? The Ulster Volunteer Force as a case study of strategic terrorism in Northern Ireland', *Studies in Conflict & Terrorism*, Vol. 32, No. 2 (2009): 146–66.

——, 'Democratic socialism and sectarianism: the Northern Ireland Labour Party and the Progressive Unionist Party compared', *Politics*, Vol. 27, No. 1 (2007): 24–31.

——, 'Democratising the mindsets: progressive Loyalism and conflict transformation', *The Other View*, Autumn/Winter (2005): 16–17.

——, *Signposts to the New Ulster?: Unionist Government Administration, the Labour Opposition, and the Protestant Working Class in Northern Ireland, 1965–1972* (M.A. Thesis, Belfast: Queen's University Belfast, 2002).

——, 'The Northern Ireland Labour Party and Loyalist paramilitary politics in the 1970s' (paper presented at the Political Science Association of Ireland Conference, Cork, 20–22 October 2006).

Edwards, Aaron, and Stephen Bloomer, *Conflict Transformation Papers: Volume 8: A Watching Brief? The Political Strategey of Progresive Loyalism Since 1994* (Belfast: Linc Resouces Centre, 2004).

——, eds, *Transforming the Peace Process in Northern Ireland: From Terrorism to Democratic Politics* (Dublin: Irish Academic Press, 2008).

——, eds, *Democratising the Peace Process: Progressive Loyalism and the Transformation of the Peace Process* (Belfast: Linc Resource Centre, 2005).

Edwards, Aaron, and McGrattan, Cillian, *The Northern Ireland Conflict* (Oxford: OneWorld Publishers, 2010).

Edwards, Ruth Dudley, *The Faithful Tribe: An Intimate Portrait of the Loyal Institutions* (London: Harper Collins Publishers, 1999).

Ellis, P. Berresford, *A History of the Irish Working Class* (London: Victor Gollancz, Ltd., 1972).

——, 'The Floodlights Have Shifted', *The Other View*, Autumn/Winter (2005): 4–5.

Farrell, Michael, *Arming the Protestants: The Formation of the Ulster Special Constabulary, 1920–27* (London: Pluto, 1983).

——, *Northern Ireland: The Orange State* (London: Pluto, 1980).

Farrington, Christopher, *Ulster Unionism and the Northern Ireland Peace Process* (Basingstoke: Palgrave, 2006).

Fearon, Kate, *The Conflict's Fifth Business: A Brief Biography of Billy Mitchell* (Belfast: Linc Resource Centre, 2002).

Féin, Sinn, and Northern Republican Clubs, *Britain's White Paper: Republican Statement and Demands for all Ireland* (Dublin, 1973).

Flackes, W. D., and Elliott Sydney, *Northern Ireland: A Political Directory, 1968–1993* (Belfast: Blackstaff Press, 1994).

Foot, Paul, *Who Framed Colin Wallace?* (London: Macmillan, 1989).

Gaffifkin, Frank, and Mike Morrissey, *Northern Ireland: The Thatcher Years* (London: Zed Books Ltd., 1990).

Gallaher, Carolyn, *After the Peace: Loyalist Paramilitaries in Post-Accord Northern Ireland* (Ithaca, NY: Cornell University Press, 2007).

Garland, Roy, *Gusty Spence* (Belfast: Blackstaff Press, 2001).

——, *The Ulster Volunteer Force: Negotiating History* (M.S.Sc thesis in Irish Studies, Belfast: Queens University Belfast, 1991).

Geraghty, Tony, *The Irish War: The Hidden Conflict Between the IRA and British Intelligence* (Baltimore, MD: Johns Hopkins University Press, 2000).

Gillespie, Gordon, *Years of Darkness: The Troubles Remembered* (Dublin: Gill and Macmillan, 2008).

Gilmore, George, preface to *The Irish Republican Congress*, by George Gilmore (Cork: An Eochair Clondara Historical & Cultural Group and LINC Resource Centre, 2006).

Goldring, Maurice, *Belfast: From Loyalty to Rebellion* (London: Lawrence and Wishart, 1991).

Grayson, Richard, *Belfast Boys: How Unionists and Nationalists Fought and Died in Together in the First World War* (London: Continuum Press, 2009).

Green, Marion, *The Prison Experience – A Loyalist Perspective* (Belfast: EPIC Print, 1998).

Hall, Michael, *Ulster's Protestant Working Class: A Community Exploration* (Belfast: Island Pamphlets, 1994).

——, ed., *Sacrifice on the Somme: Ulster's 'Cross-community' Sacrifice in the First World War* (Newtonabbey: Island Publications, 1993).

——, ed., *Ulster's Protestant Working Class: A Community Exploration* (Newtonabbey: Island Publications, 1994).

——, ed., *A New Beginning: Shankill Think Tank* (Newtonabbey: Island Publications, 1995).

Hanley, Brian, and Scott Millar, *The Lost Revolution: The Story of the Official IRA and the Workers Party* (Dublin: Penquin, 2009).

Harris, Lyndsey, 'The Power of Perception – Duck or Rabbit?: The Strategic Tradition of Loyalist Paramilitaries in Northern Ireland' (paper presented at the 45th Annual Biennial International Conference of the Inter-University Seminar on Armed Forces and Society, Chicago, IL, 21–23 October 2005.

Hayden, Tom, *Trial* (New York, NY: Holt, Rinehart and Winston, 1970).

Hayes, Mark, *Loyalism and the Protestant Working Class: Beyond Ethnicity* (Southampton: Southampton Institute, 1996).

'"PROTESTANTISM BEFORE PARTY!": THE ULSTER PROTESTANT LEAGUE IN THE 1930s', *The Historical Journal*, Vol. 28, No. 4 (1985): 961–7.

Hobsbawm, E. J., *Nations and Nationalism Since 1870: Programme, Myth, Reality* (Cambridge: Cambridge Universtiy Press, 1994).

Howe, Stephen, 'Mad dogs and Ulstermen: The crisis of Loyalism (part one)', *Open Democracy,* last modified 27 September 2005, www.opendemocracy.net/ globalization-protest/Loyalism_2876.jsp (accessed 19 July 2010).

Hume, David, *The Ulster Unionist Party: 1972–92* (Lurgan: Ulster Society, 1996).

Jordan, Hugh, *Milestones in Murder: Defining Moments in Ulster's Terror War* (London: Mainstream Publishing, 2002).

Jordan, Hugh, and David Lister, *Mad Dog: The Rise and Fall of Johnny Adair and 'C' Company* (Edinburgh: Mainstream Publishing, 2004).

Longford, Lord, and Anne McHardy, *Ulster* (London: Weidenfeld and Nicolson, 1981).

Lynch, Robert, 'The People's Protectors? The Irish Republican Army and the Belfast Pogrom, 1920–1922', *Journal of British Studies*, Vol. 47, No. 2 (2008): 375–91.

Lynn, Brendan, *Introduction to the Electoral System in Northern Ireland*, last modified 14 March 2011, cain.ulst.ac.uk/issues/politics/election/electoralsystem.htm (accessed 30 May 2011).

MacGiolla, Tomas, 'Where We Stand: The Republican Position' (speech at Republican Clubs Conference, Carrickmore: OIRA, July 1972).

MacIntyre, Brian, 'David Ervine: Both Sides Need to Give Up Violence', *Salt Lake Tribune* (Salt Lake City, UT: Media News Group, 27 July 1997).

Mallie, Eamonn, and David McKittrick, *Endgame in Ireland* (London: Holder and Stoughton, 2001).

McAuley, James, *Bury Me Under the Red Hand: Loyalist Paramilitary Group Politics in Contemporary Belfast* (Occasional Paper No. 8, Staffordshire: North Staffordshire Polytechnic Department of Sociology, September 1988).

——, *The Politics of Identity: A Loyalist Community in Belfast* (Aldershot: Avebury, 1994).

——, *Ulster's Last Stand?: (Re) Constructing Ulster Unionism after the Peace Process* (Dublin: Irish Academic Press, 2010).

McAuley, James, and Scott Hislop, 'Many roads forward: Politics and ideology within the Progressive Unionist Party', *Etudes Irlandes* (2000): 172–88.

McBride, Ian, *The Siege of Derry in Ulster Protestant Mythology* (Dublin: Four Courts Press, 1997).

McCann, Eamonn, *War and an Irish Town* (London: Pluto Press, 1993).

McClenaghan, Pauline, *Spirit of '68: Beyond the Barricades* (Derry: Guildhall Press, 2009).

McCormick, Jonathan, *A Directory of Murals – Album 31*, last modified 14 March 2011, cain.ulst.ac.uk/mccormick/album31.htm (accessed 24 May 2011).

McDermott, Jim, *Northern Divisions: The Old IRA and the Belfast Pogroms, 1920–22* (Belfast: Beyond Pale Publications, 2001).

McDonald, Henry, *Gunsmoke and Mirrors: How Sinn Féin Dressed Up Defeat as Victory* (Dublin: Gill & Macmillan Ltd., 2008).

McDonald, Henry, and Jim Cusack, *UVF: The Endgame* (Dublin: Poolbeg, 2008).

McEvoy, Sandra, 'Loyalist women paramilitaries in Northern Ireland: Beginning a feminist conversation about conflict resolution', *Security Studies*, Vol. 18, No. 2 (2009): 262–86.

McGuffin, John, *The Guineapigs* (Middlesex: Penguin Books Ltd., 1974).

McKay, Susan, *Bear in Mind These Dead* (London: Faber and Faber, 2008).
——, *Northern Protestants: An Unsettled People* (Belfast: Blackstaff Press, 2000).
McKearney, Tommy, *The Provisional IRA: From Insurrection to Parliament* (London: Pluto Press, 2011).
McKee, Sean, *The Real Voice of Ulster Loyalism?* (B.A. [Hon] Dissertation, Belfast: University of Ulster Jordanstown, 1995).
McKittrick, David, and David McVea, *Making Sense of the Troubles: A History of the Northern Ireland Conflict* (Chicago, IL: New Amsterdam Press, 2002).
McKittrick, David, Seamus Kelters, Chris Thornton and David McVea, *Lost Lives: The Stories of the Men, Women and Children who Died as a Result of the Northern Ireland Troubles* (Edinburgh: Mainstream Publishing, 2004).
McMahon, Sean, *A Short History of Ireland* (Bessbrook: Mercier Press, 1996).
McMichael, Gary, *Ulster Voice: In Search of Common Ground in Northern Ireland* (Boulder, CO: Roberts Rinehart Publishers, 1999).
McMillen, Liam, *Annual Bodenstown Speech* (speech, Belfast: OIRA, 1973).
Millar, Frank, *Northern Ireland: A Triumph of Politics* (Dublin: Irish Academic Press, 2009).
Miller, David W., *Queen's Rebel* (Dublin: University College Dublin Press, 1978).
Moloney, Ed, *Paisley: From Demagouge to Democrat?* (Dublin: Poolbeg, 2008).
——, *The Secret History of the IRA* (New York: W.W. Norton & Co., 2003).
——, *Voices from the Grave: Two Men's War in Ireland* (London: Faber and Faber Ltd., 2010).
Moloney, Ed, and Andy Pollak, *Paisley* (Dublin: Poolbeg, 1986).
Moore, Chris, *The Kincora Scandal: Political Cover-up and Intrigue in Northern Ireland* (Cork: Mercier Press, 1996).
Morgan, Austen, *Labour and Partition: The Belfast Working Class 1905–23* (London: Pluto Press, 1991).
Munck, Ronnie, and Bill Rolston, *Belfast in the Thirties: An Oral History* (Belfast: Blackstaff Press Ltd., 1997).
Murtagh, Brendan, *The Politics of Territory: Policy and Segregation in Northern Ireland* (Basingstoke: Palgrave, 2002).
Nelson, Sarah, 'Developments in Protestant working class politics', *Social Studies*, Vol. 5, 3 & 4, February Winter (1976–77): 202–24.
——, 'The Ulster Independence Debate: Background and Present Arguments' (paper presented to the Institute of Irish Studies, Queen's University, Belfast, January 1977).
——, *Ulster's Uncertain Defenders: Protestant Political, Paramilitary, and Community Groups, and the Northern Ireland conflict* (Belfast: Appletree Press Ltd, 1984).
O'Leary, Brendan, and McGarry, John, *The Politics of Antagonism: Understanding Northern Ireland* (London: Athlone Press, 1994).
O'Malley, Padraig, *Biting at the Grave: The Irish Hunger Strikes and the Politics of Despair* (Boston, MA: Beacon Press, 1990).
——, *The Uncivil Wars: Ireland Today* (Boston: Houghton Mifflin Company, 1983).
O'Neill, Brendan, 'How the Peace Process divided Ireland', *The Blanket: A Journal of Protest and Dissent*, last modified 25 July 2002, indiamond6.ulib.iupui.edu:81/peaceprocessdivide.html (accessed 31 May 2011).
O'Rawe, Richard, *Afterlives: The Hunger Strike and the Secret Offer that Changed Irish History* (Dublin: Lilliput, 2010).
——, *BLANKETMEN: An untold story of the H-Block Hunger Strike* (Dublin: New Island, 2005).

O'Ruairc, Liam, *The League of Communist Republicans: 1986–1991*, available at www.scribd.com/doc/58615490/League-of-Communist-Republicans, uploaded 24 April 2011 (accessed 3 September 2012) (2001).

Parkinson, Alan F., *Belfast's Unholy War: The Troubles of the 1920s* (Dublin: Four Courts Press, 2004).

Patterson, Henry, and Eric Kaufmann, *Unionism and Orangeism in Northern Ireland Since 1945: The Decline of the Loyal Family* (Manchester: Manchester University Press, 2007).

Pattterson, Henry, *The Politics of Illusion: A Political History of the IRA* (London: Serif, 1997).

Pincher, Chapman, *The SpycatcherAffair* (New York, NY: St. Martin's Press, 1988).

Porter, Norman, *Rethinking Unionism: An Alternative Vision for Northern Ireland* (Belfast: Blackstaff Press, 1996).

Powell, Jonathan, *Great Hatred, Little Room: Making Peace in Northern Ireland* (London: Bodley Head, 2009).

Pringle, D. G., 'Electoral systems and political manipulation: A case study of Northern Ireland in the 1920s', *Economic and Social Review*, Vol. 11, No. 3 (1980): 187–205.

Probert, Belinda, *Beyond Orange and Green: The Northern Ireland Crisis in a New Perspective* (London: The Academy Press, 1978).

Ramsay, Robert, and Dorril, Stephen, *Smear! Wilson and the Secret State* (London: Fourth Estate, 1991).

Reed, Richard, 'Blood, thunder and rosettes: The multiple personalities of paramilitary Loyalism between 1971 and 1988', *Irish Political Studies*, Vol. 26, No. 1 (2011): 45–71.

Rees, Merlyn, *Northern Ireland: A Personal Perspective* (London: Meuthen, 1985).

Rolston, Bill, *Children of the Revolution: The Lives of Sons and Daughters of Activists in Northern Ireland* (Derry: Guildhall Press, 2011).

Rowan, Brian, *Behind the Lines: The Story of the IRA and Loyalist Ceasefires* (Belfast: Blackstaff Press, 1995).

——, *How the Peace was Won* (Edinburgh: Mainstream Publishing, 2008).

——, '"New evidence" may clear Gusty Spence of 1966 gun killing', *Belfast Telegraph*, last modified 24 January 2011, www.belfasttelegraph.co.uk/news/local-national/northern-ireland/lsquonew-informationrsquo-may-clear-gusty-spence-of-1966-gun-killing-15062647.html (accessed 24 January 2011).

——, *The Armed Peace: Life and Death after the Ceasefires* (Edinburgh: Mainstream Publishing, 2003).

Scott, Kirsty, 'Men of letters, men of arms', *Guardian Online*, 2 December 2000, www.guardian.co.uk/books/2000/dec/02/society.politics (accessed 24 May 2011).

Shankill Think Tank, *At the Crossroads* (Newtonabbey: Island Publications, 1998).

Shirlow, Peter, and Kieran McEvoy, *Beyond the Wire: Former Prisoners and Conflict Transformation in Northern Ireland* (London: Pluto Press, 2008).

Shirlow, Peter, and Mark McGovern, *Who are 'THE PEOPLE'? Unionism, Protestantism and Loyalism in Northern Ireland* (London: Pluto Press, 1997).

Shirlow, Peter, Jon Tonge, James McAuley, and Catherine McGlyn, *Abandoning Historical Conflict? Former Political Prisoners and Reconciliation in Northern Ireland* (Manchester: Manchester University Press, 2010).

Sinnerton, Henry, *David Ervine: Uncharted Waters* (Dingle: Brandon, 2002).

Sluka, Jeffrey, 'For God and Ulster: The culture of terror and Loyalist death squads in Norhern Ireland'. In *Death Squad: The Anthropology of State Terror* by Jeffrey Sluka, ed., (Philadelphia, PA: University of Pennsylvania Press, 2000), 127–57.

Smyth, Marie, and Marie-Therese Fay, eds., *Personal Accounts from Northern Ireland's Troubles* (London: Pluto Press, 2000).

Spencer, Graham, 'Constructing Loyalism', *Contemporary Politics*, Vol. 10, No. 1 (2004): 37–55.

——, 'Containing dialogue: The British Government and early talks in the Northern Ireland Peace Process', *The British Journal of Politics and International Relations*, Vol. 10, Issue 3 (2008): 452–71.

——, 'Sinn Féin and the Media in Northern Ireland: The New Terrain of Policy Articulation', *Irish Political Studies* (2006): 355–82.

——, *The State of Loyalism in Northern Ireland* (Basingstoke: Palgrave and Macmillan, 2008).

Stewart, A. T. Q., *Edward Carson* (Dublin: Gill and Macmillan, 1981).

——, *The Narrow Ground: Aspects of Ulster: 1609–1969* (Belfast: Blackstaff Press, 1977).

Stone, Michael, *None Shall Divide Us* (London: Blake Publishing, 2004).

'Sutton Index of Deaths', *CAIN: Web Service,* last modified 14 March 2011, cain.ulst.ac.uk/sutton/chron/1972.html (accessed 14 August 2010).

Taylor, Peter, *Brits: The War Against the IRA* (London: Bloomsbury Press, 2002).

——, *Loyalists*, online video, directed by Peter Taylor, produced by Peter Taylor and Sam Collyns (1999).

——, *Loyalists: War and Peace in Northern Ireland* (New York, NY: TV Books, L.L.C., 1999).

——, *Provos: The IRA and Sinn Féin*, online video, directed by Peter Taylor, produced by BBC, Andrew Williams and Peter Taylor (1997).

——, *Provos: The IRA and Sinn Féin* (London: Bloomsbury, 1997).

Todd, Jennifer, 'Two Traditions in Unionist Political Culture', *Irish Political Studies*, Vol. 2 (1987): 1–26.

Tonge, Jonathan, *Northern Ireland* (Malden: Polity Press, 2006).

Toolis, Kevin, *Rebel Hearts: A Journey within the IRA's Soul* (New York, NY: St. Martin's Press, 1996).

Walker, Graham, *A History of the Ulster Unionist Party: Protest, Pragmatism and Pessimism* (Manchester: Manchester University Press, 2004).

Weiner, Ron, *The Rape and Plunder of the Shankill Community Action: The Belfast Experience* (Belfast: Nothems Press, 1976).

'Westminster General Election: 10 October 1974', *ElectionsIreland.org*, 26 July 2011, www.electionsireland.org/result.cfm?election=1974octUK&cons=714 (accessed 26 July 2011).

Wheeler, Brian, 'Wilson "plot": The secret tapes', *BBC*, 9 March 2006, news.bbc.co.uk/2/hi/uk_news/politics/4789060.stm (accessed 19 August 2010).

Wilson, Tom, *Ulster: Conflict and Consent* (Oxford: Wiley-Blackwell Press, 1989).

Wood, Ian S., *Crimes of Loyalty: A History of the UDA* (Edinburgh: Edinburgh University Press, 2006).

——, *Gods, Guns and Ulster: A History of Loyalist Paramilitaries* (London: Caxton, 2003).

## PRIMARY SOURCES

### Archival

*Civil Authorities (Special Powers) Act (Northern Ireland)*, 14 March 2011, cain. ulst.ac.uk/hmso/spa1922.htm (accessed 30 May 2011).

Gardiner, Lord, 'Report of a Committee to consider, in the context of civil liberties and human rights, measures to deal with terrorism in Northern Ireland', *CAIN Web Service*, January 1975, cain.ulst.ac.uk/hmso/gardiner.htm (accessed July 23, 2011).

Gibson, Robert, and Vivian Simpson, 'Approach to Secretary of State for NI, RE: Continuing discussions at Crumlin Road Prison with Political Prisoners', D3233/2/1/1,8.Belfast: PRONI, May 1972.

Government of Northern Ireland, 'Violence and Civil Disturbances in Northern Ireland in 1969 Report of Tribunal of Inquiry Chairman: The Hon. Mr Justice Scarman Presented to Parliament by Command of His Excellency the Governor of Northern Ireland April, 1972', *CAIN*, n.d., CAIN Web Service, cain.ulst.ac.uk/ hmso/scarman.htm#3 (accessed 14 December 2011).

n.a., 'Background Paper B: Paramilitary Organisations in Northern Ireland,', paper presented to the Working Party on Law and Order in Northern Ireland (PRONI Public Records CENT/1/5/5; Belfast: PRONI, 1976).

Secretary of State for Northern Ireland, 'Northern Ireland Constitutional Proposals', *CAIN*, 14 March 2011, CAIN Web Service, cain.ulst.ac.uk/hmso/cmd5259.htm (accessed 26 July 2011).

### Books

Hutchinson, Billy, *Hard Man Honourable Man: My Loyalist Life*, unpublished manuscript, 2009.

### Interviews

Catney, Tony, interview by Tony Novosel. Suffolk (1 June 2009).

Cosgrove, Robert, interview by Tony Novosel. PUP Office, East Belfast (16 June 2009).

David Ervine, Monica McWilliams, Phillip McGuigan, interview by University of Pittsburgh Students. Pittsburgh, PA, and Belfast (9 October 2004).

Donaghy, Harry, interview by Tony Novosel. BURC, Belfast (6 June 2009).

Ervine, David, interview by Tony Novosel. City Hall, Belfast (23 June 2005).

Ervine, David, interview by Tony Novosel. PUP Headquartes, East Belfast (27 June 2006).

Hutchinson, Billy, interview by An Phoblacht/Republican News. *Billy Hutchinson – A Loyalist Perspective*, Belfast (2 February 1995).

Hutchinson, Billy, interview by Tony Novosel (2 June 2009).

Hutchinson, Billy, followup interview by Tony Novosel (7 July 2009).

McDonald, Jim, interview by Aaron Edwards (4 May 2005).

Mitchell, Billy, interview by Aaron Edwards (27 September 2005).

Purvis, Dawn, interview by Tony Novosel (10 July 2009).

Rea, Elizabeth, interview by Tony Novosel (6 June 2009).

Rea, Winston Churchill, interview by Tony Novosel (7 July 2009).

Roberts, Tom, interview by Tony Novosel (16 June 2009).

Sandford, Tommy, interview by Tony Novosel (5 June 2009).

Smith, Willam 'Plum', interview by Tony Novosel (10 July 2009).
Smyth, Hugh, interview by Tony Novosel (26 May 2009).
Smyth, Hugh, follow up interview by Tony Novosel (19 June 2009).

## Loyalist Journals (UVF and RHC)

*Combat* (Microfiche), 1974–85.
*Loyalist News* (RHC) (Microfiche), 1970–75.
*Orange Cross* (Microfiche), 1970–75.

## Newspapers and Periodicals (online and print)

*Belfast Telegraph*
*The Blanket: A Journal of Dissent*
*The Daily Mail*
*The Daily Post*
*The Daily Telegraph*
*Fortnight*
*Guardian*
*Independent UK*
*IndyMedia*
*Irish News*
*Irish Times*
*Irish Voice*
*The Newsletter*
*New York Times*
*Salt Lake Tribune*
*Sunday News*
*Times of London*
*The United Irishmen*
*Workers' Life*

## Pamphlets, Papers, Proposals and Speeches

Bleakley David (Northern Ireland Labour Party), 'The Evolution of an agreed constitution for Northern Ireland' (Belfast, 1975).
Ervine, David, 'Briefing paper from the Progressive Unionist Party' (Belfast, 1995).
——, *Redefining Loyalism: A Political Perspective* (Dublin: Institute for British-Irish Studies, University College Dublin, 2001).
Féin, Sinn, and Northern Republican Clubs, *Britain's White Paper: Republican Statement and Demands for all Ireland* (Dublin, 1973).
Hutchinson, Billy, *Untitled*, speech (Belfast: St. Columb's Park House, 1995).
——, 'Transcendental art', unpublished paper (Belfast, 2010).
MacGiolla, Tomas, 'Where We Stand: The Republican Position' (speech at Republican Clubs Conference, Carrickmore: OIRA, July 1972).
McCusker, Harold, Frank Millar, Jr, and Peter Robinson, 'An End to Drift', *CAIN Web Services*, last modified 14 March 2011, cain.ulst.ac.uk/events/aia/taskforcereport87.htm (accessed 26 July 2011).
Mitchell, Billy, 'Principles of Loyalism', *Progressive Unionist Party*, last modified 2002. progressiveunionistparty.org/articles/principles-of-Loyalism/ (accessed 20 May 2011).
——, 'Discussions with Provisional I.R.A.' (1977).

New Ulster Political Research Group, *Beyond the Religious Divide* (report, Belfast, 1979).

——, *The People and the State: A Proposed Constitution and Political Structures* (Belfast, 1979).

Northern Ireland Labour Party, 'Supplementary N.I.L.P. Paper on Power Sharing' (Belfast, 1972).

Progressive Unionist Group, 'Proposed Democratic Devolved Administration for Northern Ireland', No. 2 (Belfast: PUP, May 1979).

Progressive Unionist Party, 'Movement Towards a Devolved Democratic Administration for Northern Ireland: Presentation to the Secretary of State for Northern Ireland the Rt. Hon. James Prior, M.P.' (Belfast: PUP, 1981).

——, 'Policy Document' (Belfast: PUP, 1987).

——, 'Sharing Responsibility' (Belfast: PUP, 1985).

——, 'Submission to the Northern Ireland Office on Policing and Related Matters' (Belfast: Stormont, 1995).

——, *War or Peace? Conflict or Conference? Policy Document of the Progressive Unionist Party* (Political Proposal, Belfast: PUP, 1986).

——, *What is the Progressive Unionist Party?*, n.d., www.pup-ni.org.uk/home/whatisthepup.aspx (accessed 10 August 2010).

Red Hand Commando, *Within the Context of Northern Ireland* (Belfast: Red Hand Commando, 1974).

Sinn Féin – Official, *Fianna Fail: The I.R.A. Connection* (Dublin: n.p., 1971).

Sinn Féin, 'Annual Bodenstown Speech 1992 Address by Jim Gibney June 1992', 18 June 1992, www.sinnfein.ie/files/Speech_Bodenstown92.pdf (accessed 7 May 2011).

——, 'Éire Nua, The Sinn Féin Policy – The Social, Economic and Political Dimensions (1979)', *CAIN Web Service*, last modified 14 March 2011, cain.ulst.ac.uk/issues/politics/docs/sf/sinnfein79.htm (accessed 8 May 2011).

Spence, Gusty, 'Speech to the PUP Conference' (speech, Belfast, 11 February 1995).

——, 'Remembrance Day Speech' (speech, Lisburn, 1975).

——, 'Remembrance Day Speech' (speech, Lisburn, 1977).

——, 'The Spence Oration' (speech, Lisburn, 12 July 1977).

Tara, 'Tara Proclamantion', *CAIN Web Service*, last modified 14 March 2011, cain.ulst.ac.uk/othelem/organ/docs/tara73.htm (accessed 19 August 2010).

Ulster Political Research Group, *Common Sense* (Belfast, 1987).

UVF, 'Statement by the Ulster Volunteer Force (UVF), (27 June2009', *CAIN Web Services*, last modified 14 March 2011, cain.ulst.ac.uk/othelem/organ/uvf/uvf270609.htm (accessed 26 July, 2011).

——, 'U.V.F. Military Policy' (Belfast: UVF, November 1974).

'Ulster Workers' Council Strike', *CAIN Web Service*, last modified 14 March 2011, cain.ulst.ac.uk/uwc/chr.htm (accessed August 12, 2010).

'Ulster Workers' Council Strike-Details of Source Materials', *CAIN Web Service*, last modified 14 March 2011, cain.ulst.ac.uk/events/uwc/soc.htm (accessed 12 August 2010).

Ulster Workers Council, 'The Ulster General Strike: Strike bulletins of the Workers Association' (Belfast, 1974).

Volunteer Political Party, *Manifesto of the Volunteer Political Party* (Political Programme, Belfast: Volunteer Political Pary, 1974).

## Primary Documents (various)

Alliance Party, 'Integrated Education Alliance Party Policy Document', *Alliance Party*, 2006, www.allianceparty.org/pages/policy-integratededucation.html (accessed 5 August 2010).

Biographicon, 'Colin Wallace – Biography', Letter from Colin Wallace to Tony Stoughton, the Chief Information Officer of the British Army Information Service at Lisburn, last modified 14 August 1975', www.biographicon.com/view/h13we/ Colin_Wallace (accessed 19 August 2010).

'Clause IV', *thecitizen.org*, n.d., www.thecitizen.org.uk/views/clause4.htm (accessed August 11, 2010).

Department of Education, 'Integrated Education', *Department of Education Northern Ireland*, 2011, www.deni.gov.uk/index85-schools/10-types_of_schools_ pg/16-schools-integratedschools_pg.htm (accessed 26 July 2011).

*Northern Ireland Parliamentary Election Results*, n.d., www.election.demon.co.uk/ stormont/totals.html (accessed 10 August 2010).

*Northern Ireland Parliamentary Election Results*, n.d., www.election.demon.co.uk/ stormont/totals.html (accessed 30 May 2011).

OFMDFM, *Structure and Operation (Civic Forum)*, n.d., www.ofmdfmni.gov.uk/ index/making-government-work/civic-forum-review/background/civic-forum- structure-operation.htm (accessed 26 July 2011).

# Index

*Compiled by Sue Carlton*